My Second Picture Dictionary

William A. Jenkins
Andrew Schiller

ST. JOHN'S SCHOOL
COR. MONROE & THIRD STREETS
GOSHEN, INDIANA

Scott, Foresman and Company
Editorial Offices: Glenview, Illinois

Regional Offices:
Sunnyvale, California •
Tucker, Georgia • Glenview, Illinois •
Oakland, New Jersey • Dallas, Texas

Contents

ISBN 0-673-12484-3   ISBN 0-673-12485-1
Copyright © 1987, 1982, 1975, 1971
Scott, Foresman and Company, Glenview, Illinois
All Rights Reserved.
Printed in the United States of America.

56789WAK9190898887

The contents of the dictionary entries in this book
have been adapted from the *Thorndike Barnhart Beginning Dictionary*,
copyright © 1979, 1974 by Scott, Foresman and Company.

Lexicon

Lexicon is
just another word for **dictionary.**

A dictionary is a book of words. The
words are listed in alphabetical order.
A dictionary tells you what those
words mean.

A a

A or **a** the first letter of the alphabet. **A's** or **a's.**

a 1. any: *Is there a book for me?* 2. one: *Here is a pen.* 3. each: *Flag Day comes once a year.*

aard vark a strange-looking animal with claws and long ears. It lives in Africa. Aardvarks eat ants. See the picture. **aard varks.**

ab bre vi a tion a short form of a word, such as *St.* for *Street.* **ab bre vi a tions.**

able having power: *Some animals are able to see well in the dark.* **abler, ablest.**

about 1. of; having something to do with: *This book is about trains.* 2. nearly; almost: *It is about ten o'clock.* 3. around: *He splashed about in the water.* 4. **About to** means on the point of; going to; ready to: *The bus is about to leave.*

above 1. in a higher place: *Read the line above the picture.* 2. higher than; over: *The sun is above the trees.*

ab ra ca dab ra a word supposed to have magic power.

ac cent 1. the loud tone of voice you give to certain syllables or words. 2. a mark (′) to show the loud syllable. 3. say with an accent: *You accent "rabbit" on the first syllable.* **ac cents; ac cent ed, ac cent ing.**

ac ci dent something bad or unlucky that happens: *Breaking the vase was an accident.* **ac ci dents.**

ac count 1. a story about what happened: *The girl gave an account of the ball game when she got home.* 2. **On account of** means because of: *The game was called off on account of rain.* **ac counts.**

aardvark

ac cuse say that someone did something: *Dad
accused us of waking him.* **ac cused, ac cus ing.**

ache 1. a steady pain: *a stomach ache.* 2. have a
steady pain: *My tooth aches.* **aches; ached,
ach ing.**

acorn the nut of an oak tree. See the picture. **acorns.**

ac ro bat a person who can walk on a tight rope
or wire, swing in the air, or do other acts of
skill. See the picture. **ac ro bats.**

across 1. from one side to the other: *It is two miles
across this lake.* 2. on the other side of: *My
house is across the road.*

act 1. a thing done: *Slapping your brother was a
stupid act.* 2. the doing: *She caught me in the
act of cutting the pie.* 3. behave: *The boy acted
like a baby.* 4. play a part: *We acted in the
play.* 5. one part of a play or program: *The
dog act was great.* **acts; act ed, act ing.**

ad an advertisement: *I saw an ad for a used
bicycle in the newspaper.* **ads**

add 1. put together: *Add 5 and 3 to make 8.*
2. **Add to** means put with: *Dad added milk to
the batter.* 3. say more: *She said good-by and
added that she'd see us later.* **add ed, add ing.**

ad dress 1. the place to which mail is sent: *Write
your address on this card.* See the picture.
2. write on an envelope or package the place to
which it is being sent. **ad dress es; ad dressed,
ad dress ing.**

ad mire look at with wonder and pleasure: *We all
admire a brave person. He was admiring the
beautiful picture.* **ad mired, ad mir ing.**

ad mit 1. say something is true: *Ed admitted that
I was right.* 2. allow to enter: *The bus driver
admitted us first.* **ad mit ted, ad mit ting.**

acorn

acrobats

address 1.

aerial on a car

Africa

ad ven ture a bold action or task, usually exciting and somewhat dangerous. **ad ven tures.**

ad ver tise 1. give public notice of; announce: *Stores advertise goods for sale.* 2. **Advertise for** means ask by public notice: *They advertised for a helper.* **ad ver tised, ad ver tis ing.**

ad vice a suggestion about what should be done: *The doctor's advice was to go to bed early.*

aer i al a radio or television antenna. See the picture. **aer i als.**

afraid 1. frightened; feeling fear: *Are you afraid of snakes?* 2. sorry: *I'm afraid I must ask you to go.*

Af ri ca one of the large masses of land on the earth; a continent. See the picture.

af ter 1. later than: *After school we'll go.* 2. behind: *Do you come after Bill in line?* 3. following: *The dog ran after the cat.*

af ter noon the time of day from noon to evening. **af ter noons.**

again another time; once more: *Come again. Please say that again.*

against 1. not on the same side: *The two teams played against each other.* 2. upon: *The rain beat against the house.*

age 1. the number of years you have lived: *What is your age? Sue entered school at the age of five.* 2. a period in history: *During the Stone Age people lived in caves.* **ag es.**

agent a person who acts for another: *My father is an agent for an insurance company.* **agents.**

ago 1. gone by; past: *I saw him two weeks ago.* 2. in the past: *Long ago people lived in caves.*

agree 1. have the same idea about something: *We all agree that it is a good story.* 2. say yes: *She agreed to go with us.* **agreed, agree ing.**

a gree ment an understanding reached by two or more persons, groups of persons, or nations. **a gree ments.**

ahead 1. in front; before: *Please go ahead of me.* 2. forward: *Go ahead with your work.* 3. farther on: *Beth is ahead of everybody in reading.*

aid 1. help: *The patient needs aid when she walks.* 2. give aid or help: *He aided the man to a chair.* 3. **First aid** is help given right away to someone who is hurt or sick. **aids; aid ed, aid ing.**

aim 1. point a gun or direct a blow or throw something at an object: *He aimed at the tree.* 2. the act of aiming at something: *His aim was so bad, he missed the tree.* 3. try; plan: *She aimed to be on time for school.* 4. a plan: *Her aim was to be a singer.* **aimed, aim ing; aims.**

air what we breathe: *Fresh air is good.*

air craft any airplane, airship, helicopter, or balloon. See the picture. **air craft.**

Air Force one part of the armed forces of the United States. See the picture.

air plane a flying machine driven by propellers or jet engines. **air planes.**

air port a field for airplanes to land on and start from. See the picture. **air ports.**

aisle a space between rows of seats: *The bride walked down the aisle.* **aisles.**

Al a bama one of the fifty states of the United States. See page 328.

alarm 1. sudden fear: *The deer ran off in alarm.* 2. make uneasy; frighten: *A noise alarmed the deer.* 3. a bell or signal that warns you: *a fire alarm.* **alarmed, alarm ing; alarms** (for 3.).

Alas ka one of the fifty states of the United States. See page 329.

aircraft

seal
of the U. S. Air Force

airport

alfalfa

alligator

Al ber ta one of the ten provinces of Canada. See the map on page 382.

al fal fa a plant used as a food for animals. See the picture. **al fal fas.**

alike like one another: *Twins usually look alike.*

alive living: *Is the bird alive or dead?*

all 1. the whole of: *We ate all the cake.* 2. every one of: *All these books are funny.* 3. everyone: *All of us are going.* 4. completely: *The candy is all gone.* 5. **All at once** means suddenly.

al ley a narrow back street in a city or town. **al leys.**

al li ga tor a large animal that lives in rivers and swamps. See the picture. **al li ga tors.**

al low 1. let: *No one is allowed to run in the hall.* 2. give; let have: *Our parents allow us fifty cents for lunch.* **al lowed, al low ing.**

al most just a little less than; not quite: *I have saved almost a dollar.*

alone 1. apart from others: *Our house stood alone on the hill.* 2. without anyone else: *One person alone can cook this dinner.* 3. without anything more: *This song alone made the show a success.*

along 1. from one part of to another part of: *Many people walked along the street.* 2. together with someone or something: *Come along with us.*

aloud loud enough to be heard: *She read the story aloud to them.*

al pha bet all the letters of a language put in a certain order. The English alphabet is a b c d e f g h i j k l m n o p q r s t u v w x y z. **al pha bets.**

al pha bet i cal arranged in the order of the alphabet: *Here is an alphabetical list of cities.*

al pha bet i cal ly in alphabetical order: *The names were arranged alphabetically.*

al ready before this time; by this time: *Don has already read this book.*

al so too: *He has a brother and sister also.*

al though even though: *Although it was true, they did not believe it.*

al ways at all times; all the time: *Winter always follows summer. The baby is always cheerful.*

am *I am here. I am going to be late. I am glad.*

Amer i ca 1. the United States. See the map on page 380. 2. North America. See the map on page 379. 3. North America and South America. **Amer i cas** (for 3.).

Amer i can 1. of or belonging to the United States: *The American flag is red, white, and blue.* 2. a citizen of the United States. 3. a person born or living in North or South America. **Amer i cans.**

ami a ble friendly; pleasant: *She is an amiable person to be with.*

among 1. surrounded by: *The house is among the trees.* 2. to each of: *Divide the candy among you.*

amount a sum: *No amount of coaxing would make Mother change her mind. What is the amount he owes you?* **amounts.**

am phib i an 1. an animal that lives both on land and in water: *Frogs are amphibians.* 2. any vehicle that can go on either land or water. See the picture. **am phib i ans.**

amuse 1. cause to laugh or smile: *The puppy amused us.* 2. keep pleased and interested: *Amuse yourself while I'm gone.* **amused, amus ing.**

amuse ment anything that amuses: *Baseball is a healthy amusement.* **amuse ments.**

an 1. any: *Is there an orange in the dish?* 2. one: *He is an inch taller than I am.* 3. each: *She earns fifty cents an hour for baby-sitting.*

an

amphibian 2.

ant

Antarctica

antelope

and 1. as well as: *You can run and jump in the park.* 2. added to; with: *3 and 4 make 7.*

an gri ly in an angry way: *"Wait!" he said angrily.*

an gry feeling or showing that you are not pleased about something: *Dad was very angry when I broke the window.* **an gri er, an gri est.**

an i mal any living thing that is not a plant. **an i mals.**

an kle the part of the leg between the foot and the calf. **an kles.**

an nounce give notice of; state; make known: *Today they will announce the names of those who won prizes.* **an nounced, an nounc ing.**

an nounc er a person who announces. **an nounc ers.**

an noy tease; make angry: *Does a crying baby annoy you?* **an noyed, an noy ing.**

an oth er 1. one more: *Eat another apple.* 2. a different: *Here's another picture.* 3. a different one: *I don't like that song; sing me another.*

an swer 1. speak or act after someone asks a question or wants something: *He didn't answer my question. Answer the door.* 2. words or action after someone asks a question: *Her answer was "no." A smile was her answer.* 3. words or action to end a problem or a puzzle: *What is the correct answer to this puzzle?* **an swered, an swer ing; an swers.**

ant a small insect that lives in the ground or in wood. See the picture. **ants.**

Ant arc ti ca one of the large masses of land on the earth; the continent around the South Pole. See the picture.

an te lope a wild animal that looks somewhat like a deer. See the picture. **an te lope.**

an tique 1. of times long ago; from times long ago. 2. something made long ago: *This carved chest is a genuine antique.* **an tiques.**

ant ler the horn of a deer. See the picture. Some other animals also have antlers. **ant lers.**

anx ious 1. uneasy because of what may happen: *Mother felt anxious about the children when they were late.* 2. wishing very much; eager: *She was anxious to get home.*

any 1. one out of many: *Choose any game you like.* 2. some: *Have you any fresh flowers?*

any body any person.

any more at present; now; currently.

any way in any case.

any where in, at, or to any place.

apart 1. in separate parts or pieces: *When I dropped the chair, it fell apart.* 2. away from each other: *Keep the boys apart.* 3. to one side: *That house stood apart from the other houses.*

apart ment a group of rooms to live in: *There are ten apartments in our building.* **apart ments.**

aphid a very small insect that takes the juice from plants for food. See the picture. **aphids.**

apiece each; for each one: *These bananas are five cents apiece.*

apos tro phe a sign (') used to show that one or more letters have been left out of a word: *Can't you come?* It can also show who owns something: *It is the boy's book.* **apos tro phes.**

ap pear 1. be seen; come in sight: *When will the stars appear?* 2. seem; look: *The apple appeared perfect, but it was rotten inside.* **ap peared, ap pear ing.**

ap ple 1. a fruit that is good to eat. 2. the tree it grows on. See the picture. **ap ples.**

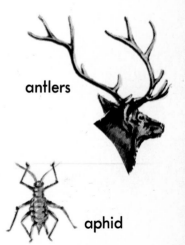

antlers

aphid

apple

apricot

aquarium **2.**

armadillo

ap pli ance a tool or a small machine that helps do something. Many appliances, such as a toaster, are run by electricity. **ap pli anc es.**

ap proach come near or nearer to: *Slow down as you approach the river. Summer is approaching.* **ap proached, ap proach ing.**

apri cot 1. a fruit like a peach but smaller. 2. the tree it grows on. See the picture. **apri cots.**

April the fourth month of the year. It has 30 days. **Aprils.**

apron a covering worn over the front of the body to protect clothes: *Wear an apron when you cook.* **aprons.**

aquar i um 1. a tank or glass bowl in which fish are kept. 2. a building where you can see living fish: *The aquarium is open today.* See the picture. **aquar i ums.**

Ar bor Day a day when many people plant trees. **Ar bor Days.**

are *We are here. You are my friend. You are all my friends. They are coming.*

aren't are not.

arith me tic the study of numbers. You learn to add, subtract, multiply, and divide.

Ar i zo na one of the fifty states of the United States. See page 330.

Ar kan sas one of the fifty states of the United States. See page 331.

arm 1. the part of your body between the shoulder and the hand. 2. something shaped or used like an arm: *the arm of a chair.* **arms.**

ar ma dil lo a small animal with a hard shell. See the picture. **ar ma dil los.**

armed forc es the army, navy, and air force of a country.

ar my 1. a group of soldiers trained for war: *Many armies fight in a war.* 2. a very large number: *an army of ants.* 3. The U.S. Army is one of the armed forces of the United States. See the picture. **ar mies.**

around 1. in a circle: *He swam around the pool.* 2. on all sides: *There were clouds all around.*

ar range 1. put in the correct order: *The words were arranged alphabetically.* 2. plan; form plans: *Can you arrange to go by six o'clock?* **ar ranged, ar rang ing.**

ar rive come to a place: *We arrived in the city a week ago.* **ar rived, ar riv ing.**

ar row 1. a kind of pointed stick. An arrow is shot from a bow. 2. a sign (→) used to show a direction on maps and road signs. See the picture. **ar rows.**

art drawing, painting, and sculpture: *Pupils in second grade are studying art.* **arts.**

ar ti choke a plant. The flower is eaten as a vegetable. See the picture. **ar ti chokes.**

art ist a person who draws or paints pictures or does sculptures. **art ists.**

as 1. equally: *Sue is as tall as Jane.* 2. doing the work of: *Ann will act as your guide.* 3. while: *As we walked, we talked.* 4. in the same way that: *Treat others as you would like them to treat you.*

ash what remains after a thing has been burned: *Take the ashes from the fireplace.* **ash es.**

ashamed 1. feeling shame because one has done something wrong or silly: *I was ashamed after I laughed in class.* 2. unwilling because of shame: *He was ashamed to admit that he had failed.*

Asia part of the largest mass of land on the earth; a continent. See the picture.

army

Asia

seal of the U. S. Army

arrow 1.

arrow 2.

artichoke

Asia

aside

---

audience

asparagus

astronaut

a side   on one side; to one side; away: *He stepped aside to let me pass.*

ask   1. try to find out by words: *Why don't you ask the way?*   2. look for the answer to: *Ask questions if you don't know.*   3. invite: *She asked six girls to her party.* **asked, ask ing.**

asleep   sleeping: *The cat is asleep on the bed.*

as par a gus   a plant. Its tender shoots are eaten as a vegetable. See the picture.

as tro naut   a member of the crew of a space ship. See the picture. **as tro nauts.**

at   1. *At* is used to show where: *Mother is at work.*   2. *At* is used to show when: *Bill goes to bed at eight o'clock.*

ate   See **eat.** *I ate five cookies.*

ath lete   a person who is trained by exercise to be strong and fast. Baseball players and boxers are athletes. **ath letes.**

At lan tic   the ocean east of North and South America.

at tack   1. begin to hurt or fight; go against as an enemy: *The cat attacked the mouse.*   2. the act of attacking: *He had an attack of sneezing.*   **at tacked, at tack ing; at tacks.**

at ten tion   the act of giving thought and care to: *The teacher asked us to pay attention. He called my attention to the cat in the tree. The boy gives his dog much attention.*

at tract   1. pull or draw to itself: *A magnet attracts metal.*   2. be pleasing to: *A smile will attract friends.*   **at tract ed, at tract ing.**

au di ence   1. people gathered in one place to hear or see something: *The audience liked the circus.*   2. any people who can see or hear: *a radio audience, a television audience.* **au di enc es.**

14

au di om e ter a machine that helps find out how
many sounds a person can hear. See the picture.
au di om e ters.

au di to ri um a large room for an audience.
au di to ri ums.

Au gust the eighth month of the year. It has 31
days. **Au gusts.**

aunt your father's sister or your mother's sister or
your uncle's wife. **aunts.**

Aus tral ia one of the large masses of land on the
earth; a continent. See the picture.

au thor a person who writes books or stories.
au thors.

au to an automobile. **au tos.**

au to graph 1. a person's name written by himself.
2. write one's name on or in: *She autographed
her book for me.* **au to graphs; au to graphed,
au to graph ing.**

au to mo bile a vehicle used on roads and streets:
An automobile carries people. **au to mo biles.**

au tumn 1. fall; the season of the year after summer
and before winter. 2. coming in autumn: *Autumn
rains are cold.* **au tumns.**

av e nue a wide street. **av e nues.**

awake 1. wake up: *He awoke from a sound sleep.*
2. not asleep: *He is still awake.* **awoke** or
awaked, awaked, awak ing.

awaked See **awake.** *She had awaked early.*

away 1. from a place: *Stay away from the street.*
2. at a distance: *The rabbit was far away from
home.* 3. absent; gone: *Our teacher is away today.*

aw ful 1. causing fear: *an awful storm, the awful
power of a hurricane.* 2. very bad: *an awful fall.*

aw ful ly 1. terribly: *Her broken arm hurt awfully.*
2. very: *I'm awfully sorry that I broke your mirror.*

audiometer

Australia

awoke

---

badly

ax

azalea

badger

awoke See **awake.** *He awoke early.*

ax or **axe** a tool for chopping wood. See the picture. **ax es.**

ax le a bar on which a wheel turns. **ax les.**

azal ea a bush bearing many flowers. See the picture. **azal eas.**

B   b

B or **b** the second letter of the alphabet. **B's** or **b's.**

baa the sound a sheep makes; bleat.

ba by 1. a very young child. 2. for a baby: *baby shoes.* 3. young or small: *baby chickens.* **ba bies.**

back 1. the part of your body opposite the front. 2. the side of anything away from you: *the back of the picture.* 3. part of a chair that a person leans against when sitting down. 4. move away from the front: *He backed his car slowly. He backed away from the snake.* **backs; backed, back ing.**

back ward 1. toward the back: *Walk backward.* 2. with the back first: *The baby tumbled over backward.*

bac te ria simple forms of life so tiny they can be seen only through a microscope. Some bacteria cause diseases.

bad 1. not good; not as it ought to be: *Teasing animals is a bad habit.* 2. rotten; spoiled: *This is a bad egg.* 3. sorry: *I feel bad about being late for the parade.* 4. sick: *I felt bad after eating that candy.* **worse, worst.**

badg er an animal that digs holes in the ground to live in. See the picture. **badg ers.**

bad ly in a bad manner: *She dances badly.*

bag a container made of paper, cloth, plastic, or leather, that can be closed at the top. **bags.**

bag gage the trunks, bags, and suitcases that people take when they travel.

bait 1. anything used to attract fish or other animals so they may be caught: *Worms are good fishing bait.* 2. put bait on a hook or in a trap to catch something. **baits; bait ed, bait ing.**

bake cook in an oven: *The cook bakes bread.* **baked, bak ing.**

bak er a person who makes or sells bread, pies, and cakes. **bak ers.**

bak ery a baker's shop; a place where bread and cakes are made or sold. **bak er ies.**

bal ance 1. being steady; not falling over: *He lost his balance and fell.* 2. keep or put in a steady position: *She balanced the jar on her head.* **bal anced, bal anc ing.**

bal co ny 1. a platform that sticks out from a building. 2. a floor above the first floor in a theater or hall. See the picture. **bal co nies.**

bale 1. a large bundle of material such as cotton or hay wrapped and tied. See the picture. 2. make into bales; tie in large bundles. **bales; baled, bal ing.**

ball¹ 1. anything round: *a ball of string.* 2. a round object thrown, kicked, or batted in games. 3. a game in which some kind of ball is used: *Let's play ball.* **balls.**

ball² a large party for dancing: *The prince went to the ball.* **balls.**

bal loon 1. a toy; a brightly colored rubber bag that is filled with air. 2. a kind of aircraft; a large bag filled with some gas that makes it float in the air. See the picture. **bal loons.**

bag

balloon

balcony 1.

balcony 2.

a bale of cotton

balloon 2.

bamboo

banker

bamboo

banana

boy playing a banjo

bam boo a kind of tall grass that grows in warm places. Its hollow stems are used to make many things. See the picture. **bam boos.**

ba nana 1. a fruit that grows in large bunches. 2. the tree it grows on. See the picture. **ba nan as.**

band 1. a group of persons acting together: *A band of bad men robbed the train.* 2. a group of musicians playing together: *The band played music for an hour.* 3. a thin, flat strip: *Put a rubber band around the papers. The plate had a band of gold around the edge.* **bands.**

band age 1. a strip of cloth or other material used to cover a wound: *Put a bandage on that cut.* 2. wrap up a wound: *The nurse gently bandaged my arm.* **band ag es; band aged, band ag ing.**

bang 1. a sudden, loud noise: *We heard the bang of the car door.* 2. make a sudden, loud noise: *The back door banged in the wind.* 3. shut with noise; slam: *He banged the desk drawer.* **bangs; banged, bang ing.**

bangs a fringe of hair across the forehead.

ban jo a musical instrument with strings. You play it with your fingers. See the picture. **ban jos** or **ban joes.**

bank¹ 1. a pile: *a bank of snow.* 2. ground along a river or lake: *He fished from the river bank.* 3. slant to one side when making a turn: *The airplane banked and turned north.* **banks; banked, bank ing.**

bank² a place for keeping money: *Mom and Dad put money in the bank every week. Rosa has a bank for nickels and pennies.* **banks.**

bank er a person that helps run a bank. **bank ers.**

18

bar 1. a piece of something such as iron, soap, or chocolate, longer than it is wide or thick. 2. a pole or rod across a door or gate to fasten or shut off something. 3. put a bar across something: *Bar the door.* 4. not allow: *All talking is barred in the halls.* **bars; barred, bar ring.**

bar be cue 1. meat roasted before an open fire. 2. roast meat over an open fire: *Dad barbecued the meat.* 3. cook meat in a sauce seasoned with spices. **bar be cues; bar be cued, bar be cu ing.**

bar ber a person whose business is cutting people's hair and shaving men's faces. **bar bers.**

bare without covering or clothes. **bar er, bar est.**

bar gain 1. a trade: *We made a bargain to wash the car for fifty cents.* 2. something for sale or bought for less than it is worth: *This chair is a bargain for five dollars.* **bar gains.**

barge a large boat with a flat bottom. It carries things like sand or coal. See the picture. **barg es.**

bark[1] the outside covering of the trunk, branches, and roots of a tree. **barks.**

bark[2] 1. a sound such as that made by a dog. 2. make this sound. **barks; barked, bark ing.**

bar ley 1. the grain of a plant, used for food. 2. the plant. See the picture.

barn a building for storing hay and grain and for sheltering farm animals. **barns.**

bar rel a large container with a round, flat top and bottom and with curved sides. See the picture. **bar rels.**

base 1. the part of a thing on which it rests: *The base of the statue is cement.* 2. a goal in some games: *I stopped on third base.* **bas es.**

bar

---

base

barge

barley

barrel

baseball

---

batter

basket 1.

basket 3.

bass²

bat²

girl twirling a baton

base ball 1. a game played with a bat and ball by two teams of nine players each. 2. the ball used in this game. **base balls.**

base ment the bottom story of a building. It is often below ground. **base ments.**

bas ket 1. a container made of dry grass or strips of wood woven together. 2. anything that looks like a basket: *a waste basket.* 3. a ring and net through which a basketball drops. See the picture. **bas kets.**

bas ket ball 1. a game played with a large leather ball between two teams of five players each. 2. the ball used in this game. **bas ket balls.**

bass¹ having a deep, low sound: *He has a bass voice.* (Bass¹ rhymes with race.)

bass² a fish used for food. See the picture. **bass es** or **bass.** (Bass² rhymes with mass.)

bat¹ 1. a thick stick or club, used to hit a ball. 2. hit with a bat. **bats; bat ted, bat ting.**

bat² an animal that looks like a mouse and can fly. See the picture. **bats.**

bath 1. a washing of the body: *I took a bath last night.* 2. a room for bathing: *The bath is upstairs.* **baths.**

bathe 1. take a bath: *Have you bathed yet?* 2. give a bath to: *Mother is bathing the baby.* 3. go in swimming: *We bathed at the beach.* **bathed, bath ing.**

bath ing suit a short, tight piece of clothing worn for swimming. **bath ing suits.**

bath room a room for bathing. **bath rooms.**

ba ton a long metal rod with a ball at one end: *Joy can twirl a baton.* See the picture. **ba tons.**

bat ter¹ flour, milk, eggs, or the like, mixed together to make things like cake. **bat ters.**

bat ter[2] in baseball, a player whose turn it is to bat. **bat ters.**

bat tery a set of electric cells that produce electricity. See the picture. **bat ter ies.**

be *Can you be here all day? She tries to be on time. They will be hungry. He will be an athlete some day. Be good to animals.*

beach a strip of land at the edge of the water, covered with sand or stones. **beach es.**

bead a small bit of glass or other material, with a hole so it can be strung on a thread. **beads.**

beady small and shiny like beads: *The animal had beady eyes.* **bead i er, bead i est.**

bea gle a hunting dog. See the picture. **bea gles.**

beam 1. a large, long piece of timber or metal, ready for use in building. 2. a line of light: *the beam of a flashlight.* **beams.**

bean 1. a smooth, flat seed used as a vegetable. 2. the shell also used as a vegetable. 3. the plant beans grow on. See the picture. **beans.**

bear[1] 1. carry: *It will take two people to bear that heavy load.* 2. hold up: *The ice is too thin to bear a sled.* 3. suffer: *He cannot bear any more pain.* 4. bring forth: *That grapefruit tree bears good fruit. They were both born in June.* **bore, borne** or **born, bear ing.**

bear[2] a large animal with coarse hair and a very short tail. See the picture. **bears.**

beard the hair growing on a man's face. **beards.**

beast any four-footed animal. **beasts.**

beat 1. hit again and again: *The cruel man beats his dog.* 2. do better than: *Our team beat yours.* 3. mix by stirring: *Beat three eggs for the cake.* **beat, beat en, beat ing.**

beat en See **beat.** *Have you beaten the cream?*

battery

beagle

bean

bear[2]

beaver

beech tree

beet

beetle

beau ti ful very pleasing to see or hear.

beau ti ful ly in a beautiful manner: *She plays the piano beautifully.*

beau ty 1. being good to look at: *We were thrilled by the beauty of the sunset.* 2. that which pleases: *There is beauty in a smile.* **beau ties.**

bea ver a mammal that lives both in water and on land. Beavers build dams across streams. See the picture. **bea vers.**

be came See **become.** *It became dark very soon.*

be cause for the reason that; since: *Pat called us in because supper was ready.*

be come 1. come to be; grow to be: *It is becoming warmer. He has become wiser as he has grown older.* 2. **Become of** means happen to: *What has become of her book?* **be came, be come, be com ing.**

bed 1. anything to sleep or rest on. 2. a piece of ground in which plants are grown: *The flower bed is beautiful.* **beds.**

bed room a room to sleep in. **bed rooms.**

bed time time to go to bed.

bee an insect that has four wings. **bees.**

beech a tree with smooth gray bark and shiny leaves. It has a nut that is good to eat. See the picture. **beech es** or **beech.**

beef the meat from a steer or cow, used for food.

been *This boy has been here for hours. The books have been read by everyone. We have been friends for years. You have been good to me.*

beet a plant. Its thick, red root and its leaves are eaten as vegetables. See the picture. **beets.**

bee tle an insect that has hard, shiny cases to cover its wings. See the picture. **bee tles.**

be fore 1. earlier than: *Wash your hands before you eat.* 2. in time past: *You have been here before.* 3. in front of; ahead of: *Your turn comes before mine.*

beg 1. ask for something, such as food, clothes, or money: *The dog was begging for some meat.* 2. ask politely: *I beg your pardon.* **begged, beg ging.**

be gan See **begin.** *He began to sing.*

be gin 1. do the first part; start: *The party will begin soon.* 2. start to be or happen: *The storm began yesterday.* **be gan, be gun, be gin ning.**

be gin ning 1. the first part of something such as a book. 2. the time when anything starts: *Can you be here at the beginning of the program?* **be gin nings.**

be gun See **begin.** *It has begun to rain.*

be have 1. act: *Some people behave badly.* 2. do what is right: *The little boy behaves in school.* **be haved, be hav ing.**

be hind 1. at the back of: *Who is behind me?* 2. not on time; late: *Her class is behind in its work.* 3. not as good as: *He is behind the others in his class.*

be ing a living creature. *People are human beings.* **be ings.**

be lief something you believe. **be liefs.**

be lieve 1. think something is true: *We believe the earth is round.* 2. think someone tells the truth: *Did her friends believe her?* **be lieved, be liev ing.**

bell a hollow object, usually made of metal, shaped like a cup, that makes a ringing sound when struck by another piece of metal inside it. See the picture. **bells.**

bell

belt 1.

belt 2.

bend 2.

be long 1. be the property of: *Do these mittens belong to you?* 2. be a part of: *She belongs to a club.* 3. have a place: *That chair belongs in the other room.* **be longed, be long ing.**

be low 1. in a lower place: *From the mountain we could see the valley below.* 2. less than: *The temperature is below zero.*

belt 1. a strip of leather or other material, worn around the body. 2. a loop that passes over wheels and moves them. See the picture. **belts.**

bench 1. a long seat. 2. a strong, heavy table on which you work with tools: *A carpenter works at a bench.* **bench es.**

bend 1. a part that is not straight: *Watch for the bend in the road.* 2. become crooked: *The board began to bend as she walked on it.* See the picture. 3. make crooked: *Try to bend this rod.* 4. move the top of your body toward the ground: *Bend over and touch your toes.* **bends; bent** or **bend ed, bend ing.**

be neath below; under; in a lower place: *Lee's coat is beneath that pile of books.*

bent 1. See **bend.** *He bent the fork. I have bent and touched the floor.* 2. not straight: *I used a bent pin for a hook.*

ber ry a small fruit, such as a strawberry or raspberry, having many seeds. **ber ries.**

be side by the side of; near: *Let's camp beside the river.*

be sides 1. also: *He didn't want to hurry home; besides he was having fun.* 2. more than: *Others came to the picnic besides our family.*

best 1. most good or excellent: *Who is the best swimmer?* See **good.** 2. in the most excellent way: *Who swims best?* See **well.**

bet say you will give something to someone if that person is right and you are wrong: *He bet that he could beat me to the corner. I have bet that he couldn't.* **bet** or **bet ted, bet ting.**

bet ter 1. more than good: *This cake is good, but that cake is better.* See **good.** 2. in a more than good way: *She sang that song well, but she sang this one better.* See **well.**

be tween in the space or time from one thing to another: *There is a rock between two trees. We'll be home between two and three o'clock.*

be yond 1. farther away: *Look beyond the fence for your ball.* 2. farther than: *Don't go beyond the corner.*

bib 1. a cloth worn under the chin by a baby. 2. the top part of an apron. See the picture. **bibs.**

Bi ble a holy book. **Bi bles.**

bi cy cle a vehicle with two wheels, one behind the other. You ride it by pushing two pedals. **bi cy cles.**

big 1. much in size or many in amount: *a big dog, a big class.* 2. grown up: *a big brother or sister.* 3. important: *big news.* **big ger, big gest.**

bike a bicycle. **bikes.**

bill[1] 1. an account of how much money a person owes someone: *Send me a bill for what I bought.* 2. a piece of paper money: *a dollar bill.* **bills.**

bill[2] the mouth of a bird. See the picture. **bills.**

bin a box or place shut in on all sides, for holding such things as grain and coal. See the picture. **bins.**

bind 1. tie together; hold together; fasten: *Bind the package with string.* 2. wrap a wound: *The doctor will bind your wound.* **bound, bind ing.**

bib 1.

bib 2.→

bill[2]

a coal bin

birch tree

bitterroot

blackberry

bi og ra phy the story of a person's life written by someone else. **bi og ra phies.**

birch a tree with smooth bark and hard wood. See the picture. **birch es.**

bird an animal that has wings and feathers. Most birds can fly. **birds.**

bird bath a shallow basin for birds to bathe in or drink from. **bird baths.**

bird house a small box for birds to nest in. **bird hous es.**

birth being born: *We heard about the birth of the baby.* **births.**

birth day the day on which a person was born. **birth days.**

bit[1] 1. a piece of metal put in a horse's mouth so its driver can control it. 2. part of a tool for boring or drilling. **bits.**

bit[2] a small piece; a small amount. **bits.**

bit[3] See **bite.** *He bit into the candy bar.*

bite 1. cut with the teeth: *Did she bite her tongue?* 2. the amount you bite off: *I only ate a bite of my apple.* 3. hurt with teeth; sting: *My dog won't bite.* 4. a sore made by biting or stinging **bit, bit ten** or **bit, bit ing; bites.**

bit ten See **bite.** *Someone has bitten this apple!*

bit ter having a sharp, unpleasant taste. The skin of an orange tastes bitter.

bit ter root a small plant with thick roots and pink flowers. See the picture.

black 1. the opposite of white; the color of coal or burned toast. 2. without light; very dark: *Without a moon the night was black.*

black ber ry 1. a small black or purple fruit. 2. the bush it grows on. See the picture. **black ber ries.**

black bird any of various American birds so named because the male is mostly black. **black birds.**

black-eyed Su san a yellow flower that looks like a daisy. See the picture. **black-eyed Su sans.**

black smith a person who works with iron, mends tools, and puts horseshoes on horses. See the picture. **black smiths.**

blade 1. the cutting part of a knife or scissors: *This knife has a very sharp blade.* 2. a leaf of grass. 3. part of a propeller. See the picture. **blades.**

blame 1. think a person or thing is the cause of something bad: *Why blame the fog for your accident?* 2. find fault with: *He can't blame us if we do our best.* **blamed, blam ing.**

blank 1. a space left empty: *Write the correct word in each blank.* 2. a paper with spaces to be filled in: *Fill out this blank and return it to me.* 3. not written on: *This is a blank page.* **blanks.**

blan ket 1. a soft, warm covering for a bed. 2. something like a blanket: *A blanket of leaves covered the ground.* **blan kets.**

blaze 1. a bright flame or fire: *You could see the blaze for miles.* 2. burn with a bright flame: *The fire blazed up, then died.* **blaz es; blazed, blaz ing.**

bleat 1. the cry made by a sheep, goat, or calf, or a sound like it. 2. make the cry of a sheep, goat, or calf, or a sound like it: *The sheep bleated loudly.* **bleats; bleat ed, bleat ing.**

bled See **bleed**. *Her nose bled for a minute. It had bled once before.*

bleed lose blood. **bled, bleed ing.**

blest See **bless**.

blew See **blow**. *The wind blew the tree down.*

black-eyed Susan

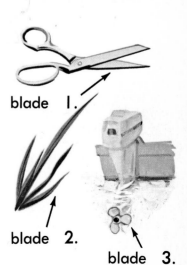

blacksmith
making a horseshoe

blade 1.

blade 2.

blade 3.

blueberry

blind²

blueberries

blind 1. not able to see. 2. something that keeps out light. See the picture. **blind er, blind est; blinds.**

blind ing making blind or as if blind: *The blinding snowstorm kept us from finding the road.*

bliz zard a storm with wind and snow. **bliz zards.**

block 1. a thick piece of wood or other material. 2. fill so nothing can pass by: *The car was blocking traffic.* 3. a square of land: *We walked around the block.* **blocks; blocked, block ing.**

blond 1. light in color. 2. having yellow or light-brown hair: *My mother's hair is blond.*

blood the red liquid in your body.

blood bank a place for storing blood until it is needed. **blood banks.**

bloom 1. a blossom. 2. have flowers: *This plant blooms often.* **blooms; bloomed, bloom ing.**

blos som 1. a flower, usually of a plant that produces fruit: *apple blossoms.* 2. have flowers: *The plum trees are blossoming.* **blos soms; blos somed, blos som ing.**

blow¹ 1. a fist or an object brought hard against something: *A blow from a boxer's fist can hurt. The man gave his horse a blow with a stick.* 2. something that suddenly upsets you: *It was a blow to see that everyone was gone.* **blows.**

blow² 1. send forth a strong current of air: *Blow out the match.* 2. move fast: *The wind is blowing hard.* 3. make a sound by a current of air: *The whistle blows at noon.* **blew, blown, blow ing.**

blown See **blow.** *She has blown up the balloon.*

blue 1. the color of the clear sky during the day. 2. having this color. **blues; blu er, blu est.**

blue ber ry 1. a small, blue berry. 2. the bush it grows on. See the picture. **blue ber ries.**

Blue Bird a member of the Camp Fire Girls. A Blue Bird is between six and eight years old. See the picture. **Blue Birds.**

blue bird a small bird that sings. See the picture. It is the state bird of several states. **blue birds.**

blue bon net a plant with blue flowers. See the picture. **blue bon nets.**

blue jay a noisy, chattering blue bird. See the picture. **blue jays.**

bluff a high, steep bank or cliff. **bluffs.**

board 1. a broad, thin piece of wood. 2. cover with boards: *The windows were boarded up.* 3. a group of persons who manage something: *the school board.* 4. get on a ship, train, or plane: *Board the plane quickly.* **boards; board ed, board ing.**

boast speak too well of yourself or of what you own: *He boasts about his new bike every day.* **boast ed, boast ing.**

boat a vehicle that floats on water and can be moved by motor, by sail, or by oars. **boats.**

bob o link a common American bird that sings. **bob o links.**

body 1. the whole of a person or animal. 2. the main part of anything. 3. the outside part of an automobile. 4. a mass: *a body of water.* **bod ies.**

boil[1] 1. send up bubbles and give off steam: *Will the water boil soon?* 2. cook by boiling: *Boil the egg three minutes.* **boiled, boil ing.**

boil[2] a red sore on the skin. **boils.**

boil er 1. a container for heating liquids. 2. a tank for holding hot water. **boil ers.**

bold without fear; showing courage: *The bold boy faced the barking dog.* **bold er, bold est.**

Blue Bird

bold

Blue Bird

bluebird

bluebonnet

blue jay

boomerang

telephone booth

bold ly in a bold way: *The firefighter ran boldly into the burning building.*

bone one of the parts of the skeleton of a person or animal: *He broke a bone in his arm.* **bones.**

bon go a small drum played with flattened hands. Bongos usually come in pairs and are held between the knees. **bon gos.**

book written or printed sheets of paper bound together: *She read half of her book.* **books.**

book case a piece of furniture with shelves for holding books. **book cas es.**

book mo bile a truck fitted out with bookshelves, that serves as a traveling branch of a library. **book mo biles.**

boo me rang a curved piece of wood. You can throw it in the air so that it will come back to you. See the picture. **boo me rangs.**

boot a heavy covering for the foot and leg: *Wear your boots when it rains.* **boots.**

booth 1. a place at a fair or market where things are sold. 2. a small closed place: *a telephone booth.* See the picture. **booths.**

bore[1] make a hole by pushing a tool in or through: *The drill bored through the wall.* **bored, bor ing.**

bore[2] See **bear**[1]. *She bore the pain bravely.*

bor ing not interesting or amusing; dull.

born See **bear**[1]. *The baby was born today.*

bor row get something from a person to use just for a while: *He has borrowed my book.* **bor rowed, bor row ing.**

boss 1. a person who hires people to work or who watches over and directs them. 2. be the boss of; direct; control. **boss es; bossed, boss ing.**

both 1. the one and the other: *Both houses are pink.* 2. the two together: *Both dogs are mine.*

both er 1. worry; trouble: *That was a lot of bother for nothing.* 2. take trouble; concern yourself: *Don't bother about getting breakfast.* 3. annoy: *Do not bother me while I work.* **both ers; both ered, both er ing.**

bot tle a container, usually made of glass and without handles, used for liquids. **bot tles.**

bot tom 1. the lowest part: *There are cookies at the bottom of the basket.* 2. the part on which anything rests: *The bottom of that bottle is wet.* **bot toms.**

bought See **buy**. *She bought a coat. She has bought a pair of shoes.*

bounce 1. spring back after hitting something: *The ball bounced.* 2. make a thing bounce: *She bounced her ball.* **bounced, bounc ing.**

bound[1] See **bind**. *The doctor bound up the cut. Has he bound the book yet?*

bound[2] 1. bounce. 2. spring lightly: *The deer can bound through the woods.* **bound ed, bound ing.**

bound a ry a line or something at the edge to show where something ends: *There is a boundary between Mexico and the United States.* **bound a ries.**

bou quet a bunch of flowers. See the picture. **bou quets.**

bow[1] 1. bend your head or body: *He bowed to us.* 2. a bending of your head or body: *The singer made a deep bow as we clapped.* **bowed, bow ing; bows.** (Bow[1] rhymes with how.)

bow[2] 1. a strip of wood bent by a string: *A bow shoots arrows.* 2. a rod with horse hairs stretched on it for playing the violin. 3. a knot; a bow of ribbon. See the picture. **bows.** (Bow[2] rhymes with so.)

bouquet

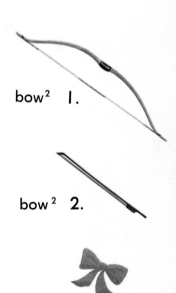

bow[2] 1.

bow[2] 2.

bow[2] 3.

31

bow

_____

branch

boxer 1.

boxer 2.

Boy Scout

girl wearing braids

bow³ the forward or front part of a ship, boat, or airplane. **bows.** (Bow³ rhymes with <u>how</u>.)

bowl¹ a hollow, deep dish. **bowls.**

bowl² play a game by rolling a heavy ball at wooden pins to knock them down. **bowled, bowl ing.**

box¹ a container made of wood, metal, or paper to put things in. **box es.**

box² fight another person with the fists, wearing heavy gloves and following special rules. **boxed, box ing.**

box er 1. a person who boxes. 2. a kind of dog. See the picture. **box ers.**

boy a male child. **boys.**

Boy Scout a member of the Boy Scouts of America. See the picture. **Boy Scouts.**

brace let a band or chain usually worn on the arm. **brace lets.**

braces metal wires used to straighten crooked teeth.

braid 1. a band of hair formed by weaving hair together: *She liked to wear her hair in braids.* See the picture. 2. weave hair together: *Every morning Mother braids my hair.* 3. a narrow band of material. Braid is used to trim clothing and other things. **braids; braid ed, braid ing.**

brain the part of the body used to feel and think. **brains.**

brake anything used to stop or slow something down: *Bicycles and automobiles need brakes.* **brakes.**

branch 1. a part of a tree that grows out from the trunk. 2. one part of something that is divided: *The river divides into two branches.* **branch es.**

brand 1. a certain kind: *Do you like this brand of mustard?* 2. a mark made on cattle and horses to show who owns them. See the picture. 3. mark with a hot iron: *Cowboys brand cattle.* **brands; brand ed, brand ing.**

brass 1. a yellow metal. 2. made of brass: *The brass bowl is filled with flowers.*

brave without fear. **brav er, brav est.**

brave ly in a brave way: *The men fought bravely.*

bread food made from flour or meal mixed with milk or water and baked.

break 1. make come to pieces by a blow or a pull: *The ball will break a window.* 2. come apart; burst: *The bag broke.* 3. fail to keep: *She broke her promise.* 4. a breaking: *A break in the water pipe caused the leak.* 5. a short stop in work: *We had a milk break.* **broke, bro ken, break ing; breaks.**

break fast the first meal of the day: *What did you have for breakfast?* **break fasts.**

breath air drawn into and forced out of the lungs: *Take a deep breath.* **breaths.**

breathe draw air into the lungs and then force it out. **breathed, breath ing.**

breeze a stirring of air; a light wind. **breez es.**

brick 1. a block of clay baked in an oven. 2. made of bricks: *The boy climbed a brick wall.* **bricks.**

bride a woman just married or about to be married. **brides.**

bride groom a man just married or about to be married. **bride grooms.**

bridge something built above water or land so that people or vehicles can cross over. See the picture. **bridg es.**

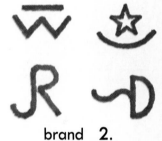

brand 2.

bridge

brook

Brownie[1] 2.

bright 1. giving much light: *The moon is bright tonight.* 2. clever: *The bright boy knew the answer.* **bright er, bright est.**

bright ly in a bright way: *The fire burned brightly.*

bring come with something from another place: *Please bring me a napkin.* **brought, bring ing.**

Brit ish Co lum bia one of the ten provinces of Canada. See the map on page 382.

broad wide; large across: *The wagons crossed a broad river.* **broad er, broad est.**

broad cast 1. a radio or television program. 2. send out a signal or program by radio or TV: *The radio station broadcasts news. Yesterday it broadcast a ball game. It has broadcast music all night long.* **broad casts; broad cast** or **broad cast ed, broad cast ing.**

broke See **break.** *Who broke this dish?*

bro ken 1. See **break.** *The football has broken a window.* 2. in pieces: *Pick up the broken cup.*

brood er a closed place that can be heated, used in raising chicks: *a new brooder for the farm.* **brood ers.**

brook a small stream. See the picture. **brooks.**

broom a brush with a long handle. **brooms.**

broth er a boy with the same parents as another. **broth ers.**

brought See **bring.** *He brought two cookies. She has brought an orange.*

brown 1. a dark color like that of toast or coffee. 2. having that color: *Many horses are brown.* **browns; brown er, brown est.**

brown ie[1] 1. in stories, a good-natured, helpful elf or fairy. 2. **Brownie,** a Girl Scout. Brownies are seven or eight years old. See the picture. **brown ies, Brown ies.**

brown ie[2] a small, flat, sweet chocolate cake with nuts. **brown ies.**

brush[1] 1. a tool made of coarse hairs, bristles, or wire, set in a stiff back or fastened to a handle. 2. clean, rub, or paint with a brush; use a brush on: *Brush your teeth.* **brush es; brushed, brush ing.**

brush[2] bushes and small trees growing in the woods.

bub ble a round drop of water that is full of air. **bub bles.**

buck et a pail. **buck ets.**

buck eye a tree with large brown seeds. See the picture. **buck eyes.**

buck le 1. an object to hold together two loose ends of a belt, strap, or ribbon. 2. fasten together with a buckle: *Buckle your belt.* **buck les; buck led, buck ling.**

buck skin strong, soft leather, made from the skin of deer or sheep.

bud the beginning of a flower or of a leaf or of a branch. **buds.**

budge move just a little bit: *We pushed hard but couldn't budge the door.* **budged, budg ing.**

buf fa lo a large animal with a shaggy head. American buffaloes are called bison. See the picture. **buf fa loes, buf fa los,** or **buf fa lo.**

bug 1. a crawling or a flying insect. 2. any animal that looks like an insect. Ants, flies, and spiders are often called bugs. **bugs.**

bug gy 1. a vehicle with wheels: *We rode in a buggy pulled by a horse.* See the picture. 2. a vehicle to carry a baby or doll. **bug gies.**

bu gle a musical instrument that you play by blowing into it. See the picture. **bu gles.**

brownie

---

bugle

buckeye

buffalo

buggy   1.

boy
playing
a bugle

bulb 1.

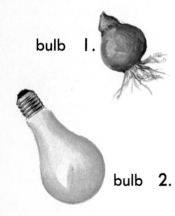

bulb 2.

bulldog

bumblebee

build make by putting materials together: *It takes many people to build a bridge.* **built, build ing.**

build ing a thing built, such as a barn or house. **build ings.**

built See **build.** *They built a sand castle. They have built two castles today.*

bulb 1. a round bud or stem from which plants such as onions, tulips, and lilies grow. 2. any round object shaped like a bulb: *a light bulb.* See the picture. **bulbs.**

bull dog a heavily built dog with a large head. See the picture. **bull dogs.**

bul let a piece of metal that is shot from a gun. **bul lets.**

bul le tin board a board for putting up notices. **bul le tin boards.**

bum ble bee a large bee with a thick body. See the picture. **bum ble bees.**

bump 1. push or throw against something: *Don't bump against the table.* 2. hit or come against: *She bumped her arm on the door.* 3. a heavy blow or knock: *He got a bump on the head.* 4. a spot that becomes bigger because it has been bumped: *The bump on his head turned black and blue.* **bumped, bump ing; bumps.**

bun bread or cake, sometimes sweet, baked in a small piece. **buns.**

bunch a group of things of the same kind growing or fastened together, put together, or thought of together: *a bunch of grapes, a bunch of flowers.* **bunch es.**

bun dle 1. a number of things tied together or wrapped together: *a bundle of newspapers.* 2. a parcel; a package. **bun dles.**

bun ny a rabbit. **bun nies.**

bun ting a small bird something like a sparrow. See the picture. **bun tings.**

burn 1. be on fire; be very hot. 2. set on fire: *Please burn the trash.* 3. a sore caused by heat: *She got a burn on her arm from the hot iron.* **burned** or **burnt, burn ing; burns.**

burnt See **burn.**

bur ro a kind of small donkey. See the picture. **bur ros.**

bur row 1. a hole dug in the ground. Rabbits live in burrows. 2. dig a hole in the ground: *A mole burrowed under the porch.* **bur rows; bur rowed, bur row ing.**

burst 1. fly apart suddenly with force: *That balloon will burst. The last one burst when I blew it too full. Have you ever burst a paper bag?* 2. go or come suddenly: *He had burst into the room without knocking.* **burst, burst ing.**

bury 1. put in the ground: *The children wanted to bury their dead pet.* 2. cover up; hide: *She buried her head under the covers.* **bur ied, bur y ing.**

bus a large automobile that carries passengers along certain streets or roads. **bus es** or **bus ses.**

bush a plant like a tree but smaller, with branches starting from near the ground. **bush es.**

bush el a measure for things such as grain, fruit, and vegetables: *Dad bought a bushel of potatoes.* **bush els.**

bushy spreading out like a bush: *Squirrels have bushy tails.* **bush i er, bush i est.**

busi ness the thing one is busy at; work: *A butcher's business is cutting and selling meat.* **busi ness es.**

bunting

burro

butterfly

button   1.

button   3.

bus sta tion a place where buses pick up passengers and start on a trip. Passengers buy tickets and wait for a bus in the bus station. **bus sta tions.**

busy 1. working: *a busy man.* 2. full of work: *a busy day.* **bus i er, bus i est.**

but 1. on the other hand: *You may go, but you may not stay late.* 2. except: *The restaurant is open every day but Monday.*

butch er a person who sells meat or gets meat ready to sell. **butch ers.**

butt strike by pushing or knocking hard with the head: *A goat butts.* **butt ed, butt ing.**

but ter 1. the yellow food formed by churning cream. 2. put butter on: *Please butter this cracker for me.* 3. something like butter: *Peanut butter is good on bread.* **but tered, but ter ing.**

but ter fly an insect with a small, thin body and four large, bright-colored wings. See the picture. **but ter flies.**

but ton 1. a knob or object on clothing to hold edges closed. 2. fasten the buttons of. 3. a knob to take hold of, push, or turn: *When I pushed the button, the bell rang.* See the picture. **but tons; but toned, but ton ing.**

buy get by paying some money: *You can buy a pencil for school.* **bought, buy ing.**

buzz 1. the humming sound made by flies, mosquitoes, or bees. 2. make a steady humming sound. **buzz es; buzzed, buzz ing.**

by 1. near; beside: *Stand by the door.* 2. along; over: *They went by the river road.* 3. through using: *He travels by bus.* 4. not later than: *Be here by twelve o'clock.* 5. **By and by** means after a while or later.

C c

California

cabbage

C or **c** the third letter of the alphabet. **C's** or **c's.**

cab a taxicab. **cabs.**

cab bage a plant. Its leaves are folded into a round head. The head is eaten as a vegetable. See the picture. **cab bag es.**

cab in 1. a small house: *a log cabin.* 2. a place for passengers in an airplane or ship. **cab ins.**

ca ble a strong, thick rope, often made of wires twisted together. See the picture. **ca bles.**

cable

ca boose a small car on the end of a freight train. The train crew can rest in the caboose. See the picture. **ca boos es.**

cac tus a desert plant with thorns. There are many kinds of cactus in the desert. See the picture. **cac tus es** or **cac ti.**

caf e te ria a place to eat. You choose your food and carry it to a table. **caf e te rias.**

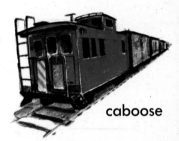
caboose

cage a frame or place closed in with wire or bars. Wild animals are kept in cages. **cag es.**

cake 1. a kind of food made of flour, sugar, and eggs. 2. food or other material pressed into the shape of a cake: *a cake of soap.* **cakes.**

cactus

cal en dar a table or chart showing the months, weeks, and days of the year. **cal en dars.**

calf[1] 1. a baby cow, elephant, or whale. 2. leather made of the skin of a calf: *My new shoes are made of calf.* **calves** (for 1.).

calf[2] the back of the leg below the knee. See the picture. **calves.**

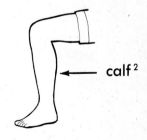
calf[2]

Cal i for nia one of the fifty states of the United States. See page 332.

camel

camellia

Camp Fire Girl

call 1. speak loudly; cry; shout: *He called for help.* 2. a shout: *Did you hear a call for help?* 3. the cry an animal or bird makes. 4. give a name: *I call my dog King.* 5. telephone to: *Call me when you get home.* **called, call ing; calls.**

calm quiet; still; not windy; not stirred up; not excited. **calm er, calm est.**

calm ly in a calm way: *She faced him calmly.*

calves more than one calf.

came See **come.** *Dad came home early.*

cam el a large animal that can go a long time without water. See the picture. **cam els.**

ca mel lia a plant with shiny leaves and a flower that looks like a rose. See the picture. **ca mel lias.**

cam era a machine for taking pictures or movies. **cam eras.**

camp 1. a group of tents or huts where people live for a while: *We set up camp near the river.* 2. live in a tent or a hut or outside: *The Boy Scouts camped out.* **camps; camped, camp ing.**

Camp Fire Girl a member of a group for girls. See the picture. **Camp Fire Girls.**

can¹ 1. be able to: *She can run fast.* 2. know how to: *She can read.* 3. have the right to: *Anyone can enter the contest.* **could.**

can² 1. a container of metal or glass. 2. keep by sealing tightly: *Did your aunt can some peaches?* **cans; canned, can ning.**

Can a da the country north of the United States. See the map on page 382.

Ca na di an 1. of Canada: *The Canadian flag has a maple leaf on it.* 2. a person born or living in Canada. **Ca na di ans.**

ca nary a small yellow bird. Canaries are good singers. **ca nar ies.**

can dle a stick of wax with a kind of string in it called a wick. As the wick burns, the candle gives light. **can dles.**

can dle nut tree a kukui. **can dle nut trees.**

can dy 1. sugar boiled with water or milk and cooled: *Most people like chocolate candy.* 2. a piece of candy: *One candy is on the plate.* **can dies.**

cane 1. a stick used to help you walk. 2. a plant with a long hard stem: *sugar cane.* See the picture. **canes** (for 1.).

ca noe a light boat moved with paddles. **ca noes.**

can't cannot.

can ta loupe or **can ta loup** a kind of sweet melon, having lots of juice. See the picture. **can ta loupes** or **can ta loups.**

can vas 1. a strong, coarse cloth. 2. made of canvas: *I am wearing canvas shoes.*

can yon a narrow valley with high, steep sides. See the picture. **can yons.**

cap 1. a soft covering for the head. 2. anything like a cap: *Most bottles have caps.* **caps.**

cape[1] a piece of clothing worn like a coat. A cape covers your arms but has no sleeves. **capes.**

cape[2] a point of land with water almost all around it. See the picture. **capes.**

cap i tal 1. the city where the government of a nation or state is located. Washington, D.C., is the capital of the United States. Each state has a capital. 2. A, B, C, D, or any large letter. **cap i tals.**

Cap i tol the building in a capital city in which laws are made. **Cap i tols.**

cane 2.

cantaloupe

canyon

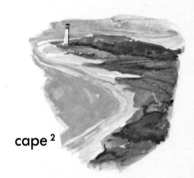
cape[2]

capsule

––––––––––

carpet

cardinal

carnation

carolers

cap sule 1. a small case or cover. Some seeds grow in capsules. 2. part of a rocket that goes into orbit. **cap sules.**

cap tain 1. the one who leads: *She is captain of the team.* 2. an officer in the armed forces. **cap tains.**

car a vehicle, such as an automobile, that can carry people and baggage. **cars.**

card a flat piece of stiff paper. **cards.**

car di nal a bright-red American bird. See the picture. The cardinal is the state bird of several states. **car di nals.**

care 1. great thought and attention: *A mother takes care of her baby. He did his school work with care.* 2. feel interest: *He cares more about football than anything.* **cares; cared, car ing.**

care ful 1. full of care for something; watching for or over: *Be careful crossing the street.* 2. done with care: *She does careful work.*

care ful ly in a careful way: *He opened the box carefully.*

care less not thinking or watching what you do: *The careless boy knocked over the vase.*

care less ly in a careless way: *She ran carelessly down the hall, bumping into people.*

car na tion a red, white, or pink flower. See the picture. **car na tions.**

car ol a song of joy. **car ols.**

car ol er one of a group of people who sing carols. See the picture. **car ol ers.**

car pen ter a person who builds things with wood. **car pen ters.**

car pet 1. a material used to cover floors. 2. a covering like a carpet: *a carpet of snow.* 3. cover with a carpet: *Leaves carpeted the ground.* **car pets; car pet ed, car pet ing.**

42

car ri er a person or thing that takes packages and messages from one place to another. **car ri ers.**

car rot a plant. Its orange-colored root is eaten as a vegetable. See the picture. **car rots.**

car ry take from one place to another: *He helped carry our packages home.* **car ried, car ry ing.**

cart 1. a wagon with two wheels. 2. a small box or frame on wheels, pushed by hand. See the picture. **carts.**

car ton a container made of heavy paper. A carton often holds smaller packages. **car tons.**

car toon a picture showing events that interest or amuse people: *The cartoon is funny.* **car toons.**

carve 1. cut into slices or pieces: *Father will carve the turkey.* 2. make by cutting: *He carved a statue from wood.* **carved, carv ing.**

case[1] some special state or time: *In case of fire, walk to the door. In case we're late, wait there.* **cas es.**

case[2] 1. something that holds or covers: *Put your glasses in this case.* 2. a box: *There is a case of canned fruit in the basement.* **cas es.**

cash 1. money. 2. give money for: *The bank will cash your check.* **cashed, cash ing.**

cash ier a person in charge of money: *Sue's mother is cashier in the bank.* **cash iers.**

cast 1. throw: *Cast your fishing line far out into the river.* 2. a case to shape something or keep it in place: *He has a cast on his broken arm.* 3. all the people in a play: *Do you know someone in the cast?* **cast, cast ing; casts.**

cas tle a large building or group of buildings with thick walls and towers. See the picture. **cas tles.**

cat a small animal often kept as a pet. **cats.**

cat

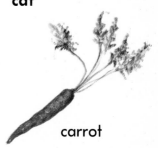

carrot

cart 1.

cart 2.

castle

caterpillar

cathedral

cauliflower

cedar tree

catch 1. take and hold something that is moving: *Try to catch the ball in the air.* 2. the act of catching: *She made a good catch in the ball game.* **caught, catch ing; catch es.**

catch er in baseball, a player who stands behind the batter. **catch ers.**

cat er pil lar the form in which insects such as the butterfly and the moth hatch from the egg. See the picture. **cat er pil lars.**

ca the dral a large or important church. See the picture. **ca the drals.**

cat sup a thick sauce made of tomatoes and spices: *Try some catsup on your hamburger.*

cat tle farm animals such as cows, steers, oxen.

caught See **catch**. *He caught more fish. He has caught many.*

cau li flow er a plant. It has a hard, white head that is eaten as a vegetable. See the picture.

cause 1. something that makes something else happen: *What was the cause of the fire?* 2. make happen: *A sudden noise caused me to jump.* **caus es; caused, caus ing.**

cave a hollow space under the ground. **caves.**

cav i ty a hole; a hollow place: *The dentist filled two cavities in my teeth.* **cav i ties.**

ce dar an evergreen tree with good-smelling wood. See the picture. **ce dars.**

ceil ing the top of a room; the part opposite the floor. **ceil ings.**

cel e brate do special things on a birthday or holiday: *We celebrated Thanksgiving by going to Grandmother's.* **cel e brat ed, cel e brat ing.**

cel e bra tion special things to do to celebrate something: *a birthday celebration.* **cel e bra tions.**

cel ery a plant. Its long green or white stalks are eaten as a vegetable. See the picture.

cell 1. a small room. 2. a small piece of living matter, from which animals and plants are made. 3. a container for materials that produce electricity: *This battery has two cells.* **cells.**

cel lar a space usually under a building and often used for storing food. **cel lars.**

cel lo a musical instrument with strings. It is like a violin, but very much larger. See the picture. **cel los.**

cent 1. the smallest amount of money of the United States and Canada: *This candy bar costs ten cents.* 2. a coin worth one cent; a penny. One hundred cents are equal to one dollar. **cents.**

cen ter 1. the point inside a circle that is the same distance from all points around the edge. See the picture. 2. the middle part: *the center of a room.* 3. a person in a middle position: *a center on the football team.* 4. a place people go: *a shopping center.* **cen ters.**

cen ti pede a small animal with many pairs of legs. See the picture. **cen ti pedes.**

ce re al 1. any grain that is used as food. Wheat, rice, and corn are cereals. 2. food made from the grain. Oatmeal and corn meal are cereals. **ce re als.**

cer e mon y a special act or set of acts to be done on special occasions such as weddings and holidays. **cer e mo nies.**

cer tain 1. sure: *I'm certain of this answer.* 2. some but not all: *Certain plants will grow in the desert.*

cer tain ly surely: *I will certainly be there.*

celery

---

certainly

celery

girl playing a cello

center 1.

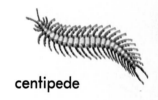

centipede

chain 1.

charm 2.

chain 1. metal rings joined together. See the picture. 2. fasten with a chain: *The dog was chained to a tree.* **chains; chained, chain ing.**

chair a seat with a back, often with arms. **chairs.**

chair man a chairperson. **chair men.**

chair per son the person who is in charge of a meeting or of a committee. **chair per sons.**

chair wom an a chairperson. **chair wom en.**

chalk a soft, white or gray limestone used for writing and drawing on a chalkboard.

chalk board a smooth surface on which you can write or draw with chalk. **chalk boards.**

chance something that may happen: *There is a chance of snow.* **chanc es.**

change 1. make different: *She changed the color of the wall from white to blue.* 2. put something in place of another: *Please change your shoes.* 3. act of changing: *There was a change in our plans.* 4. money you get back: *The clerk gave me five cents change.* **changed, chang ing; chang es.**

chap ter a part of a book. **chap ters.**

char ac ter a person in a story. **char ac ters.**

charge 1. ask as a price: *The grocer charged too much for eggs.* 2. buy now and pay for later: *Mother charged the things we bought.* 3. load; fill: *The battery in our car needs to be charged.* 4. **In charge of** means be at the head of or be the boss of. **charged, charg ing.**

charm 1. something special about a person or thing which delights or pleases: *An old-fashioned town has charm.* 2. a small object worn on a bracelet. See the picture. 3. please very much; delight: *The children were charmed by the baby ducks.* **charms; charmed, charm ing.**

charm ing very pleasant; able to charm.

chart 1. a map of the sea. 2. a picture or drawing that tells facts: *This chart tells which team won the most games.* **charts.**

chase run after to catch. **chased, chas ing.**

chat an easy, friendly talk. **chats.**

chat ter 1. talk a lot in a quick, foolish way. 2. make a rattling sound: *The cold made his teeth chatter.* **chat tered, chat ter ing.**

chauf feur a person whose work is driving a car for someone else. **chauf feurs.**

check 1. prove true or right by comparing: *Check your answers with hers.* 2. a mark (✓); a mark to show that something has been checked. 3. a written order for money from a bank account. **checked, check ing; checks.**

check er a person who checks things you buy at a supermarket. **check ers.**

cheek the side of the face below either eye. **cheeks.**

cheer 1. a good feeling; hope; joy. 2. give joy to: *Her visit cheered me.* **cheered, cheer ing.**

cheer ful 1. joyful; glad: *A cheerful person smiles a lot.* 2. pleasant: *Red is a cheerful color.*

cheer ful ly in a willing way; in a cheerful way: *He did the work cheerfully.*

cheese food made from milk. **chees es.**

cher ry 1. a small, round fruit with a pit. 2. the tree it grows on. See the picture. **cher ries.**

chest 1. the top, front part of your body. 2. a large box with a lid: *a tool chest.* **chests.**

chest nut 1. a sweet nut with a hard shell. 2. the tree it grows on. See the picture. **chest nuts.**

chew crush with the teeth. **chewed, chew ing.**

chick a dee a small bird with a cry that sounds like its name. See the picture. **chick a dees.**

cherry

chestnut

chickadee

chicken

choir

Chihuahua

chimney

chimpanzee

chipmunk

chick en 1. a young hen or rooster. 2. meat from a chicken: *We had chicken for dinner.* **chick ens.**

Chi hua hua a very small dog. See the picture. **Chi hua huas.**

child 1. a young boy or girl: *Where is that child?* 2. a son or daughter: *My parents had three children.* **chil dren.**

chim ney a tall column built to carry away smoke. See the picture. **chim neys.**

chim pan zee an animal like a large monkey. See the picture. **chim pan zees.**

chin 1. the part of your face below the mouth. 2. hang by your hands on a bar and pull your body up: *John can chin himself five times.* **chins; chinned, chin ning.**

chip 1. a small, thin piece cut or broken from something. 2. cut or break small pieces from: *She chipped the cup when she dropped it.* **chips; chipped, chip ping.**

chip munk a small, striped animal like a squirrel. See the picture. **chip munks.**

chirp 1. the short, sharp sound made by some small birds and insects. 2. make a short, sharp sound. **chirped, chirp ing; chirps.**

choc o late 1. a good-tasting powder made from the seeds of a certain tree. 2. a drink made of this powder: *hot chocolate.* 3. any kind of food with this taste: *chocolate ice cream, a chocolate cake with chocolate frosting.*

choice 1. the act of choosing: *She was very careful in her choice of friends.* 2. person or thing chosen: *This camera is my choice.* **choic es.**

choir a group of singers. **choirs.**

choke stop the breath by squeezing the throat or by blocking it with food. **choked, chok ing.**

choose take one instead of any other from a group: *Choose the color you like best.* **chose, cho sen, choos ing.**

chop 1. cut by hitting with something sharp: *The man chopped down a tree with an ax.* 2. cut into small pieces: *The cook chopped an onion.* 3. a piece of meat with a rib bone in it. **chopped, chop ping; chops.**

chose See **choose**. *I chose the biggest cookie.*

cho sen See **choose**. *Have you chosen a book?*

Christ mas December 25, a day when Christian people go to church and give gifts. **Christ mas es.**

chuck le 1. laugh to yourself. 2. a soft laugh; quiet laughter. **chuck led, chuck ling; chuck les.**

church a building in which some people worship. See the picture. **church es.**

churn 1. a machine that beats cream into butter. 2. beat cream into butter. **churns; churned, churn ing.**

ci der a drink made from the juice squeezed from apples: *Cider tastes good with a doughnut.*

cir cle 1. a line that is equally far at every point from the center. See the picture. 2. something like a circle: *Put your chairs in a circle.* **cir cles.**

cir cuit 1. a going around; a moving around: *The earth makes a circuit of the sun every year.* 2. the path or part of a path over which an electric current flows. A circuit brings electricity into your house so you can have electric light. **cir cuits.**

cir cus a show that travels from place to place. A circus has acrobats and clowns. **cir cus es.**

church

circle 1.

49

clam

boy playing a clarinet

claws of a bird

claws of an animal

city 1. a large, important town with many people living in it. 2. of or in a city: *Many city buildings are tall.* **cit ies.**

clam an animal with a soft body inside a hard shell. See the picture. **clams.**

clap 1. a sudden noise like thunder or the sound of hands struck together. 2. make such a noise with the hands: *They all clapped after the band played.* **claps; clapped, clap ping.**

clar i net a musical instrument that you play by blowing into it and pressing keys. See the picture. **clar i nets.**

class 1. a group of persons or things of the same kind. In airplanes some seats are first class. 2. a group of pupils taught together. **class es.**

class mate a member of the same class in school. **class mates.**

clat ter 1. a confused noise: *The clatter in the street woke me up.* 2. make a confused noise: *The truck clattered over the stones.* **clat tered, clat ter ing.**

claw a sharp nail like a hook on the foot of a bird or an animal. See the picture. **claws.**

clay a kind of earth that is sticky but becomes hard when it is baked.

clean 1. free from dirt: *clean clothes.* 2. make clean: *Please clean your shoes before you come in. Clean out the garage.* **clean er, clean est; cleaned, clean ing.**

clear 1. clean and free from anything that makes it hard to see: *You can see through clear glass.* 2. make clean and free: *Clear the table before you go out.* **clear er, clear est; cleared, clear ing.**

clear ing an open space in a forest. **clear ings.**

clear ly in a clear manner: *You cannot see clearly in the dark.*

clerk 1. a person who sells things in a store. 2. a person who does work in an office. 3. work as a clerk: *She clerks in a dress shop every Saturday.* **clerks; clerked, clerk ing.**

clev er 1. bright; having a good mind. 2. able to do something very well: *She is a clever artist.* **clev er er, clev er est.**

click 1. a short, sharp sound: *I heard a click as the quarter went down the coin slot.* 2. to make such a sound: *The key clicked in the lock.* **clicked, click ing; clicks.**

cliff a steep slope of rock. See the picture. **cliffs.**

climb 1. go up something too steep to walk up: *I climbed a tree.* 2. the act of climbing: *It was a long climb up the stairs.* **climbed, climb ing; climbs.**

cling stick or hold fast together: *The kitten was clinging to the narrow branch of the tree.* **clung, cling ing.**

clip¹ cut a person's hair or an animal's fur short: *The dog has been clipped.* **clipped, clip ping.**

clip² 1. fasten; hold together. 2. a thing used for holding papers together, often made of bent wire. See the picture. **clipped, clip ping; clips.**

clock an instrument for measuring time. Some clocks strike each hour. **clocks.**

clog fill up or choke up with something: *Leaves clogged the drain.* **clogged, clog ging.**

close¹ 1. shut: *Close the window.* 2. come or bring to an end: *The meeting closed with a speech.* 3. an end: *We left at the close of the meeting.* **closed, clos ing; clos es.** (Close¹ rhymes with rose.)

clearly

---

close

cliff

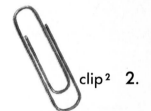

clip² 2.

cloud of dust

clover

clown

close² 1. without much space between: *The houses were built close together.* 2. near: *We live close to school.* 3. nearly equal: *We won, but it was a close game.* **clos er, clos est.** (Close² rhymes with dose.)

close ly with no difference; near: *The puppy closely followed its master.*

clos et a small room used for storing clothes and other things. **clos ets.**

cloth material woven from threads: *Clothes are made from cloth.* **cloths.**

clothes coverings for the body: *Dresses, pants, and shirts are clothes.*

cloth ing clothes.

cloud 1. a white or gray mass in the sky, made up of tiny drops of water. 2. a mass of dust or smoke: *The wind blew a cloud of dust across the field.* See the picture. **clouds.**

cloudy covered with clouds. **cloud i er, cloud i est.**

clo ver a plant with sweet-smelling red or white flowers. See the picture. **clo vers.**

clown a person whose business is making people laugh by wearing funny clothes and doing tricks. See the picture. **clowns.**

club 1. a heavy stick of wood. 2. a stick or bat used to hit a ball in some games. 3. a group of people joined together: *Kim belongs to the ski club.* **clubs.**

clue something that helps solve a mystery. **clues.**

clung See **cling.** *He clung to the boat. He has clung to it for hours.*

coach 1. a vehicle pulled by horses, used to carry passengers before railroads were built. 2. a person who teaches or trains people. 3. train or teach. **coach es; coached, coach ing.**

coal 1. black material that burns and gives off heat. 2. a piece of burned wood or coal, still red-hot: *We cooked hot dogs over the coals of our fire.* **coals** (for 2.).

coarse not fine; made up of somewhat large parts or grains: *coarse sand.* **coars er, coars est.**

coast 1. the land along the sea; the shore. See the picture. 2. slide down a hill on a sled. **coasts; coast ed, coast ing.**

coast er one of the cars on a roller coaster. **coast ers.**

Coast Guard the armed force that guards the coasts of the United States. See the picture.

Coast Guards man a member of the United States Coast Guard. **Coast Guards men.**

coat 1. a piece of clothing worn over other clothes. 2. any covering, such as a dog's hair: *Prince has a thick coat.* 3. a thin layer: *This house needs a coat of paint.* **coats.**

coax try by soft words and pleasant ways to make someone do something: *We coaxed the kitten to drink the milk.* **coaxed, coax ing.**

cob bler 1. a person whose business is mending shoes. 2. a fruit pie baked in a deep dish. **cob blers.**

cock er span iel a small dog with long, silky hair. See the picture. **cock er span iels.**

co coa 1. a powder much like chocolate. 2. a drink made from this powder.

co co nut or **co coa nut** 1. the large fruit of one kind of palm tree. It has a hard brown shell, but the inside of the shell is white and good to eat. 2. the tree it grows on. See the picture. **co co nuts** or **co coa nuts.**

coal

coconut

coast 1.

seal of
the U. S. Coast Guard

cocker spaniel

coconut

cocoon

collie

co coon the silky case spun by caterpillars to live in while they are turning into moths or butterflies. See the picture. **co coons.**

code 1. the laws of a country or of a group. 2. words or numerals used to write a secret message. 3. signals for sending messages. **codes.**

cof fee tree a tree with seeds in long, thin pods.

coin a piece of metal used as money, such as a penny, a nickel, a dime, or a quarter. **coins.**

cold 1. less warm than the body: *cold water, a cold wind.* 2. a low temperature: *Come in out of the cold.* 3. a sickness that causes your nose to run. **cold er, cold est; colds** (for 3.).

col lar the part of a coat, a dress, or a shirt that makes a band around the neck. **col lars.**

col lect bring together; come together; gather together: *He collects coins. A crowd soon collected at the fire.* **col lect ed, col lect ing.**

col lec tion 1. a group of things gathered from many places and belonging together: *a stamp collection.* 2. money given by different people: *We took up a collection for the sick man.* **col lec tions.**

col lec tor one who collects. **col lec tors.**

col lege a school beyond high school that gives degrees or diplomas. **col leg es.**

col lie a large dog. See the picture. **col lies.**

col or 1. red, yellow, blue, or any of them mixed together: *I have eight colors in my paint box.* 2. give color to; paint: *Color the sky blue and the grass green.* **col ors; col ored, col or ing.**

Col o rado one of the fifty states of the United States. See page 333.

colt a young horse or donkey. **colts.**

col um bine a plant with flowers. See the picture. **col um bines.**

Co lum bus Day a holiday in October. **Co lum bus Days.**

col umn 1. a thick, tall post or pole used to hold up a roof or a part of a building. See the picture. 2. anything like a column: *a column of numbers, a column of smoke from the chimney.* 3. a special part of a newspaper: *I always read the baseball column.* **col umns.**

comb 1. an instrument with teeth, used to arrange the hair or to hold it in place. 2. arrange with a comb: *Comb your hair every morning before you go to school.* 3. the thick, red part on the top of a chicken's head. See the picture. **combs; combed, comb ing.**

come 1. move toward: *Come over to me.* 2. get near or to a place: *Will the girls come to your house?* 3. take place; happen: *Winter has not come yet.* **came, come, com ing.**

com fort a ble 1. giving comfort: *A soft, warm bed is comfortable.* 2. free from pain or hardship: *We felt comfortable in the sun.*

com ic 1. funny. 2. **Comics** means a funny or exciting story told by pictures. **com ics.**

com ma a mark (,) of punctuation. **com mas.**

com mand 1. an order: *The dog won't move until a command is given.* 2. give an order to: *The king commanded his soldiers to halt.* **com mands; com mand ed, com mand ing.**

com mon often seen or found: *Snow is common here.* **com mon er, com mon est.**

com mu ni cate give and receive facts, news, and ideas. There are many ways to communicate. **com mu ni cat ed, com mu ni cat ing.**

columbine

---

communicate

columbine

column 1.

comb 1.

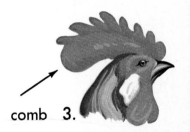

comb 3.

compass 1.

compass 2.

com mu ni ca tion 1. giving facts or news by speaking or writing: *Communication by telephone saves time.* 2. a letter or message: *She received a communication from her uncle.* **com mu ni ca tions.**

com mu ni ty a group of people living together. A neighborhood or a town or a nation can be a community. **com mu ni ties.**

com pa ny 1. a group of people joined together to run a business or put on a play. 2. a visitor or visitors: *Our company stayed for dinner.* **com pa nies.**

com pare find out or point out how persons or things are alike: *The girls compared their new red coats.* **com pared, com par ing.**

com pass 1. an instrument that shows directions. 2. an instrument for drawing circles and for measuring distances. See the picture. **com pass es.**

com pete try to win: *We are all competing for the prize.* **com pet ed, com pet ing.**

com pe ti tion 1. trying hard to win or gain something: *There is competition in many games.* 2. contest: *They won the music competition.* **com pe ti tions.**

com plain say that something is wrong; find fault: *He complains about the food.* **com plained, com plain ing.**

com plete 1. having all parts; whole: *a complete set of dishes.* 2. make whole: *They completed the puzzle.* 3. get to the end of: *She completed the task.* 4. finished; done: *My collection is complete.* **com plet ed, com plet ing.**

com plete ly in a complete way: *The glass is completely empty.*

com pute count or figure up: *We computed the number of miles we had traveled.* **com put ed, com put ing.**

com put er a machine that computes. *A computer can store many facts.* **com put ers.**

con cern 1. have to do with: *This letter does not concern you.* 2. be interested and worried: *We are all concerned about forest fires.* 3. an interest and a worry: *The teacher showed concern for pupils who were absent.* **con cerned, con cern ing; con cerns.**

con cert a performance in which musicians play or sing. **con certs.**

con crete 1. cement, sand, and water mixed and dried into a hard mass. 2. made of concrete: *a concrete sidewalk.*

con duct 1. the way someone behaves: *Her conduct was good.* 2. manage; direct: *He stepped forward to conduct the orchestra.* 3. guide or lead: *She conducted us on a trip through the building.* **con duct ed, con duct ing.**

con duc tor 1. a guide or one who leads. 2. a person in charge of a train. 3. a material through which electricity moves: *Copper wire is used as a conductor of electricity.* **con duc tors.**

cone 1. a shape having a flat, round base and a point at the top. 2. anything shaped like a cone: *an ice-cream cone.* 3. the part that bears seeds on some trees. See the picture. **cones.**

con fess admit: *He confessed that he ate all the candy.* **con fessed, con fess ing.**

con fuse 1. mix up: *The directions confused me.* 2. be unable to tell apart; mistake one thing for another: *Her jacket is often confused with mine.* **con fused, con fus ing.**

cone 1.

cone 3.

connect

---

contraction

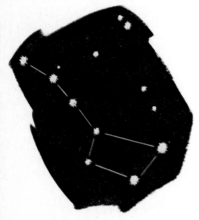

constellation
the Big Dipper

con nect join one thing to another; fasten together: *The firemen connected the hose to the hydrant.* **con nect ed, con nect ing.**

Con nect i cut one of the fifty states of the United States. See page 334.

con ser va tion protecting from being lost or being used up or being wasted: *Our class is interested in the conservation of clean air.*

con so nant any letter of the alphabet that is not a vowel. **con so nants.**

con stel la tion a group of stars such as the Big Dipper. See the picture. **con stel la tions.**

con struc tion 1. act of building; putting together: *The construction of the bridge took nearly a month.* 2. way in which a thing is constructed: *Cracks and leaks are signs of poor construction.*

con tain 1. have within itself; hold inside: *This box contains soap.* 2. be equal to: *A quart contains two pints.* **con tained, con tain ing.**

con tain er anything that can contain or hold something inside itself. Boxes, dishes, cartons, and bottles are containers. **con tain ers.**

con tent ed feel happy and satisfied: *Were you contented with the way the story ended?*

con test a test to see who will win: *I won the spelling contest.* **con tests.**

con ti nent one of the large masses of land on the earth. There are seven continents. **con ti nents.**

con tin ue 1. go on; not stop: *The baby continued to cry.* 2. take up; carry on: *Can we continue this game tomorrow?* **con tin ued, con tin u ing.**

con trac tion a short form. "Don't" is a contraction of "do not." **con trac tions.**

con trol 1. the power over: *A driver must not lose control of his car.* 2. have power over: *A driver must control his car every minute.* 3. hold back; keep down: *Please control your laughter.* 4. a lever or switch that controls a machine. 5. **The controls** of an airplane are instruments a pilot uses to fly it. See the picture. **con trols; con trolled, con trol ling.**

cook 1. prepare food by heating: *I cooked eggs for breakfast.* 2. be cooked: *Let the soup cook for an hour.* 3. a person who cooks. **cooked, cook ing; cooks.**

cook ie or **cooky** a small, flat, sweet cake. **cook ies.**

cool 1. more cold than hot: *a cool day.* 2. giving a cool feeling: *a cool dress.* 3. not excited; calm: *Keep a cool head.* **cool er, cool est.**

coop a small cage or pen for chickens or rabbits. See the picture. **coops.**

cop per 1. a somewhat red metal. 2. made of copper: *a copper kettle.*

copy 1. a thing made to be just like another: *This is a copy of a famous picture.* 2. make something like something else: *Copy this picture.* 3. one of a number of the same book or magazine: *Do you have a copy of the May magazine?* **cop ies; cop ied, cop y ing.**

cor al 1. a hard red, pink, or white material, made up of the skeletons of tiny sea animals and often used for jewelry. See the picture. 2. made of coral: *I have a coral necklace.*

cord 1. a thick, strong string; a very thin rope. 2. a pair of wires covered with rubber, used to connect an appliance or a lamp with the electric current. **cords.**

the controls
of an airplane

chicken coop

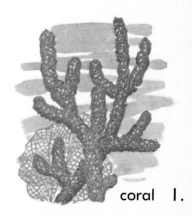

coral 1.

59

cotton

corn

girl playing a cornet

cotton   1.

cor du roy 1. a kind of thick cloth. 2. made of corduroy: *Many people wear corduroy jackets.*

cork 1. the bark of a kind of oak tree. 2. a piece of cork or other material that keeps liquid from running out of a bottle. **corks** (for 2.).

corn 1. a grain. Corn is eaten as a vegetable. 2. the plant that it grows on. See the picture.

cor ner 1. the place where two lines or surfaces meet: *the corner of a room.* 2. the place where two streets meet. 3. for or in a corner: *a corner cupboard.* **cor ners.**

cor net a musical instrument that you play by blowing into it and pressing keys. See the picture. **cor nets.**

cor ral a pen for horses and stock. **cor rals.**

cor rect 1. without any mistakes: *the correct answer.* 2. mark the mistakes in: *The teacher corrected our papers.* **cor rect ed, cor rect ing.**

cor rect ly in a correct way: *She wrote all the words correctly.*

cor ri dor a long hall; a long space in a building. **cor ri dors.**

cost 1. the price paid: *The cost of this magazine is fifty cents.* 2. be bought at the price of; require: *This magazine costs fifty cents. The one I bought yesterday cost twenty-five cents. Some have cost a dollar.* **costs; cost, cost ing.**

cos tume clothes; what a person is wearing: *In our play I wore a king's costume.* **cos tumes.**

cot a narrow bed. Some cots fold up. **cots.**

cot tage a small house. **cot tag es.**

cot ton 1. the soft white part of a plant used in making cloth. 2. the plant. See the picture. 3. the cloth made of this soft white material. 4. made of cotton: *We bought cotton curtains.*

cot ton wood a kind of poplar tree. See the picture. **cot ton woods.**

cough 1. blow air from the lungs with sudden force and noise: *He coughed all night.* 2. the act of coughing: *He has a bad cough.* **coughed, cough ing; coughs.**

could was able; was able to: *She wouldn't sew even if she could. She could swim. They asked if I could go with them.*

could n't could not.

coun cil a group of people chosen to settle any questions or to manage a city. **coun cils.**

count 1. name numbers in order: *He can count to one hundred.* 2. add up: *He counted the pennies.* 3. be of value: *What we do counts more than what we say.* **count ed, count ing.**

count er a long table, or some shelves covered with glass. A clerk stands behind the counter to sell things. See the picture. **count ers.**

coun try 1. land: *There are farms in the country.* 2. all the land of a nation: *Mai-Ling came from a country far away.* 3. of or in the country: *country air.* **coun tries.**

coun ty a place or government larger than a town but smaller than a state. **coun ties.**

cou ple 1. two things of the same kind that go together. 2. a man and a woman who are married. 3. two partners in a dance. **cou ples.**

cou pon a slip of paper that you can trade for something. **cou pons.**

cour age being able to meet danger instead of running away from it: *It takes courage to rescue someone from a burning house.*

course 1. the direction taken: *Our course was east.* 2. **Of course** means certainly. **cours es.**

cottonwood tree

a candy counter

tennis court

cowboy

coyote

crab

court 1. a place where games such as tennis and basketball are played. See the picture. 2. a place where a king or a queen lives. 3. a place where a judge decides questions of law. **courts.**

cous in the son or daughter of your uncle or aunt. **cous ins.**

cov er 1. put something over: *Cover the child with a blanket.* 2. be over: *Dust covered the furniture.* 3. spread over: *She covered her toast with jelly.* 4. anything that protects or hides: *a book cover.* **cov ered, cov er ing; cov ers.**

cov er ing anything that covers: *A blanket is a covering for a bed. Hair is a covering for your head.* **cov er ings.**

cow 1. a large farm animal that gives milk. 2. a female elephant or buffalo. **cows.**

cow ard a person who does not have courage; one who is easily frightened. **cow ards.**

cow boy a person who looks after cattle on a ranch. See the picture. **cow boys.**

co-work er person who works with another. *You should try to get along with your co-workers.* **co-work ers.**

coy o te a small wolf. See the picture. **coy o tes** or **coy o te.**

crab a water animal, used for food. See the picture. **crabs.**

crack 1. a long, narrow break in something: *There is a crack in the window.* 2. break without separating into parts: *Who cracked this cup?* 3. a sudden, sharp noise like that made by loud thunder. 4. break with a sharp noise: *We cracked nuts all afternoon.* **cracks; cracked, crack ing.**

crack er a thin, crisp biscuit. **crack ers.**

cra dle a baby's crib, usually one that rocks.
cra dles.

crane 1. a machine for lifting and moving heavy
things. 2. a large bird that lives near water.
See the picture. **cranes.**

crash 1. a sudden, loud noise like many dishes
falling and breaking. 2. make a loud, sudden
noise: *The lamp crashed when it fell.* **crash es;**
crashed, crash ing.

crate 1. a large box made of strips of wood,
used to ship things that might break. See the
picture. 2. pack in a crate for shipping: *The
movers crated our piano.* **crates; crat ed,**
crat ing.

crawl 1. move slowly, pulling the body along:
We watched a caterpillar crawl along the leaf.
2. move slowly on hands and knees: *The
boy crawled through the tall grass.* **crawled,**
crawl ing.

cray fish a water animal that looks like a small
lobster. See the picture. **cray fish es** or
cray fish.

cray on a stick or pencil of colored chalk or wax
for drawing or writing. **cray ons.**

cra zy having a sick mind. **cra zi er, cra zi est.**

creak squeak loudly: *The door creaked when it
opened.* **creaked, creak ing.**

cream the oily, yellowish part of milk: *Put cream
on your cereal.*

crea ture any living person or animal. **crea tures.**

creek a small stream of water; a brook. **creeks.**

creep move slowly with the body close to the
ground or floor; crawl. **crept, creep ing.**

crept See **creep.** *The baby crept across the
room. She has crept through the whole house.*

cradle

_____

crept

crane 1.

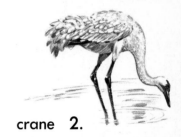

crane 2.

crate 1.

crayfish

63

crib 1.

crib 3.

cricket

crocus

crew 1. the people needed to do the work on a ship or to row a boat: *The crew takes down the sails.* 2. a group of people working together: *a train crew.* **crews.**

crib 1. a small bed with bars on the sides so a baby cannot fall out. 2. a frame to hold feed for animals. 3. a building for keeping grain. See the picture. **cribs.**

crick et a black insect that makes a loud sound. See the picture. **crick ets.**

crisp hard and thin; easy to break. Crackers are crisp. Lettuce is crisp. **crisp er, crisp est.**

croak 1. the deep, scraping, hoarse sound made by a frog or a crow. 2. make that deep, hoarse sound. **croaks; croaked, croak ing.**

cro cus a small plant that blooms early in spring and has white, yellow, or purple flowers. See the picture. **cro cus es.**

crook ed 1. not straight; bent; curved; twisted: *a crooked stick, a crooked road.* 2. not honest.

crop plants grown for people to use: *Alfalfa is a crop grown for cattle feed.* **crops.**

cross 1. a stick with another across it to form a T or an X. 2. mark with an X or draw a line through: *He crossed out his mistake.* 3. move from one side to another: *We will cross a bridge.* 4. make the sign of a cross: *The woman crossed herself.* 5. not feeling happy: *The baby was cross because he was hungry.* **cross es; crossed, cross ing; cross er, cross est.**

cross ing 1. a place at which railroad tracks cross a road. 2. a place to cross the street. **cross ings.**

cross ly in a cross manner: *She spoke crossly because we annoyed her.*

crow[1] 1. the loud cry of a rooster. 2. make this cry: *The rooster crowed and woke us up.* **crows; crowed, crow ing.**

crow[2] a large, shiny black bird with a loud cry. See the picture. **crows.**

crowd 1. a large number of people or things together. 2. collect or gather in large numbers: *Don't crowd around the swimming pool.* **crowds; crowd ed, crowd ing.**

crown a head covering for a king or queen. **crowns.**

cru el wanting to hurt others: *The dog had a cruel master.* **cru el er, cru el est.**

cru el ly in a cruel manner.

crumb a tiny bit broken from a larger piece: *A crumb of bread fell on the floor.* **crumbs.**

crunch 1. crush noisily with the teeth: *I like to crunch radishes.* 2. make such a sound: *The stones crunched under the wheels of the car.* **crunched, crunch ing.**

crush 1. squeeze or be squeezed together very hard in order to break: *The box was crushed in the mail.* 2. break into fine pieces by grinding, pounding, or pressing. **crushed, crush ing.**

crust 1. the hard outside part of bread. 2. the bottom and top coverings of pies. 3. any hard covering: *The snow had a crust on top.* **crusts.**

cry 1. call loudly: *She cried, "Look out!"* 2. a loud call: *We heard the child's cry for help.* 3. make a noise, usually with tears: *Babies cry.* **cried, cry ing; cries.**

cub a baby bear, lion, or other large animal. See the picture. **cubs.**

cube a block with six square faces, or sides, all of equal size. See the picture. **cubes.**

crow

---

cube

crow[2]

bear cub

cube

---

currant

Cub Scout

cupboard

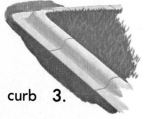

curb 3.

currants

Cub Scout a member of the Boy Scouts of America. Cub Scouts are between eight and eleven years old. See the picture. **Cub Scouts.**

cud dle 1. hold close in one's arms or lap: *I cuddled the kitten*. 2. lie close; curl up: *The two puppies cuddled together in front of the fire*. **cud dled, cud dling.**

cun ning 1. smart or sly in getting what you want, or in escaping from an enemy: *The cunning fox hid under a bush*. 2. clever in doing: *With cunning hands he shaped the clay*. **cun ning er, cun ning est.**

cup 1. a dish to drink from, usually with high sides and a handle. 2. something shaped like a cup. **cups.**

cup board a closet or piece of furniture with shelves. See the picture. **cup boards.**

cup cake a very small round cake. **cup cakes.**

curb 1. a chain or strap fastened to a horse's bit. The curb makes the horse stop. 2. hold back: *That child can't curb his laughing in class.* 3. the raised edge of a sidewalk or street. See the picture. **curbs; curbed, curb ing.**

cu ri ous 1. eager to know: *The curious kitten poked its nose into the basket.* 2. strange; odd: *I found a curious old hat in the attic.*

curl 1. twist into rings: *Please help Ann curl her hair.* 2. twist out of shape: *Curl up in a big chair.* 3. a lock of hair twisted into rings. **curled, curl ing; curls.**

curly curling: *curly hair.* **curl i er, curl i est.**

cur rant 1. a small, sour, red, white, or black berry, used for jelly. 2. the bush it grows on. See the picture. **cur rants.**

cur rent 1. a flow: *The river has a strong current.* 2. a flow of electricity through a wire. **cur rents.**

cur tain 1. cloth or other material hung at windows or doors. 2. in a theater, a screen that hangs between the stage and the audience. See the picture. **cur tains.**

curve 1. a line that has no straight part. 2. form a line that has no straight part: *The road curves to the left.* 3. a bend: *That curve in the road is dangerous.* **curves; curved, curv ing.**

cush ion 1. a soft pillow or pad for a bed or chair, used to sit, lie, or kneel on. 2. anything that makes a soft place: *Falling in a cushion of snow is fun.* **cush ions.**

cus to di an a person who takes care of a building or guards something. **cus to di ans.**

cus tom er a person who buys items in a store or supermarket. **cus tom ers.**

cut 1. separate or take away with something sharp: *Cut the grass.* 2. make by cutting: *He cut a hole through the paper.* 3. a hole made by a knife or sharp tool. 4. make such a hole; hurt with a sharp tool: *She has cut her thumb.* 5. A **short cut** is a quicker way. **cut, cut ting; cuts.**

cute 1. pleasant and dear: *He is a cute baby.* 2. clever; cunning. **cut er, cut est.**

cy clone 1. a storm with very strong wind. 2. a storm moving around a calm center. **cy clones.**

cym bal one of a pair of brass plates that are struck together to make a ringing sound. See the picture. **cym bals.**

cy press an evergreen tree that grows in swamps. See the picture. **cy press es.**

cypress

curtains

boy playing cymbals

cypress tree

dangerously

dachshund

daffodil

daisy

dam

D   d

D or **d** the fourth letter of the alphabet. **D's** or **d's.**

dachs hund a small dog with a long body. See the picture. **dachs hunds.**

dad another word for father. **dads, dad dy.**

daf fo dil a yellow or white spring flower grown from a bulb. See the picture. **daf fo dils.**

dai ly 1. done or happening every day: *a daily walk, a daily newspaper.* 2. every day; day by day: *We go to school daily.*

dairy a place where milk, cream, butter, and cheese are made or sold. **dair ies.**

dai sy a wild flower, usually white with a yellow center. See the picture. **dai sies.**

dam a wall built to hold back water. See the picture. **dams.**

damp a little wet: *Use a damp cloth to dust the furniture.* **damp er, damp est.**

dance 1. move in time with music: *Does she dance well?* 2. steps taken in time with music: *She learned a new dance.* 3. a party where people dance. **danced, danc ing; danc es.**

danc er a person who dances. **danc ers.**

dan de li on a weed with bright-yellow flowers. **dan de li ons.**

dan ger 1. a chance of harm; being near to harm: *The men were in danger when rocks fell.* 2. a thing that may cause harm: *Cars and trucks are a danger to children.* **dan gers.**

dan ger ous able to cause harm; not safe.

dan ger ous ly in a dangerous way: *The car skidded dangerously.*

dare 1. be bold; be bold enough: *He would not dare to climb the tree.* 2. ask someone to prove that he or she is not afraid to do something: *I dare you to dive into the pool.* **dared** or **durst, dared, dar ing.**

dark 1. without light: *Our closet is dark.* 2. nearly black in color: *She has dark hair.* 3. gloomy: *It was a dark day because the sun didn't shine.* 4. darkness: *Come back after dark.* **dark er, dark est.**

dark ness being dark; having no light.

dart 1. a thin, pointed object thrown by the hand. See the picture. 2. move suddenly and swiftly: *The fish darted away.* **darts; dart ed, dart ing.**

dash 1. rush: *They dashed down the street to catch the bus.* 2. a small bit: *We put a dash of pepper in the soup.* **dashed, dash ing; dash es.**

date[1] 1. the day, month, or year: *What is the date today? October 12, 1492, is the date on which America was discovered.* 2. put the date on: *I dated my letter January 3.* 3. a plan for a certain time: *She made a date to see the dentist.* **dates; dat ed, dat ing.**

date[2] 1. the sweet fruit of a kind of palm tree. 2. the tree it grows on. See the picture. **dates.**

daugh ter a girl who is the child of her father and mother: *Mr. and Mrs. Jones have three daughters.* **daugh ters.**

dawn the first part of day; the first light in the east: *In summer dawn comes early.* **dawns.**

day 1. the time of light between sunrise and sunset: *Days are getting shorter in November.* 2. the 24 hours between two midnights. **days.**

day light light of day; dawn.

dart 1.

date[2]

day time the time of day when it is light.

dead with life gone: *Why are the flowers in my garden dead?*

deaf 1. not able to hear. 2. not willing to hear: *The ruler was deaf to all that the people asked.* **deaf er, deaf est.**

deal 1. carry on business; buy and sell: *This store deals in clothing and furniture.* 2. a bargain: *Mom and Dad got a good deal on a car.* 3. part; amount: *A great deal of her time is spent reading.* **dealt, deal ing; deals.**

dear much loved: *His goldfish was very dear to him. She is a dear friend of our family.* **dear er, dear est.**

dear ly very much: *She loves her sister dearly.*

De cem ber the twelfth month of the year. *December has 31 days.* **De cem bers.**

de cide settle or agree on something: *We decided to stay home.* **de cid ed, de cid ing.**

deck one of the floors of a ship. **decks.**

de clare say; make known; say openly or strongly: *She declared that she'd do the job herself.* **de clared, de clar ing.**

de code translate secret writing from code into ordinary language. **de cod ed, de cod ing.**

deep 1. going a long way down from the top: *The snow is deep in our back yard.* 2. low: *The man had a deep voice.* **deep er, deep est.**

deep ly in a deep manner: *The boys breathed deeply as they ran.*

deer

deer a fast-moving animal. *The male deer has antlers.* See the picture. **deer.**

de fense anything that guards or protects: *A shot is a defense against measles. The bear came to the defense of her cub.* **de fens es.**

def i nite ly 1. in a definite manner: *Say definitely what you have in mind.* 2. certainly: *I definitely want to go.*

def i ni tion the words that tell what something is or what a word means. **def i ni tions.**

Del a ware one of the fifty states of the United States. See page 335.

de lay 1. put off: *Shall we delay our vacation until spring?* 2. putting off until a later time: *This delay will make us late for school.* 3. make late: *Rain delayed the game for ten minutes.* **de layed, de lay ing; de lays.**

de li cious very pleasing or satisfying to taste or smell: *We bought a delicious cake.*

de light 1. great pleasure; joy: *Her visit was a delight to the patients.* 2. please greatly: *A picnic delights children.* **de lights; de light ed, de light ing.**

de liv er 1. carry and give out: *The girl delivers newspapers.* 2. give up; hand over: *He delivered the birthday present.* **de liv ered, de liv er ing.**

de mand ask for in a firm manner: *My parents demand the truth.* **de mand ed, de mand ing.**

den 1. a wild animal's home: *a bear's den.* See the picture. 2. a small room. **dens.**

dent 1. a hollow made by a blow or pressure: *A blow of the hammer made a dent in the steel door.* 2. make a dent in: *That car dented the fender of the car behind.* **dents; dent ed, dent ing.**

den tist a person whose business is to care for people's teeth. **den tists.**

de part ment a separate part of some store, government, or business. The fire department is a part of a city government. **de part ments.**

den 1.

71

depend

---

develop

depot 1.

desert

desk

de pend 1. trust: *You can depend on the alarm clock to ring.* 2. be a result of: *Health depends on many things.* 3. get help from: *Children depend on their parents.* **de pend ed, de pend ing.**

de pot 1. a railroad station. See the picture. 2. a place where things are stored. **de pots.**

de scribe tell in words how someone or something looks, feels, or acts. **de scribed, de scrib ing.**

des ert land without water and trees, usually hot in the daytime. See the picture. **des erts.**

de serve have a right to; be worthy of: *A hard worker deserves good pay.* **de served, de serv ing.**

de sire 1. a wish: *Her desire is to be a great scientist.* 2. wish for very much: *You may have what you desire.* **de sires; de sired, de sir ing.**

desk a piece of furniture with a slanting or flat top on which to write. See the picture. **desks.**

des sert sweet food such as pie, cake, ice cream, or fruit served at the end of a meal. **des serts.**

de stroy 1. break to pieces; spoil; make no good: *The car was destroyed when the tree fell on it.* 2. kill: *The fire destroyed the trees and plants.* **de stroyed, de stroy ing.**

de tec tive a person whose business is to get facts and solve mysteries. **de tec tives.**

de tour 1. a road that is used when the main road is closed. 2. use a detour: *The police detoured traffic around the accident.* **de tours; de toured, de tour ing.**

de vel op 1. grow; bring or come into being: *Will a plant develop from this seed?* 2. treat film to make the picture: *We'll see the pictures when the film is developed.* **de vel oped, de vel op ing.**

dew water that comes from the air and collects in small drops on cool surfaces during the night.

di al 1. an instrument used to measure something. It has a pointer that moves across a face like the face of a clock or compass. 2. the knob on a radio or television for tuning in to a station. 3. the part of a telephone used to call a number. See the picture. 4. call by turning a dial: *He dialed a number.* **di als; di aled, di al ing.**

dia mond 1. a stone of great value. 2. a figure (◇). 3. part of a baseball field. **dia monds.**

dic tion ary a book in which words are listed alphabetically. A dictionary tells what words mean. **dic tion ar ies.**

did See **do**. *Did he see them yesterday? Yes, he did. She said she did not do it.*

did n't did not.

die 1. stop living; become dead. 2. lose force; come to an end: *The noise died away.* **died, dy ing.**

dif fer not be like: *My ideas differed from hers.* **dif fered, dif fer ing.**

dif fer ence 1. not being alike: *There is a great difference between night and day.* 2. what is left after subtracting one number from another: *The difference between 15 and 7 is 8.* **dif fer enc es.**

dif fer ent not alike; separate: *These flowers are all different. She asked three different questions.*

dif fer ent ly not in the same way: *They all told the same story but each one told it differently.*

dif fi cult hard to do or understand: *Arithmetic is difficult for some people.*

dig 1. make a hole in or turn over the ground: *Dig a ditch.* 2. make or get by digging: *Dig clams.* **dug, dig ging.**

dial 1.

dial 2.

dial 3.

U.S. dime

Canadian dime

dinosaur

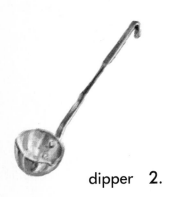

dipper 2.

dime a coin in the United States and Canada, worth ten cents. See the picture. **dimes.**

dine eat dinner: *We dined at a restaurant.* **dined, din ing.**

din ner the main meal of the day: *Some people have dinner at night.* **din ners.**

di no saur a reptile that lived many, many years ago. See the picture. No dinosaur is alive today. **di no saurs.**

dip 1. put under water or any liquid and lift out quickly. 2. go under water and come out quickly. **dipped, dip ping.**

di plo ma cy skill in getting along with people: *He used diplomacy to get what he wanted.* **di plo ma cies.**

dip per 1. a thing that dips. 2. a cup with a long handle. A dipper is used to lift water or other liquids from a pail or kettle. See the picture. **dip pers.**

di rect 1. manage; guide: *The conductor directed the orchestra.* 2. command: *The fire captain directed the people to get out of the building.* 3. show or tell the way: *Can you direct us to the zoo?* **di rect ed, di rect ing.**

di rec tion 1. the control of; the act of directing: *The school play is under the direction of our teacher.* 2. the act of telling where to go or how to do: *Can you give me directions to the park? Follow the directions on the box.* 3. any way in which one may face or point. North, south, east, and west are directions. **di rec tions.**

dirt 1. mud, dust, earth, or anything like them: *Don't get dirt on your shirt.* 2. loose earth or soil: *The dirt in our garden is very good for growing flowers.*

dirty not clean; soiled by mud, dust, earth, or anything like them. **dirt i er, dirt i est.**

dis ap pear 1. pass out of sight: *The ship disappeared in the fog.* 2. be gone or lost: *Snow disappears in the spring.* **dis ap peared, dis ap pear ing.**

dis cov er find out; see for the first time: *Someone discovered gold in California.* **dis cov ered, dis cov er ing.**

dis ease any special kind of sickness: *Measles is a disease many children have. A disease is killing all the elm trees.* **dis eas es.**

dish 1. a container for food. See the picture. *We eat from dishes.* 2. food served: *My favorite dish is pie.* **dish es.**

dis mount get off something such as a horse or a bicycle. **dis mount ed, dis mount ing.**

dis tance 1. the space in between: *The distance from our farm to the town is five miles.* 2. being far away: *The farm is at a distance from any railroad.* 3. a place far away: *The sailors saw a light in the distance.* **dis tanc es.**

dis tant 1. far away in space: *The stars are distant from the earth.* 2. not close: *a distant relative.*

Dis trict of Co lum bia the land covered by the city of Washington, capital of the United States. The District of Columbia is not part of any state. See page 378.

dis turb 1. destroy the peace, quiet, or rest of: *The bad news disturbed me.* 2. break in upon with noise or change: *If you disturb the baby, he will wake up.* **dis turbed, dis turb ing.**

ditch a long, narrow place dug along the edge of a road to carry off water. See the picture. **ditch es.**

dishes

ditch

dive

dog

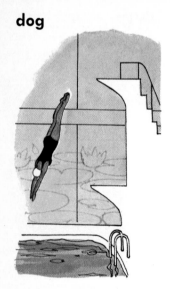

girl diving

dock   1.

dive   1. plunge head first into water. See the picture. 2. the act of diving: *a perfect dive.*
dived or **dove, dived, div ing; dives.**

div er one who dives. **div ers.**

di vide   1. separate into parts: *Divide the orange in fourths. When you divide 10 by 2, you get 5.*
2. give some to each; share: *The children divided the peanuts.* **di vid ed, di vid ing.**

di vi sion   1. being divided; dividing: *The division of the class into teams took time.* 2. dividing numbers: *I can't do long division.* **di vi sions.**

diz zy ready to fall, stumble, or spin around; not steady. **diz zi er, diz zi est.**

do   1. carry to an end an action or a piece of work: *Try to do your work quickly.* 2. act; behave: *The boys do very well in school.* **3. Do** is used to make what you say stronger or to ask questions: *I do want to hear her sing. Do you like apples?* **does, did, done, do ing.**

dock   1. a platform built out from the shore for boats to tie up. See the picture. 2. bring to a dock: *The boys docked the sailboat.* **docks; docked, dock ing.**

doc tor a person whose business is to treat and cure the sick. **doc tors.**

doe a female deer, antelope, rabbit, or hare. **does.** (Does rhymes with rose.)

does See **do.** Use *does* when you speak of *he, she,* or *it: He does his work well. Does she like milk? Does it matter? She does not want to go, does she? Will you behave as he does?* (Does rhymes with buzz.)

does n't does not.

dog an animal used as a pet, for hunting, and for guarding property. **dogs.**

dog wood a tree with white or pink flowers. See the picture. Dogwood is the state flower or the state tree of several states. **dog woods.**

doll a toy that looks like a person. **dolls.**

dol lar a large silver coin or a paper bill of United States or Canadian money; $1. **dol lars.**

dol phin 1. a small whale. See the picture. 2. a large sea fish that changes color when it is taken out of the water. **dol phins.**

done See **do.** *She has done a good job. What have you done?*

don key an animal somewhat like a small horse. See the picture. **don keys.**

don't do not.

door 1. a part that slides or turns on hinges to close an opening in a wall. 2. an opening in a wall: *He came in the front door.* **doors.**

door way opening in a wall where a door is. **door ways.**

dot 1. a small spot or point; a tiny round mark: *Put a dot over each "i" that you write.* 2. mark with a dot or dots: *Dot your "i."* **dots; dot ted, dot ting.**

dou ble 1. two times as much, as large, or as strong: *He gave me a double scoop of ice cream.* 2. become or make twice as much: *The number of people at the fire quickly doubled. She doubled her money.* 3. fold over: *Tom doubled his fists. She doubled the blanket on the bed.* **dou bled, dou bling.**

doubt 1. not believe; not be sure; feel uncertain: *The captain doubted that the ship would sink.* 2. being uncertain: *There was some doubt about going on our trip.* 3. **No doubt** means certainly. **doubt ed, doubt ing; doubts.**

doubt

dogwood

dolphin 1.

donkey

doughnut

dove[1]

dragon

dragonfly

dough nut a small, sweet cake in the shape of a ring. See the picture. **dough nuts.**

dove[1] a bird with a thick body. See the picture. **doves.** (Dove[1] rhymes with love.)

dove[2] See **dive.** *The diver dove into the water and disappeared.* (Dove[2] rhymes with stove.)

down[1] 1. to a lower place; in a lower place: *They ran down the steps. The dog was down in the basement.* 2. from an earlier time: *The story was handed down from father to son.* 3. down along: *down a hill, down a river, down a street.*

down[2] 1. soft feathers: *Baby chickens are covered with down.* 2. soft hair.

down stairs 1. down the stairs: *Bill hurried downstairs.* 2. on or to a lower floor: *She lived downstairs, and I lived upstairs.*

doz en twelve; a group of twelve things; 12. **doz ens.**

Dr. Doctor: *Dr. W. H. Smith.* **Drs.**

drag pull or move along the ground: *She dragged the big old box.* **dragged, drag ging.**

drag on in stories, a creature like a huge snake that breathes fire. See the picture. **drag ons.**

drag on fly a large insect with a long, thin body and two pairs of wings. See the picture. **drag on flies.**

drain 1. draw off; draw liquid from: *The baby drained the bottle.* 2. dry by taking away water: *Set the dishes on the sink to drain.* 3. a pipe for carrying off water or waste: *The drain is clogged.* **drained, drain ing; drains.**

drank See **drink.** *She drank all her milk.*

draw 1. pull; get or take out: *Draw money from the bank.* 2. make a picture of anything with pen, pencil, or chalk. **drew, drawn, draw ing.**

draw er a box, with handles, built to slide in and out of a table or desk or dresser. See the picture. **draw ers.**

drawn See **draw.** *The horse has drawn the wagon home. She has drawn three pictures.*

dream 1. something thought, felt, or seen during sleep: *Pilar had a bad dream.* 2. something not real: *The boy had dreams of being king.* 3. think, feel, hear, or see during sleep: *I dreamed about my uncle.* 4. form fancies; imagine: *The girl dreamed of being a doctor.* **dreams; dreamed** or **dreamt, dream ing.**

dream er 1. a person who has dreams: *The dreamer saw pink clouds in her sleep.* 2. a person whose ideas do not fit real conditions: *John is a real dreamer; he thinks his homework will get done all by itself.* **dream ers.**

dreamt See **dream.**

dreary not cheerful; gloomy: *A cloudy day is a dreary day.* **drear i er, drear i est.**

dress 1. a piece of clothing worn by women and girls. See the picture. 2. put clothes on: *He can dress himself.* 3. make ready for use or to cook: *Grandmother dressed the turkey.* 4. clean and cover a wound. **dress es; dressed, dress ing.**

dress er a piece of furniture with drawers and usually a mirror. See the picture. **dress ers.**

drew See **draw.** *He drew a bucket of water from the well. He drew a picture for her.*

drift 1. be carried along by currents of air or water: *A boat drifts.* 2. heap or be heaped by the wind: *The wind drifts the snow.* 3. snow or sand heaped by the wind: *A big drift blocked the road.* **drift ed, drift ing; drifts.**

drawer

---

drift

drawer

dress

dresser

drill[1] 1.

drill 1. a tool for boring holes. See the picture.
2. bore a hole with a drill: *The plumber drilled through the pipe.* 3. teach by having something done over and over: *We drilled each other on the spelling words.* 4. doing a thing over and over for practice: *The class needs some drill in arithmetic.* **drills; drilled, drill ing.**

drink 1. swallow liquid, such as water or milk.
2. any liquid swallowed: *a drink of water.*
drank, drunk, drink ing; drinks.

drip fall or let fall in drops: *Water drips from the roof.* **dripped, drip ping.**

drive 1. make go: *The dog will drive the cat away. Cowboys drive cattle.* 2. operate: *My mother learned how to drive a car.* 3. go in a car: *She drove to school.* 4. a ride in a car: *We went for a drive in the country.* 5. a road: *There is a drive along the river.* **drove, driv en, driv ing; drives.**

driv en See **drive.** *Dad has driven to work.*

driv er someone who drives. **driv ers.**

drive way road to drive on, often leading from a house or garage to the road. **drive ways.**

droop 1. hang down; bend down: *These flowers will soon droop if they are not put in water.* 2. become weak and discouraged: *The hikers drooped in the hot sun.* **drooped, droop ing.**

drop 1. a small amount of liquid in a round shape: *a drop of water.* 2. a very small amount: *I'll drink just a drop of cider.* 3. a sudden fall: *There was a drop of thirty feet below the cliff.*
4. fall suddenly: *The cat dropped from the tree.*
5. let fall: *She dropped a hammer.* **drops; dropped, drop ping.**

drove See **drive.** *We drove over the bridge.*

drug a kind of medicine doctors give sick people. **drugs.**

drug gist a person who works in a drugstore. **drug gists.**

drug store a store where medicines and other things are sold. **drug stores.**

drum a musical instrument that is hollow and has animal skin stretched over the ends. To make a sound you hit it with a stick. See the picture. **drums.**

drum mer a person who plays the drum. **drum mers.**

drunk See **drink.** *The dog has drunk all the water in its dish.*

dry 1. not wet; not damp: *The clothes are dry already.* 2. make dry: *She dried her hands on a towel.* 3. having little or no rain: *This was a dry summer.* 4. not interesting: *I found the book dry and boring.* **dri er, dri est; dries; dried, dry in**

dry er a thing that dries: *a hair dryer, a clothes dryer.* See the picture. **dry ers.**

duch ess 1. the wife of a duke. 2. a woman who is equal by birth or position to a duke. **duch ess es.**

duck¹ a swimming bird with a flat bill. See the picture. **ducks.**

duck² 1. dip the head or body under water and come up quickly, as a duck does; put under water for a short time. 2. bend the body quickly to keep off a blow. **ducked, duck ing.**

dug See **dig.** *He dug a ditch. He has dug ditches all day.*

duke a man of very high birth or one who has been given a high position by a king or a queen. **dukes.**

drug
_____
duke

girl playing a drum

boy using a hair dryer

duck¹

dustpan

dwarf 2.

dull 1. not sharp: *dull scissors*. 2. not bright or shiny: *a dull color*. 3. boring; not interesting: *a dull story*. **dull er, dull est.**

dumb 1. not able to speak: *Even smart animals are dumb*. 2. silent; not speaking. **dumb er, dumb est.**

dump 1. empty out; throw down: *The truck dumped the sand on the sidewalk*. 2. a place for throwing trash. **dumped, dump ing; dumps.**

dur ing 1. through the whole time of: *The boys talked during the movie*. 2. at some time in: *Come during the day*.

durst See **dare.**

dust 1. fine, dry dirt; any fine powder: *Dust covered the furniture*. 2. get dust off; brush or wipe the dust from: *The janitor dusts the floors every day*. 3. sprinkle with: *She dusted powder over the baby*. **dust ed, dust ing.**

dust pan a pan into which you can sweep dust and crumbs from the floor. See the picture. **dust pans.**

dusty 1. covered with dust; filled with dust. 2. dry and like powder. **dust i er, dust i est.**

du ty 1. the thing that is right to do; what a person ought to do: *It is your duty to obey the rules at school*. 2. the things a person has to do in a job: *The mail carrier's duties are to carry and deliver the mail*. 3. a tax on things you bring into or take out of the country: *We paid duty on the hats we brought from Mexico*. **du ties.**

dwarf 1. a person, animal, or plant that is smaller than others of its kind. 2. in fairy tales, an ugly little man with magic power. See the picture. **dwarfs.**

E   e

E or e the fifth letter of the alphabet. **E's** or **e's**.

each 1. all of a group but thought of one by one: *Each boy in the class has his lunch.* 2. for one: *These cookies are three cents each.*

ea ger wanting very much: *The children are eager to go to the picnic.*

ea ger ly in an eager way: *The puppy ran eagerly to the girl.*

ea gle a large bird that can see far and fly far. The eagle is the symbol of the United States. See the picture. **ea gles.**

ear[1] the part of the body by which people and animals hear. **ears.**

ear[2] the part of certain plants that contains the grain: *an ear of corn.* **ears.**

ear ly 1. in the beginning: *In his early years he learned another language.* 2. before the usual time: *Can you come early?* **ear li er, ear li est.**

earn be paid; get in return for doing something: *She earned money by washing cars.* **earned, earn ing.**

earth 1. the planet on which we live, a great ball that moves around the sun. See the picture. 2. the part of the earth's surface that is not rock or water: *The earth must be soft for planting seeds.*

ea sel a stand for holding a picture or chalkboard. See the picture. **ea sels.**

eas i ly without trying hard.

east 1. the direction of the sunrise; opposite of west. 2. to the east: *Walk east for two blocks.* 3. coming from the east: *An east wind is blowing.*

east

eagle

earth

easel

eel

East er a Christian holiday. Easter comes on a Sunday every spring. **East ers.**

east ern 1. toward the east: *The eastern sky looks dark.* 2. from the east: *We have some eastern visitors.*

east ward toward the east.

easy 1. not hard to do or understand: *This was an easy lesson.* 2. free from pain or trouble: *Climb this hill the easy way.* **eas i er, eas i est.**

eat chew and swallow food or have a meal. **ate, eat en, eat ing.**

eat en See **eat.** *He has eaten everything.*

edge 1. the line or place where something ends; the part farthest from the middle; the side: *The edge of the paper is straight. He stood at the edge of the road.* 2. the thin side that cuts: *This knife has a sharp edge.* **edg es.**

ed it 1. prepare writing to be printed: *The teacher edited our stories.* 2. be in charge of a newspaper and decide what shall be printed in it: *Two girls edit the class newspaper.* **ed it ed, ed it ing.**

ed i tor a person who edits. **ed i tors.**

ed u ca tion learning by going to school: *In the United States, education is free to all children.* **ed u ca tions.**

eel a long fish shaped like a snake. See the picture. **eels.**

egg 1. the object laid by female birds, fish, and reptiles. Their young are hatched from eggs. 2. the contents of an egg, used as food: *She eats two boiled eggs every morning.* **eggs.**

eight one more than seven; 8. Four and four make eight. **eights.**

eight een eight more than ten; 18. **eight eens.**

eight eenth 1. next after the seventeenth; 18th. 2. one of 18 equal parts. **eight eenths.**

eighth 1. next after the seventh; 8th. 2. one of 8 equal parts. **eighths.**

eight i eth 1. next after the seventy-ninth; 80th. 2. one of 80 equal parts. **eight i eths.**

eighty eight times ten; 80. **eight ies.**

ei ther 1. one or the other of two: *A window is either shut or open. Either leave or stay.* 2. each of two: *There are trees on either side of the street.*

el bow 1. the joint in the middle of the arm. 2. any bend with the shape of a bent arm. Some water pipes have elbows. **el bows.**

elec tric 1. having something to do with electricity: *an electric current.* 2. run by electricity: *an electric fan.*

elec tri cian a person whose business is repairing electric wires, lights, motors, and anything run by electricity. **elec tri cians.**

elec tric i ty 1. a kind of energy that makes light and heat, and that runs motors. 2. an electric current: *This radio is run by electricity.*

el e phant the largest four-footed animal. See the picture. **el e phants.**

el e va tor 1. a vehicle for carrying people or things up and down. 2. a building for storing grain: *a grain elevator.* 3. a part of an airplane tail that moves. Elevators make the plane go up. See the picture. **el e va tors.**

elev en one more than ten; 11. **elev ens.**

elev enth 1. next after the tenth; 11th. 2. one of 11 equal parts. **elev enths.**

elf in stories, a tiny being that is full of mischief. See the picture. **elves.**

eighteenth

---

elf

elephant

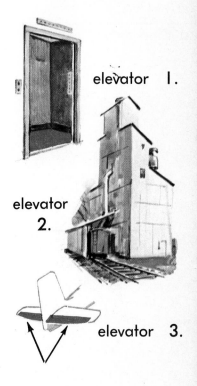

elevator 1.

elevator 2.

elevator 3.

elf

elk

elm tree

diesel engine

elk a large deer. See the picture. **elks** or **elk.**

elm a tall shade tree. See the picture. The elm is the state tree of several states. **elms.**

else other; different; instead: *Will somebody else carry this for a while? Shall we go somewhere else tomorrow? What else could I do?*

emer gen cy 1. a need to do something immediately: *In an emergency, call the fire department.* 2. for a sudden need: *Most cars have an emergency brake.* **emer gen cies.**

emp ty 1. with nothing in it: *The bird's nest was empty.* 2. pour out or take out all that is in a thing: *He emptied his cup quickly.* 3. flow out: *The river empties into the ocean.* **emp ti er, emp ti est; emp tied, emp ty ing.**

en code put into code. **en cod ed, en cod ing.**

end 1. the last part; the part where a thing begins or where it stops: *A stick has two ends.* 2. finish something: *Let's end this fight right now.* **ends; end ed, end ing.**

en e my 1. one who is against you or wishes to harm you. 2. anything that will do harm: *Pollution is our enemy.* **en e mies.**

en er gy 1. being able to work or move: *Children have so much energy they can't sit still.* 2. power. **en er gies.**

en gine 1. a machine that does work or makes something move. Many engines are run by gas or electricity. 2. the machine that pulls a railroad train. See the picture. **en gines.**

en gi neer 1. a person who plans and builds or takes care of machines, roads, bridges, and buildings. 2. the person who runs a railroad engine. **en gi neers.**

Eng land a country on an island near Europe.

Eng lish 1. the people of England. 2. the language of England.

en joy be happy or have fun with: *We enjoy games.* **en joyed, en joy ing.**

enor mous very, very large.

enough as much or as many as you need: *Do you have enough money to buy some gum? Are there enough cookies for us all? Have you watched TV long enough for one day?*

en ter go into; come into: *We enter a room through the door.* **en tered, en ter ing.**

en trance 1. the act of coming in or entering: *The fireman's entrance was swift.* 2. the place to enter: *Meet me at the main entrance to the hall.* **en tranc es.**

en try 1. the act of entering: *She made her entry last.* 2. a place by which to enter: *Leave your boots in the entry.* See the picture. 3. a word and how it is explained in a dictionary: *Look up an entry in this book.* **en tries.**

en ve lope a folded paper cover or case for a letter or for anything flat. **en ve lopes.**

equal the same in amount, size, or number: *Five nickels are equal to one quarter. The two boys are equal in size. One dozen is equal to twelve.*

equal ly in equal shares; in an equal way: *The two pictures are equally good.*

erase rub out or scrape away: *He erased the word he had written.* **erased, eras ing.**

eras er a tool used to rub out or to erase marks made with a pen or pencil. See the picture. **eras ers.**

es ca la tor moving stairs. You can go from one floor to another by standing on one step and riding up or down. See the picture. **es ca la tors.**

escalator

entry 2.

eraser

escalator

Eskimo

Europe

es cape 1. get free or get out and away: *The bird escaped from its cage.* 2. act of getting away: *His escape was made at night.* **es caped, es cap ing; es capes.**

Es ki mo one of the people who live on the most northern shores of North America and Asia. See the picture. **Es ki mos** or **Es ki mo.**

Eu rope a part of the largest mass of land on the earth; a continent. See the picture.

eve the evening or day before some holiday or special day: *New Year's Eve.* **eves.**

even 1. level, flat, smooth: *Are the edges of the paper even?* 2. at the same level: *The top of the tree is even with the roof.* 3. equal; no more nor less than: *They divided the apple in even pieces.* 4. that can be divided by two without a remainder: *Two is an even number. Three is an odd number.*

eve ning the time between sunset and bedtime. **eve nings.**

even ly in a level, smooth, or equal way: *Spread the frosting evenly on the cake. Divide the money evenly.*

event something important that happens: *The governor's visit was an exciting event.* **events.**

ev er at any time: *Does he ever sleep? Will they ever get here?*

ev er green 1. having green leaves all year round: *Pines are evergreen trees.* 2. a plant that has green leaves all year round. **ev er greens.**

eve ry 1. each: *Every child should have a box of crayons.* 2. **Every now and then** means from time to time. 3. **Every other one** means every second one.

eve ry body every person.

eve ry one each one; everybody.

eve ry thing every thing; all things: *She did everything she could to help.*

eve ry where in every place; in all places or lands: *Everywhere I looked I saw snow.*

ewe a female sheep. **ewes.**

ex act without any mistake; correct; no more nor less: *Give the waiter the exact amount of our bill.*

ex act ly in an exact way: *Do exactly as I say. He looks exactly like his twin.*

ex am ple one thing taken to show what the others are like or should be like: *Her sister is an example of a good worker. He is a good example to follow.* **ex am ples.**

ex cept other than: *This store is open every day except Sunday. Except for two people, the building was empty.*

ex change 1. give for something else: *I will exchange two dimes for twenty pennies.* 2. give and take similar things: *We exchanged letters.* **ex changed, ex chang ing.**

ex cit ed stirred up or eager: *The excited crowd clapped loudly.*

ex cit ed ly in an excited way: *The boys shouted excitedly when the ball was caught.*

ex cite ment a feeling of being excited: *When I won, there was great excitement in our family.*

ex cit ing able to cause excitement: *exciting news, an exciting game.*

ex claim speak or cry out suddenly with strong feeling: *"Oh, no!" she exclaimed as she tore her book.* **ex claimed, ex claim ing.**

ex cla ma tion something exclaimed: *Her only exclamation was "Well!"* **ex cla ma tions.**

girl exercising

expressway

ex cuse 1. give a reason: *She excused her mistake by saying she was tired.* 2. not blame: *Please excuse me for being careless.* 3. allow to leave: *May I be excused from the table?* 4. a reason given to explain something you said or did: *There is no excuse for bad manners. He brought an excuse from home.* 5. **Excuse me** means Pardon me or I'm sorry or May I have permission to go? **ex cused, ex cus ing; ex cus es.**

ex er cise 1. use; practice: *An athlete exercises every day.* See the picture. 2. something that gives practice: *Do the first exercise in your book.* **ex er cised, ex er cis ing; ex er cis es.**

ex hib it 1. show; put on display: *I will exhibit my stamps in class.* 2. things shown in public: *I have an exhibit at the science fair.* **ex hib it ed, ex hib it ing; ex hib its.**

ex pect look for or think something will probably come or happen: *We expect rain tomorrow.* **ex pect ed, ex pect ing.**

ex per i ment 1. test or try something out: *The cook experimented with a new recipe.* 2. a test to find out something: *Scientists test ideas by experiments.* **ex per i ment ed, ex per i ment ing; ex per i ments.**

ex plain 1. make plain or clear: *Our teacher explains the hard arithmetic problems.* 2. give reasons for: *Can somebody explain why she laughed at me?* **ex plained, ex plain ing.**

ex plore go over a place and examine it: *The children explored the new playground.* **ex plored, ex plor ing.**

ex press way a highway, usually without traffic lights, for fast traveling. See the picture. **ex press ways.**

ex tra beyond what is usual, expected, or needed: *The carpenters asked for extra pay.*

eye 1. the part of the body by which you see. 2. something like an eye: *the eye of a needle.* See the picture. **eyes.**

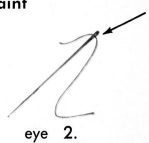

eye 2.

F   f

F or **f** the sixth letter of the alphabet. **F's** or **f's.**

fa ble a story that teaches a lesson. Many fables are about animals that talk. **fa bles.**

face 1. the front part of the head. 2. the front part; surface: *the face of a clock.* 3. to have the front toward: *Our house faces the street.* 4. meet bravely or boldly: *He faced the mad dog.* **fac es; faced, fac ing.**

fact a thing that can be proved to be true. **facts.**

fac to ry a building or group of buildings where things are made. A factory usually has machines in it. See the picture. **fac to ries.**

factory

fade 1. lose color: *My blue shirt has faded. The red sunset faded to gray.* 2. die away: *The noise faded after the jet took off.* 3. cause to fade: *Sun light faded the curtains.* **fad ed, fad ing.**

fail 1. not succeed; not be able to do: *He tried hard to win, but he failed.* 2. not do what should be done: *He failed to follow directions.* 3. **Without fail** means surely. **failed, fail ing.**

faint 1. not clear or plain; dim: *a faint idea, faint colors.* 2. weak: *a faint voice.* 3. a state in which a person lies as if asleep and does not know what is going on around him. 4. fall into a faint: *I thought I'd faint from hunger.* **faint er, faint est; faints; faint ed, faint ing.**

fan

fairground

falcon

electric fan

folding fan

faint ly in a faint or weak manner; far away: *The voice was heard faintly inside the cave.*

fair[1] 1. not liking one more than any other; honest: *A fair judge decided to let the man go.* 2. going by the rules: *Be sure to play fair.* 3. not too good and not too bad: *The crop of wheat this year is fair.* 4. not cloudy or rainy: *I hope the weather will be fair.* **fair er, fair est.**

fair[2] a show or sale, often of farm animals and such things as clothes and canned food. **fairs.**

fair ground a place outdoors where fairs are held. See the picture. **fair grounds.**

fair ly in a fair way: *She won the game fairly. The game was fairly good.*

fairy 1. in stories, a tiny make-believe person with magic power. 2. of fairies: *fairy tales.* **fair ies.**

fal con a hawk trained to hunt and kill other birds. See the picture. **fal cons.**

fall 1. come down from a higher place: *Leaves are falling.* 2. the coming down from a higher place: *She had a bad fall down the stairs.* 3. the part of the year after summer and before winter; autumn. 4. of fall: *a beautiful fall day.* **fell, fall en, fall ing; falls.**

fall en See **fall.** *Beth has fallen off the swing.*

fam i ly 1. a father, a mother, and their children. 2. all of a person's relatives: *Grandmother invited the whole family.* 3. of a family: *a family picnic.* **fam i lies.**

fa mous very well known; important.

fan 1. an instrument or appliance that stirs the air in order to cool it or to blow dust away. See the picture. 2. stir the air; stir up: *Fan the fire to make it blaze.* 3. use as a fan: *He fanned himself with his hat.* **fans; fanned, fan ning.**

fan cy 1. picture to yourself; imagine: *Can you fancy yourself a grown-up?* 2. the power to imagine: *Elves are creatures of fancy.* 3. not plain: *She won't wear a fancy dress with ruffles.* **fan cied, fan cy ing; fan cies; fan ci er, fan ci est.**

far 1. a long way; a long way off: *Is it far to the store? The moon is far away.* 2. much: *The roses are far better this year than they were last year.* **far ther, far thest.**

far a way distant; far away: *The Chang family came from a faraway land.*

fare the money that a person pays to ride. **fares.**

farm 1. the land used to raise crops or animals. See the picture. 2. work on a farm; raise crops or animals to eat or to sell: *My family farmed this land for years.* 3. of or for a farm: *a farm wagon, farm animals.* **farms; farmed, farm ing.**

farm er a person who raises crops or animals on a farm. **farm ers.**

far ther See **far.** *My house is farther from school than yours.*

far thest See **far.** *Who ran the farthest of all?*

fash ion 1. the way a thing is shaped or done: *He walks in a straight fashion.* 2. make, shape, or form: *She fashioned a cage out of wire.* **fash ions; fash ioned, fash ion ing.**

fast[1] 1. taking very little time; not slow: *a fast runner, a fast game.* 2. in a fast way; swiftly: *Airplanes go fast.* 3. showing a time ahead of the real time: *That clock is fast.* 4. firmly: *Wet leaves stuck fast to the walk.* **fast er, fast est.**

fast[2] go without food. **fast ed, fast ing.**

fas ten hold together or make something hold together: *Fasten the door tight so it won't blow open. Fasten your belt.* **fas tened, fas ten ing.**

farm 1.

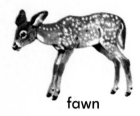

fawn

feather

fat 1. a white or yellow oily mass formed in the body of an animal. 2. having much fat: *a fat baby, a fat robin.* **fats; fat ter, fat test.**

fa ther 1. a male parent: *She called her father at the office.* 2. a priest. **fa thers.**

fault 1. something that is not as it should be: *Talking too loud is my greatest fault.* 2. **Find fault with** means find things wrong with something or someone. 3. a cause for blame: *Is it my fault that we are late?* **faults.**

fa vor ite liked best: *Which is your favorite dress?*

fawn a baby deer. See the picture. **fawns.**

fear 1. a feeling that danger or something bad is near: *The baby has no fear.* 2. feel fear; be afraid of: *We feared the storm that was coming.* **fears; feared, fear ing.**

feast 1. a big meal for some special party: *We had a big feast on Thanksgiving Day.* 2. eat many good things: *They feasted on chicken.* **feasts; feast ed, feast ing.**

feath er one of the light, thin objects that cover a bird's skin. See the picture. **feath ers.**

fea ture 1. part of your face. Your eyes, mouth, and nose are features. 2. what makes a thing different from others: *Good weather is this state's best feature.* **fea tures.**

Feb ru ary the second month of the year. It has 28 days except in every fourth year it has 29. **Feb ru ar ies.**

fed See **feed.** *I fed the dog. Dad has fed it, too.*

fee ble weak: *A feeble old man was calling for help.* **fee bler, fee blest.**

fee bly in a weak or feeble way: *The new colt raised its head feebly.*

feed 1. give food to: *I helped feed the baby.* 2. eat: *Cows feed on hay.* 3. food for animals: *chicken feed.* **fed, feed ing; feeds.**

feel 1. touch: *Feel the smooth stone.* 2. try to find by touching: *He was feeling in the dark for a flashlight.* 3. be; have in the mind: *She feels sad. I have felt sad too.* **felt, feel ing.**

feel ing how you feel about something. Joy, fear, and hate are feelings. **feel ings.**

feet more than one foot: *A person has two feet. Bill is four feet tall.*

fell See **fall.** *She fell on her knees.*

fel low a man or boy: *The old fellow sat on a bench.* **fel lows.**

felt¹ See **feel.** *The baby felt the cat's soft fur. Mom has felt better today.*

felt² 1. cloth made by rolling and pressing wool, hair, or fur together. 2. made of felt: *a felt hat.*

fe male a woman or girl; the kind of person or animal that brings forth young. **fe males.**

fence something put around a yard, garden, or field to show where it ends or to keep people and animals out or in. See the picture. **fenc es.**

fend er something that protects by being between: *Automobile fenders protect the car from stones and mud on the road.* See the picture. **fend ers.**

fern a kind of plant that has no flowers. See the picture. **ferns.**

fer ry 1. carry people and things across a river or narrow strip of water: *This ship ferries automobiles.* 2. the boat that makes the trip. See the picture. **fer ried, fer ry ing; fer ries.**

fes ti val 1. a day or special time of feasting. 2. a celebration: *Every year we go to the music festival.* **fes ti vals.**

fence

automobile fender

fern

ferry 2.

boy playing a fife

fig

few 1. not many: *There are a few pieces of cake left.* 2. a small number: *There are only a few people in the room.* **few er, few est.**

fid dle 1. a violin. 2. play a violin: *He fiddled for the dancers.* **fid dles; fid dled, fid dling.**

field 1. land used for crops or for pasture. 2. land for a special use: *a baseball field.* 3. in baseball, stop a batted ball and throw it quickly. **fields; field ed, field ing.**

fierce wild: *A fierce lion roared. A fierce wind blew many trees down.* **fierc er, fierc est.**

fierce ly in a fierce manner: *The lion roared fiercely.*

fife a musical instrument that you play by blowing into it. See the picture. **fifes.**

fif teen five more than ten; 15. **fif teens.**

fif teenth 1. next after the fourteenth; 15th. 2. one of 15 equal parts. **fif teenths.**

fifth 1. next after the fourth; 5th. 2. one of 5 equal parts. **fifths.**

fif ti eth 1. next after the forty-ninth; 50th. 2. one of 50 equal parts. **fif ti eths.**

fif ty five times ten; 50. **fif ties.**

fig 1. a small fruit that grows in warm places. 2. the tree it grows on. See the picture. **figs.**

fight 1. a struggle or contest. 2. a quarrel. 3. take part in a struggle or a quarrel. **fights; fought, fight ing.**

fig ure 1. a mark or sign that stands for a number, such as 1, 3, 4. 2. use numbers to find out the answer to a problem: *Can you figure the cost of building a doghouse?* 3. a form or shape: *She saw the figure of a man through the window.* 4. **Figure out** means think out; understand. **fig ures; fig ured, fig ur ing.**

file[1] 1. a place for keeping papers in order. 2. put away papers in order. 3. a row of persons or things one behind another: *single file.* 4. march or move in this way: *The boys filed out of the room.* **files; filed, fil ing.**

file[2] 1. a tool with many small edges or teeth in it, used to smooth or wear away hard material. See the picture. 2. smooth or wear away with a file. **files; filed, fil ing.**

file[2] 1.

fill 1. put into until there is no more room; make full. 2. take up all the space in: *Parents filled the auditorium.* 3. stop up or close by putting something in: *The farmer dug out the stump and filled the hole with dirt.* **filled, fill ing.**

fill ing material used to fill something: *a filling in a tooth.* **fill ings.**

film 1. a very thin surface or covering, often of liquid: *There was a film of oil on the water.* 2. a roll of thin material used to take pictures. 3. a movie: *We saw a film about dogs.* **films.**

fin one of the parts of a fish's body that help it swim. By moving its fins the fish swims and balances itself in water. See the picture. **fins.**

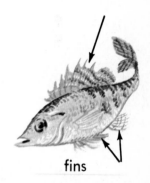

fins

fi nal coming last; deciding; closing the question: *Here is the final report.*

fi nal ly at the end; at last: *Our team finally won a game.*

finch a small bird that sings. See the picture. The finch is the state bird of several states. **finch es.**

gold finch

find 1. meet with; come upon: *She found a dime.* 2. look for and get: *Did you find your other shoe?* 3. get: *You can find the answer on page ten.* 4. **Find out** means learn about; come to know; discover. **found, find ing.**

fine

firm

fir tree

firehouse

fire truck

fine¹ 1. very small or thin: *She drew a fine line with her pen. Sugar is ground fine.* 2. excellent: *He cooked a fine meal.* **fin er, fin est.**

fine² 1. money paid for breaking a law: *a fine for speeding.* 2. make someone pay a fine: *The judge fined him five dollars.* **fines; fined, fin ing.**

fin ger one of the five end parts of the hand. **fin gers.**

fin ger print 1. a mark made by the fleshy tip of a finger. 2. take the fingerprints of. **fin ger print ed, fin ger print ing; fin ger prints.**

fin ish 1. complete; bring to an end; get to the end of: *Finish your dinner before you go.* 2. the end: *It was a close race from start to finish.* **fin ished, fin ish ing; fin ish es.**

fir a small evergreen tree. See the picture. **firs.**

fire 1. flame, heat, and light that feed upon something and destroy it: *The fire burned the wood to ashes.* 2. having something to do with fire: *a fire engine.* **fires.**

fire fight er a person whose work is putting out fires. **fire fight ers.**

fire fly a small insect that gives off flashes of light as it flies at night. **fire flies.**

fire house a building where fire trucks are kept. See the picture. **fire hous es.**

fire man 1. a firefighter. 2. a person who looks after fires in railroad engines. **fire men.**

fire truck a truck that carries a machine to throw water on a fire. See the picture. **fire trucks.**

fire works small rockets and other things that burst into bright lights or make loud noises.

firm not moving when pressed or pushed: *The horse trotted on firm ground. Mother was firm when she said I couldn't go.* **firm er, firm est.**

firm ly in a firm manner: *She held her sister firmly by the hand.*

first 1. coming before all others: *He is first in line.* 2. before anything else: *We ate first and then played ball.* 3. what is first; the beginning: *At first, I did not like him.* 4. for the first time: *When I first came into the room, I didn't see you.*

fish 1. an animal that lives and breathes in water and has fins but no legs. 2. fish used for food: *We had fish for dinner.* 3. catch fish; try to catch fish: *We fished with worms.* **fish es** or **fish; fished, fish ing.**

fist the hand closed tightly. See the picture. **fists.**

fit[1] 1. right: *A fancy dress is fit for a party.* 2. feeling well and strong: *He is fit for work.* 3. be the right size or shape: *The coat fits her well.* 4. try to make right: *I fitted the collar onto the dress.* **fit ter, fit test; fit ted, fit ting.**

fit[2] a sudden, short period of doing or feeling something: *The girls had a fit of laughing.* **fits.**

five one more than four; 5. *Five and five make ten.* **fives.**

fix 1. make firm or tight: *The farmer fixed the fence post in the ground. The girl fixed the date in her mind.* 2. put in order; arrange: *Fix your hair.* 3. mend: *Can he fix a watch?* **fixed, fix ing.**

flag a piece of colored cloth, usually almost square, that stands for some country or state or group. See the picture. **flags.**

Flag Day June 14, 1777, the day the Stars and Stripes became the flag of the United States. **Flag Days.**

flag pole pole from which a flag is flown. **flag poles.**

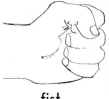

fist

the first American flag

flamingo

flap 3.

flame one of the hot, glowing tongues of light that come when a fire blazes up. **flames.**

fla min go a bird with long legs and pink or red feathers. See the picture. **fla min gos** or **fla min goes.**

flap 1. hit noisily: *The flag flapped in the wind.* 2. move wings up and down: *The duck flapped its wings.* 3. a piece hanging or fastened at one edge only: *There is a flap on his pocket.* See the picture. **flapped, flap ping.**

flare 1. blaze for a minute, sometimes with smoke: *The fire flared when I poked the log.* 2. a bright, unsteady flame: *the flare of a match.* **flared, flar ing; flares.**

flash 1. a sudden light or flame. 2. give out such a light or flame: *The light flashed, then disappeared.* 3. come and go quickly: *A deer flashed across the path.* **flash es; flashed, flash ing.**

flash light a light small enough to carry. A flashlight runs on batteries. **flash lights.**

flat[1] 1. smooth and level; even: *We spread out our lunch on a flat rock.* 2. not very deep or thick: *A plate is a flat dish.* 3. in a flat way: *The boy fell flat on the ground.* 4. in music, a tone one-half step below; the sign (♭). **flat ter, flat test; flats.**

flat[2] a set of rooms on one floor. **flats.**

flat land level land, not broken by hills and valleys. **flat lands.**

flew See **fly**[2]. *The butterfly flew away.*

flight[1] 1. act or manner of flying: *the flight of a bird.* 2. a ride in an airplane: *We had a nice flight after the weather cleared.* 3. from one landing or one story of a building to the next: *We live one flight up.* **flights.**

flight[2] running away; escape: *Their flight from jail was soon discovered.* **flights.**

fling throw; throw with force: *It's fun to fling stones into the water.* **flung, fling ing.**

flip toss or move by the snap of a finger and thumb: *The man flipped a coin in the air.* **flipped, flip ping.**

flit fly lightly and quickly: *The bird flitted from branch to branch.* **flit ted, flit ting.**

float 1. stay on top of or be held up by air or water. *A cork will float on water.* 2. anything that stays up or holds up something in water. 3. move along without trying; be moved along in or on something: *The log floated down the stream.* **float ed, float ing; floats.**

flock 1. a group of certain birds or animals of one kind: *a flock of geese.* See the picture. 2. go in a flock: *Geese flock together and fly south.* **flocks; flocked, flock ing.**

flock of geese

flood 1. flow over: *Water flooded the streets.* 2. a flow of water over what is usually dry land; a large amount of water: *We had a flood in the back yard.* **flood ed, flood ing; floods.**

floor 1. the part of a room you walk on. 2. a story or one level of a building: *Four families live on the tenth floor.* **floors.**

flop move, fall; drop loosely or heavily: *Mother was so tired she flopped into a chair.* **flopped, flop ping.**

Flor i da one of the fifty states of the United States. See page 336.

floun der a flat fish. See the picture. **floun ders** or **floun der.**

flounder

flour meal, made by grinding grain such as wheat or rye, and used in cooking.

girl playing a flute

fly[1]

flycatcher

flow 1. run like water: *Rivers flow. Electric current flows through wires.* 2. a running like water: *a flow of gas.* **flowed, flow ing; flows.**

flow er the part of a plant or tree, often beautiful in color and shape, that bears the seed. **flow ers.**

flown See **fly**[2]. *She has flown in an airplane.*

flung See **fling**. *He flung the bag of flour over his shoulder. She has flung her sweater on a chair.*

flute a musical instrument that you play by blowing into it and pressing keys. See the picture. **flutes.**

fly[1] an insect with two wings. See the picture. **flies.**

fly[2] 1. move through the air with wings: *Birds fly.* 2. float in the air: *Our flag flies every day we are in school.* 3. cause to fly: *The boys are flying model airplanes.* 4. go through the air in an airplane. **flew, flown, fly ing.**

fly catch er a bird that catches insects in the air. See the picture. **fly catch ers.**

fly speck 1. a tiny spot left by a fly. 2. any tiny speck. **fly specks.**

fog a cloud of fine drops of water just above the ground, thick and white, sometimes impossible to see through. **fogs.**

fold 1. bend or turn over upon itself. You fold a napkin. 2. a layer of something folded. 3. bend close to the body: *She folded her arms to keep warm.* **fold ed, fold ing; folds.**

folk tale an old story that has been told for many years by many people. **folk tales.**

fol low 1. go or come after: *Let's follow him. Tuesday follows Monday.* 2. go along something: *Follow this path to the river.* 3. use or act as you are told: *She has followed the directions.* **fol lowed, fol low ing.**

fond loving; liking: *He is fond of children. I am fond of milk.* **fond er, fond est.**

fond ly in a fond way: *She petted the dog fondly.*

food anything that plants, animals, or people eat or drink that makes them live and grow. **foods.**

fool 1. act foolish for fun; play; joke: *Don't fool around in school.* 2. trick: *Don't try to fool me.* **fooled, fool ing.**

foot 1. the end part of a leg; the part that you stand on. 2. the lowest part; the bottom: *Meet me at the foot of the hill.* 3. a measure of length. Twelve inches are equal to one foot. **feet.**

foot ball 1. a leather ball used in a game. 2. the game, in which two teams try to move a football past a line at either end of the field. **foot balls.**

foot print the mark made by a foot. See the picture. **foot prints.**

foot step 1. a person's step. 2. a sound of steps. 3. mark made by a foot. **foot steps.**

for 1. in place of: *He gave me a dime for two nickels. I bought a bunch of flowers for a dollar.* 2. with the idea of: *He lay down for a nap.* 3. meant to be used with: *a bank for pennies, pots for stew.* 4. because of: *He got a ticket for speeding.* 5. as far as: *We drove for twenty miles.* 6. as long as: *We talked for a minute.*

force 1. power; being strong. 2. power used against someone: *They took the dog out of the car by force.* 3. make a person act against his or her will: *Don't force me to tell.* 4. get or take by being stronger than the thing or person against you: *She forced her way to the head of the line.* 5. break through: *We forced a door that was locked.* **forc es; forced, forc ing.**

footprints

forget-me-not

fork I.

fork in a road

fort

fore at the front; toward the beginning or front.

fore head the part of your face above the eyes.
fore heads.

fore noon the time between dawn and noon.
fore noons.

for est I. thick woods, often covering many miles.
2. of the forest: *Forest fires can be stopped.*
for ests.

for ev er I. for all time; without ever coming to
an end. 2. always; all the time: *She's forever
thinking of others.*

for get I. let go out of the mind; fail to remember.
2. fail to think of; fail to do. **for got,
for got ten** or **for got, for get ting.**

for get-me-not a small blue flower. See the
picture. **for get-me-nots.**

for got See **forget.** *I forgot to thank her.*

for got ten See **forget.** *He has forgotten what
she told him.*

fork I. a tool having a handle and two or more
long points, for lifting food or other things.
2. anything that separates into two branches:
a fork in the road. See the picture. **forks.**

form I. a shape. Circles and cones are forms.
2. shape; make into a shape: *The cook formed
stars out of the cookie batter.* 3. take shape:
Ice formed in the stream. **forms; formed,
form ing.**

fort a strong building or place that can be held
against an enemy. See the picture. **forts.**

forth I. out; into view: *The winner came forth
from the crowd.* 2. forward: *He strode back and
forth on the dock.*

for ti eth I. next after the thirty-ninth; 40th.
2. one of 40 equal parts. **for ti eths.**

for tune 1. a great deal of money or property: *He made a fortune when he discovered gold.* 2. what happens or may happen: *Did you have your fortune told?* **for tunes.**

for ty four times ten; 40. **for ties.**

for ward 1. on; ahead: *She drove the car forward; then she backed up.* 2. to the front: *All pitchers step forward.* 3. a certain player on a basketball team. **for wards.**

fought See **fight.** *They fought over the last piece of candy. They have fought all day.*

found See **find.** *I found a nickel. The cat has found its way home.*

foun tain 1. water rising into the air in a spray. 2. the pipes through which the water is forced and the container the water falls into. 3. a place to get a drink: *There's a drinking fountain in the park.* See the picture. **foun tains.**

four one more than three; 4. *Four and four make eight.* **fours.**

four teen four more than ten; 14. **four teens.**

four teenth 1. next after the thirteenth; 14th. 2. one of 14 equal parts. **four teenths.**

fourth 1. next after the third; 4th. 2. a quarter; one of 4 equal parts. *One fourth of a dollar is twenty-five cents.*

Fourth of Ju ly a holiday on which Americans celebrate the birthday of the United States. **Fourth of Ju lies.**

fowl 1. any kind of bird, but specially a rooster, hen, or turkey. 2. any birds used for food. **fowls** or **fowl.**

fox a small, sly, wild animal. See the picture. **fox es.**

fra grant sweet-smelling: *Perfume is fragrant.*

fountain 1.

fountain 2.

fountain 3.

fox

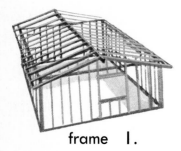

frame 1.

frankfurter

freight train

frame 1. the part over which something is stretched or built: *The frame of a house is built first.* See the picture. 2. make; put together; plan: *He framed his speech the day before.* 3. the outside edge in which a thing is set: *He put a frame on the picture.* 4. put an edge around: *I asked him to frame the picture.* **frames; framed, fram ing.**

frank furt er a red sausage made of beef or pork. See the picture. **frank furt ers.**

free 1. loose; not fastened or shut up. 2. not under another person's control. 3. not held back from acting or thinking as one pleases: *She was free to say what she thought.* 4. without paying: *free tickets.* *We got in free.* 5. make free; loose: *She freed the bird and let it fly away.* **fre er, fre est; freed, free ing.**

free ly in a free way: *She gave money away freely.*

freeze 1. turn into ice; harden by cold. 2. make or become very cold. 3. kill or hurt by frost. **froze, fro zen, freez ing.**

freight 1. the things that a train or truck carries. 2. for freight: *freight car.* 3. **Freight train** means a train that carries only freight and no passengers. See the picture.

fresh 1. newly made, grown, or gathered: *Go and pick some fresh flowers.* 2. pure; cool: *A fresh breeze was blowing.* **fresh er, fresh est.**

fresh ly just made or done: *These berries are freshly picked.*

fric tion the rubbing of one thing against another. Rubbing your hands together causes friction.

Fri day the sixth day of the week. **Fri days.**

fried 1. cooked in hot fat: *fried potatoes.* 2. See **fry.** *The Scouts fried the eggs for breakfast.*

friend a person who knows and likes you. **friends.**

friend ly of or like a friend: *She sent us a friendly letter.* **friend li er, friend li est.**

fright sudden fear of something: *I got a fright when the door slammed.* **frights.**

fright en cause fright; make afraid: *Does a storm frighten you?* **fright ened, fright en ing.**

fringe 1. an edge or trimming made of threads either loose or tied together in small bunches. See the picture. 2. anything like this: *He had a fringe of hair around his head.* 3. make or be a fringe for: *Trees fringed the lake.* **fring es; fringed, fring ing.**

frisky fond of playing; full of life: *We have a frisky puppy at our house.* **frisk i er, frisk i est.**

frog a small, leaping animal that lives near water. See the picture. **frogs.**

from 1. out of: *Steel is made from iron.* 2. beginning with: *Two weeks from today school is over.* 3. because of: *She is suffering from mosquito bites.* 4. off of: *He took a doughnut from the plate.*

front 1. the first part; the part that faces forward: *The front of the house was painted.* 2. at or in the front: *the front door, a front apartment.*

fron tier the edge of settled land, where wilderness begins. *Pioneers lived on the frontier.* **fron tiers.**

frost 1. tiny drops of water frozen on a surface, making a cold white covering like ice or snow: *There was frost on the grass this morning.* 2. cover with frost: *The window was frosted this morning.* 3. cover with something like frost: *It's my job to frost the cake.* **frosts; frost ed, frost ing.**

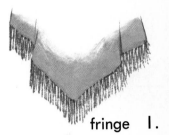

fringe 1.

frog

man moving a
lever on a fulcrum

funnel 1.

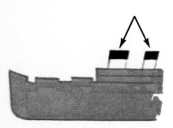

funnel 2.

frost ing a sweet mixture spread on a cake.
frost ings.

frown 1. wrinkles in the forehead, usually when a person is thinking hard or is angry: *He had a frown on his face.* 2. look as though you are angry or thinking: *You frown when you are angry.* **frowns; frowned, frown ing.**

froze See **freeze.** *The pond froze early this year.*

fro zen 1. made hard by cold; turned into ice: *a frozen river, frozen food.* 2. See **freeze.** *The water has frozen in the pool.* 3. **Frozen to the spot** means too frightened to move.

fruit 1. part of a tree, bush, or vine that is good to eat. Apples, oranges, and bananas are fruits. 2. the part of the plant the seeds are in. Acorns and tomatoes are also fruits. **fruits** or **fruit.**

fry cook in hot fat: *He is frying hamburger for supper.* **fried, fry ing.**

fu el anything that can be burned for heat or to make something go. Gas is a fuel. **fu els.**

ful crum the thing on which a lever moves as it lifts something. See the picture. **ful crums.**

full able to hold no more: *The cup is full; don't try to put more in it.* **full er, full est.**

ful ly completely: *She was fully awake.*

fun 1. a good time; amusement: *We had fun at the party.* 2. **Make fun of** means laugh at someone in an unfriendly way.

fun nel 1. a kind of cup, open at the bottom and used to pour liquid, powder, or grain into a small hole such as the neck of a bottle. 2. the chimney on a ship. See the picture. **fun nels.**

fun ny 1. causing laughter. 2. strange; queer; odd in speech or acts. **fun ni er, fun ni est.**

fur 1. the coat of hair that covers many animals: *a kitten's fur.* 2. made of fur: *a fur coat.* **furs.**

fur nace a box in which a fire is made to melt iron, make glass, or heat a building. See the picture. **fur nac es.**

fur ni ture things used in a house. Chairs, tables, beds, and dressers are pieces of furniture.

fur ther farther.

fur thest farthest.

fu ture the time to come; what is to come.

G g

G or **g** the seventh letter of the alphabet. **G's** or **g's.**

gal lon a measure for liquids. A gallon of milk is equal to four quarts. **gal lons.**

gal lop run in a fast, hopping way: *The horse galloped home.* **gal loped, gal lop ing.**

game something to play or a contest with certain rules: *This store sells games.* **games.**

ga rage 1. a place for keeping cars. 2. a building in which automobiles are repaired. **ga rag es.**

gar bage scraps of food to be thrown away.

gar den a piece of ground in which vegetables or flowers are grown. **gar dens.**

gar den er a person who takes care of a garden. **gar den ers.**

gar de nia a plant with fragrant white flowers. See the picture. **gar de nias.**

gas 1. something that is like air, not a mass or a liquid: *We filled the balloon with gas to make it go up in the air.* 2. gasoline. 3. using or burning gas: *a gas stove, a gas furnace.* **gas es.**

worker shoveling
coal into a furnace

gardenia

gas station

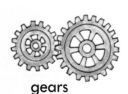

gears

gas o line the liquid fuel that makes automobiles and other engines run.

gasp 1. a catching of the breath with the mouth open: *Her answer was a loud gasp.* 2. take short, quick breaths through the mouth: *The boy gasped after running so fast.* 3. talk while breathing this way: *"Save me!" gasped the drowning girl.* **gasps; gasped, gasp ing.**

gas sta tion a place to buy gasoline and oil. See the picture. **gas sta tions.**

gate a door or an opening in a wall or fence. **gates.**

gath er 1. collect; bring or come into one place: *Tom gathered his tools and went to fix his bike.* 2. come together: *The crowd gathered to hear the governor.* 3. pull together in folds: *When I made a skirt, I gathered it at the top.* **gath ered, gath er ing.**

gave See **give**. *He gave me a cookie.*

gay 1. happy and full of fun; merry: *a gay laugh, a gay tune.* 2. bright-colored. **gay er, gay est.**

gaze 1. look long and steadily: *She gazed at the sunset.* 2. a long, steady look. **gazed, gaz ing; gaz es.**

gaz et teer a geographical dictionary. **gaz et teers.**

gear a wheel with teeth that fit into another wheel and make it turn. See the picture. **gears.**

geese more than one goose.

ge nie a powerful spirit. **ge nies.**

gen tle 1. soft or low: *The rain made a gentle sound on the roof.* 2. kind or friendly: *We had a gentle dog.* **gen tler, gen tlest.**

gen tle man a polite word for a man. **gen tle men.**

gen tly in a gentle way; softly: *The rain fell gently. She spoke gently to the baby.*

ge o graph i cal about geography.

ge og ra phy 1. the study of the earth's surface, countries, and people. 2. a book about geography. **ge og ra phies.**

Geor gia one of the fifty states of the United States. See page 337.

ger bil a small animal. Many people keep gerbils as pets. See the picture. **ger bils.**

germ a very tiny animal or plant, too small to be seen without a microscope: *Some germs make you sick.* **germs.**

get 1. be given; come to have: *I hope to get a bike for my birthday.* 2. cause to be or do: *Can you get the window open?* 3. become: *It gets hot in the summer.* **got, got** or **got ten, get ting.**

ghost in stories, one who is dead but who appears to living people. See the picture. **ghosts.**

gi ant 1. in stories, a person of great size or of very great power. 2. huge: *a giant sandwich, a giant footprint.* **gi ants.**

gift something given; a present; something you received without having to pay for: *My uncle brought me a gift from Mexico.* **gifts.**

gig gle 1. laugh in a silly way: *The children giggled in the corner.* 2. a silly laugh: *We heard a loud giggle from the back of the room.* **gig gled, gig gling; gig gles.**

gin ger bread a kind of cake or cookie, often made to look like a man or a house. See the picture.

ging ham a cotton cloth made from colored threads: *a gingham apron.*

gerbil

ghost

gingerbread house

giraffe

glass

giraffe

Girl Scout

gladiolus

drinking glass

gi raffe a large animal with a very long neck. Giraffes are the tallest living animals. See the picture. **gi raffes.**

girl 1. a female child. 2. a young, single woman. **girls.**

Girl Scout a member of a group for girls called The Girl Scouts of the United States of America. See the picture. **Girl Scouts.**

give 1. hand over as a present or gift and without receiving anything in return. 2. pay: *I will give you three dollars for the necklace.* 3. do or make: *The dog gave me a scare when it barked.* **gave, giv en, giv ing.**

giv en See **give.** *He has given his bike to me.*

glad 1. happy or pleased: *She is glad to be home.* 2. bringing joy; pleasant: *She smiled when she heard the glad news.* **glad der, glad dest.**

glad i o lus a plant with tall stalks of large, brightly colored flowers. See the picture. **glad i o li** or **glad i o lus es.**

glad ly in a happy or glad way: *I will gladly sing to you.*

glance 1. a quick look: *A glance at him told me he was angry.* 2. look quickly: *I only glanced at her.* **glanc es; glanced, glanc ing.**

glare 1. a strong, bright light that hurts the eyes. 2. shine strongly enough to hurt the eyes. 3. look at someone angrily. **glares; glared, glar ing.**

glass 1. a hard substance that you can usually see through. Windows are made of glass. 2. a container to drink from, usually made of glass. See the picture. 3. a mirror. It is also called a looking glass. 4. made of glass: *a glass vase.* 5. **Glasses** often means something to wear in front of your eyes to help you see. **glass es.**

gleam 1. a flash or beam of light: *The gleam of bright light hurt our eyes.* 2. send out a light; shine: *The flashlight gleamed in the dark.* **gleams; gleamed, gleam ing.**

glee lively joy; great delight.

glid er an airplane without a motor. A glider floats on the air currents. See the picture. **glid ers.**

globe 1. anything that is round like a ball. 2. the earth; the world. 3. a ball with a map of the earth or the sky drawn on it. See the picture. **globes.**

gloomy dark and sad: *We felt better as soon as we walked out of that gloomy room.* **gloom i er, gloom i est.**

glo ri ous 1. having or deserving glory. 2. giving glory: *Our team won a glorious victory.* 3. magnificent; splendid: *The children had a glorious time at the fair.*

glo ry 1. great praise: *The pilot of the plane got all the glory.* 2. something so magnificent or splendid that it should be praised: *They saw the glory of the sky at night.* **glo ries.**

glove a covering for the hand, with a place for each finger and for the thumb. See the picture. **gloves.**

glow 1. the shine that comes from something that is hot or bright: *There was a glow in the sky from the city lights.* 2. shine with a bright, warm color: *See how the fire glows.* **glows; glowed, glow ing.**

glue 1. something used to stick or hold things together: *We fixed the broken chair with glue.* 2. stick together with glue: *We glued the parts of the model plane.* **glues; glued, glu ing.**

glider

globe 3.

pair of gloves

goat

goblin

goldenrod

goldfish

go 1. move along: *Boats go down the river.* 2. move away: *Are you ready to go?* 3. act or work: *I can't make my watch go.* 4. pass: *Time goes slowly when you're alone.* 5. have its place; belong: *This dish goes on the first shelf.* 6. be about to: *Are you going to start now?* **went, gone, go ing.**

goal the place in a race or game that the players move toward and try to reach. **goals.**

goat an animal with horns. See the picture. **goats.**

gob ble[1] eat fast and noisily: *He gobbled his dinner.* **gob bled, gob bling.**

gob ble[2] 1. the noise a turkey makes. 2. make this noise: *We could hear the turkeys gobble.* **gob bles; gob bled, gob bling.**

gob lin in stories, a mean or ugly elf. See the picture. **gob lins.**

God the Supreme Being that many people believe in and worship.

goes See **go**. *Where I go, she goes.*

gold 1. a heavy, bright-yellow metal of great value. 2. made of gold: *a gold bracelet.*

gold en 1. made of gold: *a golden chain.* 2. shining like gold; bright-yellow: *golden hair.*

gold en rod a plant with tall stalks of small yellow flowers. See the picture.

gold fish a small fish of golden color often kept in a pool or fish bowl. See the picture. **gold fish** or **gold fish es.**

gone See **go**. *She has gone home.*

good 1. as it should be or well done: *She does good work.* 2. doing what is right: *That's a good boy.* 3. pleasant: *I hope you have a good time at the ball game.* **bet ter, best.**

good-by or **good-bye** words said when people go away. **good-bys** or **good-byes**.

good ness 1. the state of being good. 2. an exclamation: *"My goodness!" cried Grandmother.*

goods things for sale.

goose a bird that looks like a duck but is larger. See the picture. **geese**.

go pher a small animal like a rat. See the picture. **go phers**.

go ril la a very strong animal like a monkey. See the picture. **go ril las**.

got See **get**. *It got chilly. It has got much colder.*

got ten See **get**.

gourd a kind of fruit with a hard shell. You can make bowls from the shells. See the picture. **gourds**.

gov ern control; take care of; rule over: *The king governed his people well.* **gov erned, gov ern ing**.

gov ern ment the way of governing a country, a state, a county, or a city. A government is made up of different departments. **gov ern ments**.

gov er nor a person who is head of a state of the United States. **gov er nors**.

grab take suddenly or snatch: *The dog grabbed my shoe and ran.* **grabbed, grab bing**.

grade 1. a class in school: *She is in third grade.* 2. a number or letter that shows how well one has done: *Did you get a good grade on the test?* 3. give a grade to: *We graded each other's papers.* **grades; grad ed, grad ing**.

grain 1. the seed of such plants as wheat, oats, and corn. 2. one of the tiny bits of material that make up some things: *grains of sand, grains of sugar.* **grains**.

wild goose

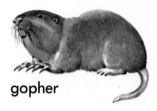
gopher

gorilla

gourds

grapes

grapefruit

grasshopper

grand large and splendid; wonderful: *The king and queen lived in a very grand palace.* **grand er, grand est.**

grand child a child of one's son or daughter. **grand chil dren.**

grand daugh ter a daughter of one's son or daughter. **grand daugh ters.**

grand fa ther the father of one's father or mother. **grand fa thers; grand pa**

grand moth er the mother of one's mother or father. **grand moth ers; grand ma**

grand par ent grandfather or grandmother. **grand par ents.**

grand son a son of one's son or daughter. **grand sons.**

grand stand a place for people to sit while they are watching a game or a sport. A fairground usually has a grandstand. **grand stands.**

grant give what is asked: *The queen granted our wish.* **grant ed, grant ing.**

grape 1. a small round fruit, red, purple, or green, that grows on a vine. See the picture. 2. tasting like grapes: *He likes grape jam.* **grapes.**

grape fruit 1. a yellow fruit like an orange, but larger and not so sweet. 2. the tree it grows on. See the picture. **grape fruits** or **grape fruit.**

grass a plant with leaves like blades. **grass es.**

grass hop per an insect with wings and strong legs for jumping. See the picture. **grass hop pers.**

grate¹ 1. rub with a squeaking sound: *The iron door grated against the floor.* 2. wear down or grind off in small pieces: *We grated cheese.* **grat ed, grat ing.**

grate² a frame of iron bars to hold a fire or cover an opening. See the picture. **grates.**

gra vy 1. the juice that comes out of meat when it is cooked. 2. a sauce made from this juice. **gra vies.**

gray 1. a color made by mixing black and white. 2. having a color between black and white: *We saw the gray clouds coming fast.* It is also spelled **grey. grays; gray er, gray est.**

graze¹ eat growing grass: *Sheep were grazing in the meadow.* **grazed, graz ing.**

graze² scrape or touch lightly in passing: *Dad grazed the garage door with the car.* **grazed, graz ing.**

grease 1. thick fat or oil. 2. put grease on or in: *Grease the cookie sheet before you bake the cookies.* **greas es; greased, greas ing.**

great 1. big; large: *a great cloud.* 2. more than usual: *in great pain.* 3. important: *a great artist.* **great er, great est.**

great ly in a great way.

greedy wanting more than your share; wanting to eat a lot. **greed i er, greed i est.**

green 1. the color of most growing plants. 2. having this color: *a green leaf, a green dress.* 3. not ripe; not fully grown: *Eating green apples made him sick.* **greens; green er, green est.**

greens the leaves and stems of some plants, used for food: *turnip greens, mustard greens.*

greet say hello to someone: *She came to the door to greet us.* **greet ed, greet ing.**

grew See **grow.** *The baby grew an inch.*

grey gray. **greys; grey er, grey est.**

grey hound a tall, slim hunting dog. See the picture. **grey hounds.**

grate²

greyhound

grin 1. a broad smile. 2. smile with teeth showing. **grins; grinned, grin ning.**

grind crush or cut into small pieces or into powder. **ground, grind ing.**

groan 1. a sound made down in the throat when one is sad or in pain: *Groans could be heard from the attic.* 2. make this sound. **groans; groaned, groan ing.**

gro cer a person who operates a grocery. **gro cers.**

gro cery 1. a store that sells food and sometimes things for the house. 2. **Groceries** may mean food and things for the house. **gro cer ies.**

ground[1] 1. the surface of the earth; soil: *The ground was hard and rocky.* 2. of or on the ground: *the ground floor of a building.*

ground[2] See **grind**. *She ground the meat. She has ground three pounds of it.*

group 1. several persons or things together: *We saw a group of children laughing.* 2. form or put several together: *The grocer grouped the apples by size.* **groups; grouped, group ing.**

grouse

grouse a bird with a thick body. See the picture. **grouse.**

grove a group of trees: *There are many pecan groves in the south.* **groves.**

grow 1. become bigger; become more: *Business will grow if we advertise.* 2. live and become big: *A cactus will grow in sand.* 3. cause to grow; raise: *We grow corn on our farm.* 4. become: *It grew darker.* **grew, grown, grow ing.**

growl 1. a sound like that made by a fierce dog; a deep, warning sound. 2. make such a sound: *The dog growled at the squirrels.* **growls; growled, growl ing.**

grown See **grow**. *The flowers have grown tall.*

grown-up 1. a grown person. 2. like a grown-up: *He acted in a grown-up way.* **grown-ups.**

gruff cross and unfriendly: *The old man spoke in a gruff voice.* **gruff er, gruff est.**

grum ble complain; find fault: *She grumbled about the weather all day.* **grum bled, grum bling.**

grum py bad-tempered; grouchy.

grunt 1. a deep, hoarse sound that a pig makes or a sound like it. 2. make this sound. **grunts; grunt ed, grunt ing.**

guard 1. take care of; keep safe: *The dog guards the house at night.* 2. keep from escaping. 3. a person who guards: *a crossing guard.* See the picture. 4. a certain player in football and basketball. **guard ed, guard ing; guards.**

guess 1. an idea you have that may not be right: *My guess is that the tree is ten feet high.* 2. think without really knowing: *I guess it will rain tomorrow.* **guess es; guessed, guess ing.**

guest a person who is visiting at another's house: *She was our guest for dinner.* **guests.**

guide 1. show the way or lead someone: *The compass will guide us back to camp.* 2. a person who leads you or shows the way: *We hired a guide to show us the cave.* **guid ed, guid ing; guides.**

guin ea hen a bird having dark-gray feathers with small white spots. See the picture. **guin ea hens.**

guin ea pig an animal often kept as a pet. See the picture. **guin ea pigs.**

gui tar a musical instrument having six strings. You play it with your fingers. See the picture. **gui tars.**

grown-up

---

guitar

crossing guard

guinea hen

guinea pig

girl playing a guitar

gull

guppy

gull a bird living on or near lakes and oceans. See the picture. **gulls.**

gulp swallow fast or noisily. **gulped, gulp ing.**

gum[1] 1. the sticky juice of certain trees. It is used for sticking things together. 2. something sweet that you chew but don't swallow. **gums.**

gum[2] the part of the mouth around the teeth. **gums.**

gun a weapon that shoots bullets. **guns.**

gup py a small, brightly colored fish. See the picture. **gup pies.**

gush 1. rush out suddenly; pour out. 2. rush of liquid from an enclosed space. **gushed, gush ing.**

gym gymnasium. **gyms.**

gym na si um a room or building in which athletes and other people exercise and play some games. **gym na si ums.**

H   h

H or h the eighth letter of the alphabet. **H's or h's.**

hab it something you do without thinking: *Biting your nails is a bad habit.* **hab its.**

had See **have.** *We had a good time at the movie. I had a dime. He had to go home. Mother had the walls washed. You had plenty of time. They had been away.*

had n't had not.

hail[1] 1. small round pieces of ice coming down like rain; frozen rain. 2. fall in frozen drops. **hailed, hail ing.**

hail[2] 1. greet: *The crowd hailed the team that won.* 2. a loud call; a shout: *The hails of the crowd pleased him.* 3. call loudly to; shout to: *We tried to hail a car.* **hailed, hail ing; hails.**

hair fine, thin pieces like threads growing from the skin of people and animals: *The little girl's hair was soft as silk.* **hair** or **hairs.**

half one of two equal parts: *Half of 6 is 3.* **halves.**

half way one half of the distance or the amount: *She walked halfway home with me. I am halfway through my supper.*

hal i but a large fish, used for food. See the picture. **hal i buts** or **hal i but.**

hall 1. a narrow space in or through a building: *Leave your boots in the hall.* 2. a large room in a building: *The hall was filled with people.* **halls.**

Hal low een or **Hal low e'en** October 31; a time for ghosts, witches, and jack-o'-lanterns. **Hal low eens** or **Hal low e'ens.**

halt stop: *The marching band halted.* **halt ed, halt ing.**

ham meat from a hog's leg. **hams.**

ham burg er 1. ground beef shaped into flat cakes. 2. a sandwich made with hamburger. **ham burg ers.**

ham mer 1. a tool used to drive nails and to beat metal into shape. 2. drive, hit, or work with a hammer. **ham mers; ham mered, ham mer ing.**

ham mock a hanging bed. See the picture. **ham mocks.**

ham ster an animal somewhat like a mouse, but larger. See the picture. **ham sters.**

hand 1. the end part of the arm. 2. something like a hand: *the hands of a clock.* 3. give with the hand; pass: *Please hand me the salt.* **hands; hand ed, hand ing.**

hand ful as much or as many as the hand can hold. **hand fuls.**

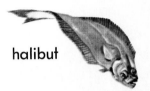
halibut

hammock

hamster

harbor

handles

hangar

harbor

hand ker chief a square of cloth used for wiping the nose, face, and hands. **hand ker chiefs.**

han dle 1. the part of the thing you take hold of. Pans, suitcases, rakes, have handles. 2. touch, feel, or use with the hand: *Don't handle the vase.* **han dles; han dled, han dling.**

hand some good-looking; pleasing to the eye: *That man is handsome.* **hand som er, hand som est.**

hand writ ing writing done by hand.

handy 1. easy to reach or use: *Find a handy place to keep the pots and pans.* 2. clever with the hands: *She is handy with tools.* **hand i er, hand i est.**

hang 1. fasten or be fastened to something above: *Hang the hammock between those trees.* 2. kill by hanging with a rope around the neck. 3. bend down. If you are sad you might hang your head. **hung (hanged** for 2.), **hang ing.**

hang ar a shed for airplanes. See the picture. **hang ars.**

Ha nuk kah a holiday, usually in December, when Jewish people give gifts and light candles. **Ha nuk kahs.**

hap pen go on; take place: *So many funny things happen at school.* **hap pened, hap pen ing.**

hap pi ly in a happy manner; with pleasure and joy: *The girls played happily in the pool.*

hap pi ness being happy or glad: *We wish the couple much happiness.*

hap py 1. feeling as you do when you are having a good time; glad; pleased. 2. showing that you are glad: *a happy smile.* **hap pi er, hap pi est.**

har bor a place of shelter for ships. See the picture. **har bors.**

hard 1. stiff; firm; not soft; not moving when touched: *Most nuts have hard shells.* 2. needing much work or time: *This was a hard job to do.* 3. not easily or lightly: *He works hard. Yesterday it snowed hard.* **hard er, hard est.**

hard ly only just; with nothing extra: *We had hardly finished eating when the telephone rang.*

hard ship something hard to bear; a hard way of living. *Hunger is a hardship.* **hard ships.**

hare an animal very much like a big rabbit, with long ears and long hind legs. **hares.**

harm 1. anything that can hurt you: *I hope no harm comes to him.* 2. hurt: *The baby's fall did not harm her.* **harmed, harm ing.**

harp a large musical instrument with strings. You play it with the fingers. See the picture. **harps.**

har vest 1. the collection of crops when they are ripe. 2. gather the crops. **har vests; har vest ed, har vest ing.**

has See **have**. *Who has my boots? He has been on vacation. What has she done?*

has n't has not.

haste 1. trying to be quick; a hurry: *Her haste in calling the fire department saved the house.* 2. **Make haste** means hurry; be quick.

hast i ly in a hurried way; quickly and perhaps not very carefully: *The boys hastily put up their tents when the rain began.*

hasty in a hurry; quick and not very careful. **hast i er, hast i est.**

hat a covering for the head. **hats.**

hatch 1. come out from an egg: *One chicken hatched today.* See the picture. 2. plan secretly; plot: *The class was hatching a surprise.* **hatched, hatch ing.**

woman playing a harp

hatch 1.

hawk

hawthorn tree

hayloft

hate not love someone or something at all.
hat ed, hat ing.

haul pull or drag with force: *Mules hauled a heavy load up the mountain.* **hauled, haul ing.**

have 1. hold: *I have a snake in my hand.* 2. own: *I have two dollars.* 3. know; understand: *You have the right idea.* 4. be forced: *I have to leave now.* 5. *Have* is also used with *en* forms of verbs. **has, had, hav ing.**

have n't have not.

Ha waii one of the fifty states of the United States. See page 338.

hawk a bird with a strong bill and large claws. See the picture. **hawks.**

haw thorn a small tree with thorns and red, pink, or white flowers. See the picture. **haw thorns.**

hay grass cut and dried, used as feed.

hay loft a place in a barn where hay is stored. See the picture. **hay lofts.**

hay mow a hayloft. **hay mows.**

he any boy, man, or male animal you are talking about: *Joe says he goes to work every day. He is strong. My dog is so old he can't see.*

head 1. the top part of the human body. 2. the front of an animal where the eyes, ears, and mouth are. 3. the top part: *the head of the stairs.* 4. the front: *the head of the line.* 5. be at the front or the top of: *His name heads the list.* 6. move toward; face toward: *After the movie we will head home.* 7. the one in charge: *the head of the family.* 8. the chief or main one: *the head nurse.* 9. **Over your head** means too hard to understand. **heads; head ed, head ing.**

head quar ters 1. the place from which orders are sent out. 2. the main office.

health being well or being sick: *The doctor is concerned about my health.*

healthy in good health: *a healthy person.* **health i er, health i est.**

heap 1. a pile. 2. form into a heap or pile. **heaps; heaped, heap ing.**

hear 1. get sounds through the ear: *Can you hear my watch?* 2. receive word or news: *Did you hear from your sister?* **heard, hear ing.**

heard See **hear.** *He heard a noise. He has heard it before.*

heart 1. the part of your body that pumps the blood. 2. feelings; mind: *She has a kind heart.* 3. the middle; the main part: *It is dark in the heart of the forest.* 4. a certain shape. See the picture. **hearts.**

hearth the floor of a fireplace where a fire is made. See the picture. **hearths.**

heat 1. being hot: *The heat of a stove feels good on a cold day.* 2. make or become warm or hot: *The furnace heats the house.* **heat ed, heat ing.**

heav i ly in a heavy way or manner: *The tired woman walked heavily.*

heavy hard to lift or carry; having much weight. **heav i er, heav i est.**

he'd 1. he had: *He'd already gone.* 2. he would: *He said he'd wait.*

hedge a thick row of bushes that makes a fence. See the picture. **hedg es.**

hedge hog a porcupine. **hedge hogs.**

heel 1. the back part of your foot, below the ankle. 2. the part of a stocking or shoe that covers your heel. 3. the part of a shoe or boot that is under your heel. **heels.**

heart 4.

hearth

hedge

helicopter

football helmet

hemlock tree

held See **hold**[1]. *She held his hand. She had held mine, too.*

hel i cop ter an aircraft with a rotor and four large blades. See the picture. **hel i cop ters.**

he'll 1. he will. 2. he shall.

hel lo a call to greet someone: *I said, "Hello!"* **hel los.**

hel met a covering usually made of metal or plastic to protect the head. See the picture. **hel mets.**

help 1. give or do what is needed or useful: *Help Grandmother put her coat on.* 2. the act of helping: *I need some help.* 3. make better: *The medicine helped my cold.* **helped, help ing.**

help ful giving help; useful: *The girls tried to be helpful at the party.*

help ful ly in a helpful way: *He helpfully carried my groceries.*

help ing the amount of food served to one person: *I ate three helpings of beans.* **help ings.**

help less without help; not able to help yourself: *A puppy is helpless.*

hem lock an evergreen tree like a pine. See the picture. **hem locks.**

hemp a plant with a strong stalk that is used to make rope. **hemps.**

hen a female chicken or other female bird. **hens.**

her 1. any girl or woman or female animal you are talking about: *Sue is here; have you seen her? Wait for her.* 2. of her; belonging to her; done by her: *Peg hurt her arm. It's her fault. Mother has finished her painting.*

herb a kind of plant with leaves, stems, or roots that are used for medicine or to season food. *Mint is an herb.* **herbs.**

herd 1. a group of animals together: *a herd of buffaloes, a herd of elephants.* 2. form into a herd: *He herded the sheep on a hill.* **herds; herd ed, herd ing.**

here in this place; at this place: *Do you live here? The sale will be held here.*

her on a bird that lives near the water. See the picture. **her ons.**

hers of her; belonging to her: *This scarf is hers.*

her self used instead of *her* or *she*: *She hurt herself when she fell. She bought that sweater herself. She herself did it.*

he's 1. he is: *He's a big boy.* 2. he has: *He's gone home.*

hey sound made to attract attention.

hi bis cus a plant with large flowers. See the picture. **hi bis cus es.**

hic cups a catching of the breath that you cannot control. Hiccups usually stop after a few minutes.

hick o ry a North American tree with nuts that are good to eat. See the picture. **hick o ries.**

hid See **hide¹**. *She hid the ring in a safe place.*

hid den 1. out of sight; secret; not clear: *The boys hoped to find the hidden caves.* 2. See **hide¹**. *The dog had hidden a bone.*

hide¹ 1. put out of sight: *Hide the candy.* 2. be in front of: *That picture hides a crack in the wall.* 3. keep secret: *She tried to hide her fear.* 4. hide yourself: *I'll hide, and you find me.* **hid, hid den** or **hid, hid ing.**

hide² an animal's skin. **hides.**

high 1. tall: *a high hill.* 2. up above the ground: *a high step.* 3. at or to a high place: *The kite was caught high in the tree.* 4. above others: *of high birth.* **high er, high est.**

heron

hibiscus

hickory

hinge

hip

hippopotamus

high ly very, very much: *She was highly amused.*

high way a main road. **high ways.**

hike 1. take a long walk; tramp; march. 2. a long walk. **hiked, hik ing; hikes.**

hill 1. a raised part of the earth's surface, not so big as a mountain. 2. a little heap or pile: *Ants make hills to live in.* **hills.**

him any boy or man or male animal you are talking about: *Did you thank him? She gave him candy. The dog is hungry; take the food to him.*

him self used instead of *him* or *he*: *The little boy put his boots on by himself. He ate the last cookie himself. He hit himself on the head.*

hind back; rear: *hind legs.*

hinge a joint on which a door or a lid moves back and forth. See the picture. **hing es.**

hint 1. a clue that helps you know something: *The thunder gave a hint of the coming storm.* 2. suggest without telling: *She hinted that she wanted to go home.* **hints; hint ed, hint ing.**

hip the joint where the leg joins the body. See the picture. **hips.**

hip po pot a mus a huge animal with thick skin. See the picture. **hip po pot a mus es** or **hip po pot a mi.**

his 1. of him; belonging to him: *His bicycle is lost.* 2. the one or ones belonging to him: *My shoes are black; his are brown.*

hiss 1. make a sound like a drop of water on a hot stove. 2. a sound like *ss.* **hiss es, hiss ing.**

his to ry 1. the story of a person or a nation: *We studied the history of the United States.* 2. an account of what has happened: *The guide gave us the history of the building.* **his to ries.**

hit 1. go hard against something: *One boy hit the other. Will the ball hit the roof? She has hit her arm on the door.* 2. a blow; a going against something sharply: *A hit on the head can hurt.* 3. in baseball, hitting the ball and running safely to first base: *The boy got a hit.* **hit, hit ting; hits.**

hive a house or box for bees to live in. See the picture. **hives.**

hoarse sounding hard and not smooth: *A cold made his voice hoarse.* **hoars er, hoars est.**

hob by something a person likes to do as a pastime. **hob bies**

hoe 1. a tool with a small blade set across the end of a long handle, used to loosen soil. See the picture. 2. loosen soil around; dig or cut with a hoe. **hoes; hoed, hoe ing.**

hog a pig raised for food. **hogs.**

hold[1] 1. take or pick up and keep: *Hold this suitcase for me. Hold my jacket while I put on my boots.* 2. the act of holding: *I took a good hold of the knob and pulled.* 3. keep back: *Hold your laughter.* 4. contain: *This carton holds books.* **held, hold ing; holds.**

hold[2] the lowest part of the inside of a ship. **holds.**

hole 1. an open place: *There is a big hole in this stocking.* 2. a hollow place: *The car hit a hole in the road.* **holes.**

hol i day a day when you do not work or go to school; a day for having fun. **hol i days.**

hol low 1. with nothing inside; empty. A tube or pipe is hollow. 2. a place lower than the parts around it. 3. take out the inside parts: *We hollowed out a pumpkin.* **hol lows; hol lowed, hol low ing.**

bee hive

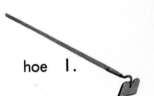

hoe 1.

hook

holly tree

honeybee

hood over a stove

horse's hoof

hook 1.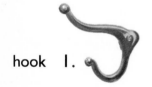

hol ly an evergreen bush or tree with shiny leaves and red berries. See the picture. **hol lies.**

ho ly coming from God or belonging to God or set apart for God. **ho li er, ho li est.**

home 1. the place where a person or a family lives. 2. the town or country where you were born or brought up: *Her home is England.* 3. a place where people who are poor, old, or sick may live. 4. in games, the place where a player can be safe: *The player ran for home.* 5. of or about home: *This is my home town.* **homes.**

hon est fair; telling the truth; not saying or doing anything that isn't true, right, or good.

hon es ty the act of being fair and honest; doing only what is right and saying only what is true.

hon ey a thick, sweet, yellow liquid, good to eat. Bees make honey of the drops they collect from flowers. **hon eys.**

hon ey bee a bee that makes honey. See the picture. **hon ey bees.**

honk 1. a sound like the cry of a wild goose: *the honk of an automobile horn.* 2. make such a sound. **honks; honked, honk ing.**

hood 1. a soft covering for the head and neck. 2. anything like a hood: *Some stoves have hoods above them.* See the picture. 3. the metal covering over an automobile engine. **hoods.**

hoof the hard part of the foot of some animals. See the picture. **hoofs** or **hooves.**

hook 1. a piece of metal, wood, or other stiff material, curved or bent, for hanging things on. See the picture. 2. catch or take hold of with a hook. 3. fasten with hooks: *Hook your tie to your collar.* 4. a bent piece of wire for catching fish. **hooks; hooked, hook ing.**

hoop 1. a ring or a flat metal circle: *Hoops hold a barrel together.* 2. a large metal or plastic circle you roll along the ground. 3. a frame used to hold out an old-fashioned skirt. **hoops.**

hoot 1. the sound that an owl makes. 2. make this sound or one like it. **hoots; hoot ed, hoot ing.**

hooves more than one hoof.

hop 1. spring, or move by springing: *How far can you hop on one foot?* 2. a hopping; a spring: *Take two hops forward and one hop back.* **hopped, hop ping; hops.**

hope 1. a feeling that what you want to happen will happen: *Her words gave me hope.* 2. look for; expect: *I hope you'll like school.* **hopes; hoped, hop ing.**

hope ful feeling or showing hope; expecting to receive what you want.

hope ful ly with hope; in a hopeful way: *The boy hopefully asked if we had found his baseball.*

hope less feeling no hope: *The lost child had a hopeless look. I wanted to catch the bird, but it was hopeless to try.*

hope less ly in a hopeless way; without hope.

hop scotch a game played by hopping in squares marked on the ground or sidewalk.

horn 1. a hard mass, usually curved and pointed, on the heads of some animals. See the picture. 2. a musical instrument played by blowing into it. 3. a signal of danger: *automobile horn.* **horns.**

hor net a large insect, like a wasp, that can sting. See the picture. **hor nets.**

horse a large animal with hoofs and a mane. People ride horses. See the picture. **hors es.**

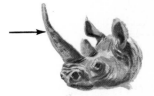

rhinoceros's horn

hornet

horse

hose 1. a long, hollow tube for carrying or moving liquid. 2. stockings. **hos es** (for 1.).

hos pi tal a place where sick people are cared for. **hos pi tals.**

hot 1. much warmer than the body; having much heat. 2. having a sharp, burning taste: *I don't like hot pepper.* **hot ter, hot test.**

hot dog 1. a frankfurter. 2. a sandwich made with a frankfurter in a bun. **hot dogs.**

ho tel a building where people can rent rooms to sleep in. **ho tels.**

hound a kind of dog used for hunting. **hounds.**

hour a period of time; one of the 24 equal parts of one day. Sixty minutes make an hour. **hours.**

house 1. a building in which people live. 2. a special building: *a doghouse, a birdhouse.* **hous es.**

house keep er person hired to manage a home and to do the housework. **house keep ers.**

how 1. in what way: *How did you get home? How can we get to her house?* 2. to what amount: *How much do you weigh? How late is it?*

how ev er nevertheless; yet; in spite of: *I was late for lunch; however, there was plenty of food.*

howl 1. give a long, loud, sad cry: *A wolf howls at night.* 2. a long, loud, sad cry: *We heard the wolf's howl.* **howled, howl ing; howls.**

hub

hub the center of a wheel. See the picture. **hubs.**

hug 1. put your arms around and hold close: *The little boy hugs his puppy.* 2. a tight pressure with the arms: *When I come home I expect a hug.* **hugged, hug ging; hugs.**

huge very, very large: *A huge shark was found on the beach.* **hug er, hug est.**

hum 1. make a steady sound like that of a bee or of a spinning top: *The sewing machine hums when it is running.* 2. a sound that doesn't stop: *We listened to the hum of bees in the field.* 3. sing with closed lips, not sounding words: *Can you hum a tune?* **hummed, hum ming; hums.**

hu man being a person or like a person: *Men, women, and children are human beings. The dog seemed almost human.*

hum ming bird a tiny, brightly colored bird. Its wings move so rapidly they make a humming sound. See the picture. **hum ming birds.**

hun dred ten times ten; 100. **hun dreds.**

hun dredth 1. the next after the ninety-ninth; 100th. 2. one of 100 equal parts. **hun dredths.**

hung See **hang.** *She hung his picture on the wall. Have you hung her picture yet?*

hun ger the pains caused by having had nothing to eat: *He ended his hunger when he ate.*

hun gri ly in a hungry manner.

hun gry feeling a need for food: *The girls are hungry.* **hun gri er, hun gri est.**

hunt 1. track animals for food or for fun: *The men were hunting deer.* 2. look for; try to find: *Don't forget to hunt for that book.* **hunt ed, hunt ing.**

hunt er a person who hunts. **hunt ers.**

hur rah a shout of joy. **hur rahs.**

hur ray hurrah. **hur rays.**

hur ri cane a fierce storm with heavy wind and very heavy rain. **hur ri canes.**

hur ry 1. drive, carry, send, or move quickly: *Hurry home after the movie.* 2. a quick move: *Her hurry caused the accident.* **hur ried, hur ry ing; hur ries.**

hummingbird

ice

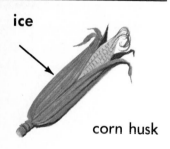

corn husk

Husky

hyacinth

hydrant

hurt 1. do harm to: *The stones will hurt your feet.* 2. a cut or sore; the breaking of a bone; any wound. 3. suffer pain: *Your head hurt, didn't it? Has it hurt all day?* **hurt, hurt ing; hurts.**

hus band a man who has a wife; a married man. **hus bands.**

husk 1. the dry, outside covering of some seeds or fruits. See the picture. 2. take the husk from: *May I help husk the corn?* **husks; husked, husk ing.**

husky[1] 1. dry in the throat; hoarse: *You certainly have a husky cough.* 2. big and strong: *He is a husky boy.* **husk i er, husk i est.**

Husky or **husky**[2] an Eskimo dog. See the picture. **Husk ies.**

hut a small cabin; a little house. **huts.**

hy a cinth a spring flower that grows from a bulb. See the picture. **hy a cinths.**

hy drant an iron pipe going up from a water main to the street above. Firemen connect a hose to a hydrant to get water. See the picture. **hy drants.**

I i

I or **i** the ninth letter of the alphabet. **I's** or **i's.**

I the person speaking: *I am here. I am running. I am a citizen.*

ice 1. frozen water. 2. of ice; having something to do with ice: *ice water, ice cubes.* 3. put ice in or around: *She iced the glasses for our lemonade.* 4. a frozen dessert, usually one made of fruit juice: *lemon ice.* 5. cover a cake with frosting: *Let's ice the cake.* **ic es; iced, ic ing.**

ice cream a dessert made of cream and sugar, and frozen. **ice creams.**

ici cle a hanging spear of ice formed when water freezes as it drips. See the picture. **ici cles.**

icy 1. covered with ice. 2. like ice; slick. **ic i er, ic i est.**

Ida ho one of the fifty states of the United States. See page 339.

idea a plan, picture, or thought in the mind: *Whose idea was it to go to the zoo? We had no idea it was true.* **ideas.**

if 1. not certain or sure: *I'll go to the park if it doesn't rain.* 2. whether: *I wonder if I should go.*

ig nore pay no attention to; disregard. **ig nored, ig nor ing.**

ill sick; not having good health. **worse, worst.**

I'll 1. I shall. 2. I will.

Il li nois one of the fifty states of the United States. See page 340.

I'm I am.

i mag i na tion 1. power of forming pictures in the mind. 2. creation of the mind; fancy.

imag ine form a picture of something in the mind; have an idea: *The boy likes to imagine he's an astronaut.* **imag ined, imag in ing.**

im i tate copy; make or do something like. **im i tat ed, im i tat ing.**

im por tant meaning a lot; valuable: *It is important to go to school. The president is an important person.*

im pos si ble something that cannot be or happen: *It is impossible for one and two to make four.*

im prove make or become better: *You could improve your handwriting with practice.* **im proved, im prov ing.**

icicle

in 1. within; not outside: *We live in the city.*
2. during: *in the winter, in an hour.* 3. into:
Go in the house. 4. on the inside: *Is Dad in?*

inch a measure of length. Twelve inches are equal
to one foot. **inch es.**

in clined 1. willing: *I'm inclined to believe your
story.* 2. slanting: *We walked up an inclined
board.*

in cu ba tor box or chamber for hatching eggs.
in cu ba tors.

in deed 1. really: *Germs are indeed dangerous.*
2. a word used to show surprise: *Indeed!*

in dex a list at the end of a book. It tells on
which pages to find each item. **in dex es.**

In di an 1. one of the first people living in
America. 2. a person living in a country in Asia.
3. of Indians: *There was an Indian camp near the
forest. The Indian prince rode an elephant.*
In di ans.

In di ana one of the fifty states of the United
States. See page 341.

In di an paint brush a plant with bright-red tips
on its leaves. See the picture.
In di an paint brush es.

in doors in or into a house or building: *Come
indoors if it rains.*

ink a colored liquid used for writing. **inks.**

inn a hotel: *We spent the night at a little inn.* **inns.**

in quire try to find out by asking questions:
*I inquired about a room. Did she inquire about
a lost child?* **in quired, in quir ing.**

in sect a small animal with a body divided into
three parts. It has three pairs of legs and usually
two pairs of wings. Mosquitoes, flies, and bees
are insects. **in sects.**

Indian paintbrush

in side 1. the part within; the surface not on the outside: *The inside of the box was covered with silk.* 2. being within: *an inside seat.* 3. in: *The astronaut is inside the module.* **in sides.**

in sist keep saying or thinking something without changing your mind or giving up: *She insists that this is her book.* **in sist ed, in sist ing.**

in stant 1. a small bit of time: *He stopped for an instant.* 2. quick: *instant coffee.* 3. at an exact moment: *The instant she arrives, call me.* **in stants.**

in stant ly at once: *The talking stopped instantly.*

in stead 1. in place of something: *Please bake a pie instead of cookies.* 2. in place of someone: *She stayed home, and I went instead.*

in stru ment any tool, machine, or special thing that helps you do or make something. See the picture. **in stru ments.**

in sur ance a kind of protection. If you have fire insurance and your house burns, you will receive money to pay for the house.

in ter est 1. a feeling of wanting to know or share in: *His main interest is cars.* 2. make someone want to know or share: *Can I interest you in a book?* 3. extra money you pay if you borrow money: *My parents pay interest on money they borrowed.* **in ter ests; in ter est ed, in ter est ing.**

in ter est ing holding your interest: *He told an interesting story.*

in to 1. to the inside of: *The cows walked into the barn.* 2. to the form of: *Heat turns ice into water.*

in tro duce 1. bring in or show for the first time: *She introduced a new idea at the meeting.* 2. make people known to each other: *May I introduce my dad?* **in tro duced, in tro duc ing.**

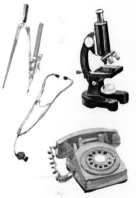

instruments

iris 1.

ironing board

island

in vent 1. make or think of something new: *Who invented the airplane?* 2. make up: *He invented an excuse for staying home.* **in vent ed, in vent ing.**

in ven tion the thing invented: *The telephone is a wonderful invention.* **in ven tions.**

in ven tor a person who invents. **in ven tors.**

in vis i ble not able to be seen: *The man was invisible in the fog.*

in vite ask someone politely to come to some place or to do something: *We invited her to go to the movies with us. Shall we invite them to stay?* **in vit ed, in vit ing.**

Io wa one of the fifty states of the United States. See page 342.

iris 1. a plant with long, pointed leaves, tall stalks, and big flowers. See the picture. 2. the colored part of your eye. **iris es.**

iron 1. a metal from which tools and machines are made. A blacksmith makes horseshoes of iron. 2. made of iron: *an iron box.* 3. an instrument that is heated and used to press clothing. 4. press with an iron: *I ironed two curtains.* **irons** (for 3.); **ironed, iron ing.**

iron ing board a flat board covered with thick cloth. Clothes are placed on it and pressed with a hot iron. See the picture. **iron ing boards.**

is *My head is cold. He is at home. She is going. It is hot inside. The house is heated with gas.*

is land a mass of land with water all around it. See the picture. **is lands.**

is n't is not.

is sue something sent out: *The last issue of our weekly paper sold out. This is the third issue of the magazine.* **is sues.**

it the thing or animal spoken about: *Your cap is where you left it. Look at that bird; is it hurt? It looks like rain. My head hurts; I bumped it.*

itch feel something on your skin that makes you want to scratch: *Don't scratch your mosquito bites even if they itch. My back itches.* **itched, itch ing.**

item one separate thing: *I had to get four items at the drugstore. I read a short item in the newspaper.* **items.**

it'll .1. it will. 2. it shall.

its of it; belonging to it: *Any cat likes to have its back rubbed. The tree lost its leaves.*

it's 1. it is: *It's going to rain.* 2. it has: *It's rained all day.*

it self *Itself* is used instead of *it* in sentences like: *The monkey sees itself in the mirror.*

I've I have.

J j

J or **j** the tenth letter of the alphabet. **J's** or **j's.**

jack et 1. a short coat. 2. an outside covering: *New books have paper jackets.* See the picture. **jack ets.**

Jack Frost in stories, a tiny fairy who paints windows with frost. See the picture.

jack-o'-lan tern a pumpkin hollowed out and cut to look like a face, to be used as a lantern at Halloween. **jack-o'-lan terns.**

jacks a game played with a ball and small metal objects. See the picture.

jade 1. a hard stone used for sculpture. Most jade is green. 2. made of jade: *a jade necklace.*

it

jade

jacket 1.

jacket 2.

Jack Frost

girl and boy playing jacks

jaguar

jar¹

jasmine

jeep

jag uar a wild animal that looks like a leopard. See the picture. **jag uars.**

jail a place where people are kept to punish them. **jails.**

jam¹ 1. press or squeeze tight: *He jammed all the socks and ties into one drawer.* 2. stick or catch so that it cannot be worked: *The door has jammed; I can't open it.* 3. fill or block the way by crowding: *Trucks jam the streets.* 4. a crowded mass: *What a traffic jam!* **jammed, jam ming; jams.**

jam² fruit boiled with sugar until it is thick. Jam can be spread on bread or toast. **jams.**

James town the first settlement built in Virginia in 1607.

jan i tor a person who takes care of a building; a custodian. **jan i tors.**

Jan u ary the first month of the year. It has 31 days. **Jan u arys.**

jar¹ a deep container usually made of stone or glass, with a wide mouth. See the picture. **jars.**

jar² shake; rattle; send a shock through something: *Don't jar the desk while I write.* **jarred, jar ring.**

jas mine a vine or bush with fragrant yellow, red, or white flowers. See the picture. **jas mines.**

jaw the lower part of the face. **jaws.**

jeans strong cotton work pants.

jeep a kind of small, sturdy automobile. See the picture. **jeeps.**

Jell-O the name of a sweet food.

jel ly a food made of fruit juice and sugar boiled together: *Jelly spread on bread is good.* **jel lies.**

jerk 1. pull or twist suddenly: *He jerked his hand out of the hot water.* 2. move with a jerk: *The train jerked along the tracks.* **jerked, jerk ing.**

jes sa mine jasmine. **jes sa mines.**

jet[1] 1. a stream of liquid forced from a small hole: *That jet of water is coming from a broken pipe.* 2. an airplane driven by jet engines. **jets.**

jet[2] a hard, black mineral that is shiny when rubbed. Jet is used for beads and jewelry.

jew el 1. a rare stone, such as a diamond. 2. a piece of jewelry. **jew els.**

jew el ry things to wear, such as bracelets, necklaces, rings.

jin gle 1. a sound like little bells ringing. 2. make such a sound: *He jingled the coins in his pocket.* 3. a verse that has a jingling sound: *She wrote a jingle.* **jin gles; jin gled, jin gling.**

job 1. work; anything a person has to do: *It was Mark's job to pass out the crayons.* 2. work done for pay: *My mom has a job in a store.* **jobs.**

jog walk or trot slowly. **jogged, jog ging.**

jog ger a person who jogs. **jog gers.**

join 1. bring or fasten things together: *We joined hands in a circle.* 2. take part with others: *He joined the Boy Scouts.* **joined, join ing.**

joint 1. the place at which two things or parts are joined together. See the picture. 2. the place where two bones move on each other. Your knee is a joint in your leg. 3. **Out of joint** means moved out of place at the joint. **joints.**

joke 1. something funny said or done to make somebody laugh. 2. make jokes; say or do something funny. **jokes; joked, jok ing.**

jol ly merry; very cheerful. **jol li er, jol li est.**

Josh ua tree a yucca plant that looks like a short tree with twisted branches. See the picture. **Josh ua trees.**

jour ney a trip. **jour neys.**

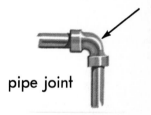

pipe joint

Joshua tree

clown juggling plates

juniper tree

joy a glad feeling; happiness. **joys.**

joy ful full of joy: *They had a joyful visit.*

joy ful ly in a joyful way: *She waved her hand joyfully at her friends.*

judge 1. one who decides questions about the law or between two people who don't agree. 2. act as a judge; decide questions of law. 3. one who decides who wins a contest. 4. decide who wins a contest. 5. one who can decide how good a thing is: *He is a good judge of horses.* **judg es; judged, judg ing.**

jug gle do tricks that require skill in balancing or catching. See the picture. **jug gled, jug gling.**

juice the liquid part of fruit or vegetable or meat. **juic es.**

Ju ly the seventh month of the year. It has 31 days. **Ju lies.**

jump 1. leave the ground by pushing the body upward or off: *Jump over that rock. Jump from the top step.* 2. a spring from the ground; a leap: *The horse made a high jump over the fence.* 3. give a sudden jerk: *A loud noise made me jump.* 4. a sudden jerk of the body when frightened. **jumped, jump ing; jumps.**

jump rope a piece of rope with handles on both ends. You swing it over your head and jump over it when it hits the ground. **jump ropes.**

jump y nervous; easily excited or frightened: *I felt jumpy until I turned on the light.*

June the sixth month of the year. It has 30 days. **Junes.**

jun gle wild land with thick bushes, vines, and trees: *There are jungles in Africa.* **jun gles.**

ju ni per an evergreen bush or tree with purple berries. See the picture. **ju ni pers.**

just 1. right; fair. 2. exactly: *The apples weighed just a pound.* 3. a very little while ago: *He just came back from vacation.* 4. only: *He is just going to the corner.*

K   k

K or **k** the eleventh letter of the alphabet. **K's** or **k's.**

kan ga roo an animal living in Australia, that carries its young in a pouch. See the picture. **kan ga roos** or **kan ga roo.**

Kan sas one of the fifty states of the United States. See page 343.

ka ty did a large green insect somewhat like a grasshopper. See the picture. **ka ty dids.**

keep 1. have forever: *Grandmother said I could keep this ring.* 2. have and not let go: *I know she can keep a secret.* 3. have and take care of: *He keeps gerbils.* 4. hold back: *We kept the dog from running away.* 5. hold in a good state: *A fan keeps our house cool.* **kept, keep ing.**

Ken tucky one of the fifty states of the United States. See page 344.

kept See **keep.** *Our teacher kept us in all day. He has kept the fire going.*

ket tle a metal pot. See the picture. **ket tles.**

key[1] 1. a small metal instrument for opening or fastening a lock. 2. the answer to a problem. 3. a set of signs used in a dictionary. 4. one of the parts you press with your fingers on a piano and other instruments. 5. in music, a scale of notes: *the key of F.* **keys.**

key[2] a low island. **keys.**

kangaroo

katydid

kettle

kid

boy and girl
wearing kimonos

kingfisher

kitten

kick 1. strike out with the foot: *The baby likes to kick his feet.* 2. strike something with the foot. 3. a blow with the foot: *She gave the door a kick.* **kicked, kick ing; kicks.**

kid 1. a young goat. See the picture. 2. a child. **kids.**

kill 1. cause to die: *A wolf killed the sheep.* 2. get rid of: *Kill the weeds.* **killed, kill ing.**

ki mo no a loose coat worn by men and women in some countries of Asia. See the picture.

kind[1] friendly; doing good rather than harm: *a kind person.* **kind er, kind est.**

kind[2] a group of things that are alike: *What kind of candy do you like best?* **kinds.**

kind ly 1. kind; friendly: *kindly faces.* 2. in a kind or friendly way. **kind li er, kind li est.**

king a man who rules or was born to rule a country and its people. **kings.**

king dom the land ruled by a king or queen. **king doms.**

king fish er a bright-colored bird. See the picture. **king fish ers.**

kiss 1. touch with the lips as a sign of love or respect. 2. a touch with the lips as a sign of love or respect. **kissed, kiss ing; kiss es.**

kitch en a room where food is prepared. **kitch ens.**

kite a wooden frame covered with paper. **kites.**

kit ten a young cat. See the picture. **kit tens; kit ty**

knee the joint between the thigh and the lower leg. **knees.**

kneel go down on your knees: *They often kneel in prayer.* **knelt** or **kneeled, kneel ing.**

knelt See **kneel**. *I knelt to tie my little cousin's shoes. He has knelt for hours.*

knew See **know.** *I knew she'd come today.*

knife a flat piece of steel or other metal with a handle and a sharp edge. **knives.**

knight a man given a title because of great service. In stories, knights often fight dragons. See the picture. **knights.**

knit 1. make a kind of cloth out of yarn, using long needles: *Will you knit a sweater for me?* 2. grow together: *The broken bone has knitted quickly.* **knit ted** or **knit, knit ting.**

knives more than one knife.

knob 1. a lump: *Some old tree trunks have knobs.* 2. the handle of a door or of a drawer. **knobs.**

knock 1. hit and cause to fall: *I knocked down the lamp.* 2. make a noise by hitting: *Knock on the door.* 3. the sound made: *a knock on the window.* **knocked, knock ing; knocks.**

knot 1. strings or ropes twisted together so they will not pull apart: *He tied the ends of the rope in a knot.* 2. tie or fasten in a knot: *Knot the string; it won't slip.* **knots; knot ted, knot ting.**

know 1. tell apart from others: *How many kinds of cars do you know?* 2. have as a friend: *Do you know my aunt?* 3. have the facts about; be skilled in: *She knows baseball.* 4. have the facts and be sure that they are true: *We know that 3 and 3 are 6.* **knew, known, know ing.**

knowl edge what you know or what is known.

known See **know.** *We have known her for years.*

ko a la a small gray animal that carries its young in a pouch. See the picture. **ko a las.**

ku kui a large tree grown for its oil. It is also called a candlenut tree. See the picture. **ku ku is.**

kum quat 1. a fruit like a small orange. 2. the tree it grows on. See the picture. **kum quats.**

knight

koala

kukui tree

kumquat

lame

lace 1.

ladybug

lady's slipper

lake

lamb 1.

L l

L or **l** the twelfth letter of the alphabet. **L's** or **l's.**

lab o ra to ry a building or room where scientists work and do experiments. **lab o ra to ries.**

La bor Day a holiday, the first Monday in September. **La bor Days.**

lace 1. fine threads woven to make a delicate net. See the picture. 2. a cord, string, or strip for holding the edges of something together: *My ice skates have new laces.* 3. pull or hold together with laces: *The ice skate was laced tightly.* **lac es; laced, lac ing.**

lad a boy; a young man. **lads.**

lad der a set of rungs or steps fastened into two long poles, for climbing up and down. **lad ders.**

la dy a polite word for a woman. **la dies.**

la dy bug a small, red beetle with black spots. See the picture. **la dy bugs.**

la dy's slip per a moccasin flower. See the picture. **la dy's slip pers.**

laid See **lay.** *He laid the heavy book down.* (Laid always means "laid something" down.)

lain See **lie².** *He has lain on the floor watching television for an hour.* (Never say, "He has laid on the floor.")

lake water with land all around it. See the picture. **lakes.**

lamb 1. a young sheep. See the picture. 2. meat from a lamb: *roast lamb.* **lambs.**

lame 1. not able to walk very well; having a hurt leg or foot: *a lame horse.* 2. stiff and sore: *He has a lame arm.* **lam er, lam est.**

lame ly in a lame way: *She walked lamely.*

lamp a thing that gives light, usually by burning oil or electricity: *We have a new bulb for this lamp.* See the picture. **lamps.**

land 1. the hard part of the earth's surface. 2. ground; soil: *Our farm has good land.* 3. a country: *He came from a distant land.* 4. come to land: *The ship landed at the dock.* **lands; land ed, land ing.**

lane 1. a path or narrow road in the country. 2. any narrow way: *This road has three lanes of traffic.* **lanes.**

lan guage human speech, spoken or written. **lan guag es.**

lan tern a light that can be carried. See the picture. **lan terns.**

lap the front part of a person sitting down, from the waist to the knees. **laps.**

large big; of great size, amount, or number: *Canada is a very large country.* **larg er, larg est.**

lar i at a long rope with a knot that slides tight. It is used by cowboys for catching horses and cattle. See the picture. **lar i ats.**

lass a girl; a young girl. **lass es.**

last¹ 1. coming after all others: *Z is the last letter in the alphabet.* 2. after all others: *Mickey was last in line.* 3. latest: *last night.*

last² hold out; continue: *Do you think our money will last until the end of our trip? The movie lasted three hours.* **last ed, last ing.**

latch 1. something for fastening a door, gate, or window. See the picture. 2. fasten with a latch. **latch es; latched, latch ing.**

late 1. after the usual time: *We had a late supper.* 2. near the end: *late at night.* **lat er, lat est.**

oil lamp

electric lamp

oil lantern

lariat

latch 1.

launch[1]

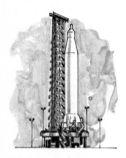

launching pad

laurel

late ly not long ago: *Have you been there lately?*

Lat in the language of the ancient Romans.

laugh 1. the sounds you make when you hear or see something funny: *Bert had a loud laugh.*
2. make those sounds: *We laughed at the silly story.* **laughs; laughed, laugh ing.**

laugh ing ly while laughing; with laughter: *She told the story laughingly.*

laugh ter the sounds of laughing.

launch[1] a small boat run by a motor. See the picture. **launch es.**

launch[2] 1. cause to slide into the water to float.
2. start or set going. **launched, launch ing.**

launch ing pad a place from which a rocket or space ship is shot into the air. See the picture. **launch ing pads.**

laun dry 1. a place where clothes are washed and ironed. 2. clothes washed or to be washed. **laun dries.**

lau rel a small tree or bush with shiny leaves and bunches of pink or white blossoms. See the picture. **lau rels.**

lav en der light purple. **lav en ders.**

law 1. a rule for all the people: *Everyone must obey the law.* 2. the study of such rules: *Did he study law?* **laws.**

lawn a piece of land covered with grass. **lawns.**

law yer a person who studies and knows the laws and gives advice about the law. **law yers.**

lay[1] 1. put something down: *Lay the book on the desk.* 2. put something in place: *Lay the bricks.*
3. bring something forth: *Hens lay eggs.* (You always lay something somewhere.) **laid, lay ing.**

lay[2] See **lie**[2]. *She lay down and fell asleep.* (Never say, "She laid down.")

lay er one fold or a flat mass: *My birthday cake has two layers. I am wearing three layers of clothes—a shirt, a sweater, and a coat.* **lay ers.**

la zy not willing to work or move fast: *I was too lazy to work today.* **la zi er, la zi est.**

lead[1] 1. show the way by going along with or in front of: *She will lead the horses to the river.* 2. be first: *Ted leads the class in writing.* **led, lead ing.** (Lead[1] rhymes with <u>seed</u>.)

lead[2] 1. a heavy gray metal. 2. made of lead: *He used a lead weight on his fishing line.* (Lead[2] rhymes with <u>bed</u>.)

leaf 1. one of the thin, flat, usually green parts of a plant. 2. a thin sheet; a page. **leaves.**

leak 1. a hole or crack not meant to be there that lets something in or out: *a leak in the roof.* 2. let something in or out: *My boots leak and my feet are wet.* **leaks; leaked, leak ing.**

leaky having a leak: *Rain dripped on my head through the leaky roof.* **leak i er, leak i est.**

lean[1] 1. stand slanting or bent: *Snow caused the bushes to lean over almost to the ground.* 2. rest against something: *Lean against the wall.* **leaned, lean ing.**

lean[2] thin or having little fat: *lean meat.* **lean er, lean est.**

leap 1. a jump off the ground: *She took one leap over the creek.* 2. jump: *The dog leaped over the fence.* **leaps; leaped** or **leapt, leap ing.**

leapt See **leap.**

learn find out about something; come to know how to do something. **learned, learn ing.**

least 1. less than any other: *He is the least friendly of the puppies.* 2. the smallest thing: *The least you can do is say you're sorry.*

girl wearing a lei

lemon

leath er 1. a strong material made by tanning hides. 2. made of leather: *leather gloves.* **leath ers.**

leave[1] 1. go away: *Our family will leave on a fishing trip tomorrow.* 2. stop being in or working for: *Why did you leave the Boy Scouts?* 3. go without taking; let stay behind: *Don't leave your book on the table.* **left, leav ing.**

leave[2] permission: *May I have your leave to go?* **leaves.**

leaves more than one leaf.

led See **lead**[2]. *The band led the parade. Have you ever led one?*

left[1] 1. belonging to the side with the arm and hand most people use less than the other: *the left hand, the left foot.* 2. on or to the left side: *Turn left at the corner.*

left[2] See **leave**[1]. *I left early. They have left too.*

leg 1. one of the limbs on which people and animals stand and walk. 2. anything shaped or used like a leg: *a chair leg.* **legs.**

lei a necklace made of flowers or nuts. See the picture. **leis.**

lem on 1. a sour, light-yellow fruit. 2. the tree it grows on. See the picture. **lem ons.**

lem on ade a drink made of lemon juice, sugar, and water. It is usually iced.

lend let someone use something you own: *Will you lend me your skates?* **lent, lend ing.**

length 1. the longest way a thing can be measured: *My rug is six feet in length.* 2. how long a thing lasts: *The length of the speech was an hour.* 3. distance: *The length of this race is one mile.* **lengths.**

lent See **lend.** *She lent me a nickel. I have lent her my bicycle.*

leop ard a fierce, spotted animal like a cat, but larger. See the picture. **leop ards.**

less 1. smaller: *less width, less important.* 2. not so much: *Less rain and more sun would give us better crops.* 3. with something taken away; without: *Five less two equals three.*

les son something to be learned or taught. **les sons.**

let not stop someone or something from doing something: *She let the kitten play by itself. I had let him go yesterday. Will your parents let you stay?* **let, let ting.**

let's let us.

let ter 1. a mark or sign that stands for any one of the sounds that make up words. There are 26 letters in our alphabet. 2. a written message: *He wrote his grandmother a letter.* **let ters.**

let ter car ri er a mail carrier. **let ter car ri ers.**

let tuce a plant. Its large green leaves are used for salad. See the picture.

lev el 1. flat; equally high everywhere: *This floor is not level; it slants.* 2. a surface that is equally high everywhere: *We stopped at three different levels in the mine.* 3. an instrument that shows whether a surface is level. See the picture. **lev els.**

lev er a bar on a fulcrum for moving something heavy. See the picture. **lev ers.**

lex i con a book of words and their meanings in alphabetical order; a dictionary. **lex i cons.**

li brar i an a person who has been trained for work in a library. **li brar i ans.**

li brary 1. a collection of books: *I started my library with three books.* 2. a room or building where a collection of books is kept. **li brar ies.**

leopard

library

leopard

lettuce

level 3.

man using a lever

lid

lifeguard

li cense 1. being allowed by law to do something; permission. 2. a paper, a plate, or a card that shows you have this permission: *a fishing license, a bicycle license.* **li cens es.**

lick pass the tongue over or lap up with the tongue: *The kitten licked its paw.* **licked, lick ing.**

lic o rice 1. the sweet root of a certain plant, dried and used in candy. 2. tasting like licorice: *licorice candy.*

lid a cover that can be taken off or lifted. See the picture. **lids.**

lie¹ 1. something said that is not true: *His lie was discovered.* 2. say something that is not true: *Don't lie about it.* **lies; lied, ly ing.**

lie² 1. have your body in a flat position: *I want to lie down.* (Never say, "I want to lay down.") 2. rest on a surface: *The maps were lying on the table* (never laying). **lay, lain, ly ing.**

life the state of living; being alive, not dead. People, animals, and plants have life; rocks and metals do not. **lives.**

life guard a person who works at a beach or swimming pool to guard swimmers. See the picture. **life guards.**

lift 1. move something up into the air; take up or pick up: *Can you lift this box?* 2. a ride: *We got a lift to school.* **lift ed, lift ing; lifts.**

light¹ 1. that by which we see: *The sun gives light.* 2. something that gives light: *Bring a light into this room.* 3. give light to; fill with light: *One window lights the room. Dad lighted the candles.* 4. become light: *The sky lights up at dawn.* 5. almost white: *My dress is light blue.* **lights; light ed** or **lit, light ing; light er, light est.**

light² easy to lift; not heavy. **light er, light est.**

light³ come down to the ground: *He lighted from the bus.* **light ed** or **lit, light ing.**

light ly in a light, not a heavy, way: *He tapped her lightly on the shoulder.*

light ning a flash of electricity in the sky.

like¹ 1. the same as: *Sue is like her mother. This tastes like candy.* 2. giving promise of: *It looks like snow.*

like² be pleased with; be satisfied with: *Most children like to play games.* **liked, lik ing.**

li lac a bush with fragrant lavender or white blossoms. See the picture. **li lacs.**

lily a plant that has flowers shaped like bells. See the picture. **lil ies.**

limb 1. a leg, arm, or wing. 2. a large branch of a tree. **limbs.**

Lim bur ger a soft, creamy cheese having a strong smell and flavor.

lime¹ a powder made of limestone. It is used in building and in gardening.

lime² 1. a fruit like a lemon, but green. 2. the tree it grows on. See the picture. **limes.**

limp¹ 1. a lame step or walk: *The horse had a limp.* 2. walk with a lame step: *Pat limped after he hurt his leg.* **limps; limped, limp ing.**

limp² ready to bend; not stiff. **limp er, limp est.**

Lin coln's Birth day a holiday. Abraham Lincoln was born February 12, 1809. **Lin coln's Birth days.**

line¹ 1. a piece of string or rope: *a fishing line.* 2. a long, narrow mark: *Draw two lines on the paper.* 3. an edge: *Here is the line between your yard and ours.* 4. mark with lines: *Line your papers.* 5. arrange in line: *Line up along the fence.* **lines; lined, lin ing.**

lilac

lily

lime²

lion

line² put a layer of material on the inside surface of something: *Her boots are lined with fur.* **lined, lin ing.**

lin ing material used to line: *My coat lining is torn.* **lin ings.**

li on a large, strong, wild animal. The lion is sometimes called the king of beasts. See the picture. **li ons.**

lip either of the two edges of the mouth. **lips.**

liq uid 1. something that flows like water; not a hard mass or a gas. 2. in the form of a liquid: *We use liquid soap to wash dishes.* **liq uids.**

list 1. items written one below the other: *a shopping list.* 2. make a list of: *Will you list these books?* **lists; list ed, list ing.**

lis ten try to hear: *Listen for the phone. I listen to music a lot.* **lis tened, lis ten ing.**

lit¹ See **light**¹. *He lit a candle. He has lit two lights.*

lit² See **light**³. *She lit from her bicycle. The bird has lit on the fence.*

lit ter 1. little bits left about in disorder: *We picked up the litter.* 2. scatter things about; make untidy: *You have littered the room with your papers.* **lit tered, lit ter ing.**

lit tle 1. not big: *A grain of sand is little.* 2. short; not long in time or in distance: *It will be dark in a little while. Let's go for a little walk.* 3. not much: *The child eats little food.* **lit tler, lit tlest.**

live¹ 1. be alive; have life. *All animals and plants live; rocks do not.* 2. make your home: *Where do you live?* **lived, liv ing.** (Live¹ rhymes with give.)

live² 1. having life; alive: *a live pet.* **2.** burning: *We cooked food over live coals.* **3.** carrying an electric current: *Don't touch a live wire.* (Live² rhymes with dive.)

lives more than one life. (Lives rhymes with dives.)

liz ard a small animal somewhat like a snake, but having four legs and a long tail. See the picture. **liz ards.**

load 1. what is being carried: *a load of furniture.* **2.** put in or put on what is to be carried: *He loaded the truck with bricks.* **loads; load ed, load ing.**

loaf¹ 1. bread baked as one piece: *We cut the loaf into slices.* **2.** anything like a loaf in shape: *We ate meat loaf for dinner.* **loaves.**

loaf² spend time doing nothing important: *Can we loaf tomorrow if we work now?* **loafed, loaf ing.**

loaves more than one loaf.

lob ster a sea animal with two big claws. See the picture. **lob sters.**

lo cal having something to do with just one certain place: *our local weather report, local news.*

lo cal ly only in a local place: *Her father is well known locally.*

lo cate 1. stay or settle down in a place: *The settlers located near the river.* **2.** find out the position of: *The boy tried to locate his friend's house.* **lo cat ed, lo cat ing.**

lo ca tion the place where something is located: *Our tent was in a good location.* **lo ca tions.**

lock¹ 1. something that holds doors, lids, or windows so they cannot be opened. Many locks must be opened with keys. **2.** fasten with a lock: *Lock the door.* **locks; locked, lock ing.**

lock² a curl of hair. See the picture. **locks.**

lizard

lobster

lock²

locket

loon

loop 1.

lock et a little metal case for holding a picture or a lock of hair. A locket is worn around the neck. See the picture. **lock ets.**

log 1. a long piece from the trunk or branches of a tree. 2. made of logs: *a log cabin.* **logs.**

lone ly 1. feeling alone and wanting company: *The old woman was lonely.* 2. without many people around: *a lonely street.* **lone li er, lone li est.**

lone some 1. feeling lonely. 2. making one feel lonely: *a lonesome afternoon.* **lone som er, lone som est.**

long[1] having great distance from end to end or from beginning to end: *An inch is short; a mile is long. This table is four feet long. Spring will come before long.* **long er, long est.**

long[2] wish very much or want badly: *He longed for his family. She longed to go home.* **longed, long ing.**

look 1. see; turn your eyes toward: *Look at me.* 2. search; try to find: *Did you look in the closet for your cap?* 3. the act of looking: *He gave me an angry look.* 4. give the feeling of being: *She looks happy. It looked cold outside.* 5. **Look after** means take care of. **looked, look ing; looks.**

loon a bird like a duck, but larger. See the picture. **loons.**

loop 1. a curved line that crosses itself. See the picture. 2. make a loop: *She looped the ribbon to make a bow.* **loops; looped, loop ing.**

loose not tight; not firmly fastened: *a loose button, a loose tooth.* **loos er, loos est.**

loose ly in a loose way: *The package was easy to open because I tied it loosely.*

loos en make or become loose: *Why don't you loosen your tie? The knot loosened.* **loos ened, loos en ing.**

lope run with long, easy steps: *The tall boy loped along the road.* **loped, lop ing.**

Lord God.

lose 1. not have any longer: *Try not to lose your key.* 2. not be able to find: *Did you lose a book?* 3. not win: *We may lose the game.* **lost, los ing.**

lost 1. See **lose.** *I lost my candy. I have lost my lunch box too.* 2. not found: *a lost glove.* 3. not won: *a lost race.*

lot 1. a piece of land: *an empty lot.* 2. a great many; very much: *a lot of fish, a lot of milk.* **lots.**

loud not quiet or soft; making a great sound. **loud er, loud est.**

loud ly in a loud way: *He spoke loudly.*

Lou i si ana one of the fifty states of the United States. See page 345.

love 1. a deep feeling for a person or a thing. 2. have this feeling for. **loves; loved, lov ing.**

love ly beautiful; good: *What lovely manners! She is a lovely girl.* **love li er, love li est.**

low[1] 1. not high or tall: *This is a low stool.* 2. in a low place: *The plane is flying low.* See the picture. 3. not loud: *a low voice.* **low er, low est.**

low[2] 1. the sound a cow makes. 2. make the sound of a cow: *The cows were lowing in the field.* **lows; lowed, low ing.**

luck what seems to happen or come to you: *good luck, bad luck.*

luck i ly by good luck; by good fortune.

lucky having or bringing good luck: *Three is my lucky number.* **luck i er, luck i est.**

plane flying low

lumber[1]

lumberyard

mackerel

lum ber[1] wood that is cut and ready for sale; boards. See the picture.

lum ber[2] move along heavily and noisily: *The old bear lumbered along.* **lum bered, lum ber ing.**

lum ber yard a place where lumber is kept and sold. See the picture. **lum ber yards.**

lump 1. a hard mass: *a lump of coal, a lump of sugar.* 2. a bump: *I have a lump on my head from falling down the stairs.* **lumps.**

lu nar of or like or about the moon: *a lunar orbit.*

lunch a light meal. **lunch es.**

lung the part of your body that holds the air you breathe. People have two lungs. **lungs.**

lus cious very pleasing to taste, smell, hear, see, or feel: *This is a luscious peach.*

ly ing See **lie**[2]. *Uncle Ben is lying down (never laying down).*

M   m

M or **m** the thirteenth letter of the alphabet. **M's** or **m's.**

ma'am a title that shows respect to a woman.

mac a ro ni hollow tubes made of a mixture of flour and water. Macaroni is a food.

ma chine an object with moving parts for doing some kind of work: *Levers and pulleys are machines.* **ma chines.**

mack er el a salt-water fish used for food. See the picture. **mack er el** or **mack er els.**

mad 1. out of your head; crazy. 2. angry: *He will be mad when he sees me wearing his new necktie.* **mad der, mad dest.**

made See **make.** *My sister made my birthday cake. She has made one every year.*

mag a zine a paper-covered book that is printed weekly or monthly. **mag a zines.**

mag ic 1. in stories, making things happen by secret charms and power: *Witches use magic.* 2. done by this power: *She had a magic wand.*

ma gi cian 1. in stories, one who has magic power. 2. a person who does tricks that seem to be magic. See the picture. **ma gi cians.**

mag net a stone or piece of iron or steel that attracts or pulls toward it anything made of iron or steel. See the picture. **mag nets.**

mag nif i cent beautifully colored; grand; splendid: *The king had a magnificent palace.*

mag nif i cent ly in a magnificent way: *She was magnificently dressed.*

mag ni fy make something look or seem larger than it really is. **mag ni fied, mag ni fy ing.**

mag ni fy ing glass a glass that causes things to look larger. **mag ni fy ing glass es.**

mag no lia a tree with large white or pink flowers. See the picture. **mag no lias.**

mag pie a noisy, black-and-white bird. See the picture. **mag pies.**

maid 1. a young girl. 2. a woman servant. **maids.**

mail 1. letters and parcels sent from one person to another by the post office department. 2. send by mail: *Please mail this letter.* **mailed, mail ing.**

mail box 1. a public box from which mail is collected. 2. a private box to which mail is delivered. **mail box es.**

mail car ri er a person who carries or delivers mail. **mail car ri ers.**

mail man a mail carrier. **mail men.**

mailman

magician 2.

magnet

magnolia tree

magpie

mallard

mammoth   1.

boy playing a mandolin

main   1. most important: *Where is the main road?*
2. a large pipe for water, gas, and so on:
There is a water main under the street. **mains.**

Maine   one of the fifty states of the United States.
See page 346.

maj es ty   a title given to a king or queen: *His
Majesty, Her Majesty.* **maj es ties.**

make   1. put together; build; shape: *make a cake,
make a boat, make a poem.* 2. cause; bring
about: *make a noise.* 3. force to: *Make him sit
down.* 4. become; turn out to be: *She will make
a good dentist.* 5. arrange: *Make the beds.*
6. earn; gain: *make money.* 7. add up to: *Two
and two make four.* 8. **Make believe** means
pretend: *Let's make believe we're acrobats.*
9. **Make fun of** means laugh at: *The boys
made fun of me.* 10. **Make up** means become
friends again after a quarrel. **made, mak ing.**

male   a man or boy. The kind of person or animal
that can be a father. **males.**

mal lard   a kind of wild duck. See the picture.
mal lards or **mal lard.**

ma ma   mother. **ma mas.**

mam mal   an animal that gives milk to its young.
mam mals.

mam moth   1. a kind of elephant that lived many
years ago. See the picture. 2. very big:
What a mammoth tree! **mam moths.**

man   a male human being. A man is a boy grown
up. **men.**

man age   control and guide: *They hired a woman
to manage the business.* **man aged, man ag ing.**

man do lin   a musical instrument with strings.
You play it with your fingers. See the picture.
man do lins.

mane the long hair on the neck of a horse and some other animals. See the picture. **manes.**

man go 1. a fruit with a thick skin. 2. the tree it grows on. See the picture. **man goes** or **man gos.**

Man i to ba one of the ten provinces of Canada. See the map on page 382.

man ner 1. the way someone behaves: *Her rude manner annoyed me.* 2. Having **good manners** means being polite. **man ners.**

many a great number of: *Many years ago the house was new.* **more, most.**

map a drawing of the earth's surface or part of it. Some maps show countries, cities, rivers, oceans, mountains, lakes, and so on. **maps.**

ma ple 1. a tree that gives much shade. 2. its wood. See the picture. **ma ples.**

mar a thon a long foot race or contest, usually lasting about 26 miles. **mar a thons.**

mar ble 1. a hard stone with streaks of color in it. 2. made of marble: *a marble statue.* 3. a small ball of marble, clay, or glass, used in games. **mar bles.**

march[1] 1. walk as soldiers do, in line taking steps of the same length at the same time: *The school band marched up the field.* 2. the act of marching: *It was a long march to the Capitol.* 3. a piece of music to march by: *The band played a march.* **marched, march ing; march es.**

March[2] the third month of the year. It has 31 days. **March es.**

mar ga rine something like butter but made from vegetable oils instead of animal fats; oleomargarine.

horse's mane

mango

maple tree

the seal of
the U.S. Marine Corps

marionette

marlin

mask

Ma rine Corps one part of the armed forces of the United States. See the picture.

mar i o nette a doll or puppet moved by strings. See the picture. **mar i o nettes.**

mark 1. any line or dot made on a surface. 2. a grade: *My mark in spelling was good.* 3. put your name on: *Mark the towels you will take to camp.* 4. make a line to show where a place is: *He is marking all cities on this map.* 5. **Mark off** means make lines to show where something is. 6. **Mark time** means move your feet as if you are marching but without going forward. **marks; marked, mark ing.**

mar ket 1. a place where people buy and sell things. 2. a store: *She went to the meat market.* **mar kets.**

mar lin a large fish with a big fin on its back. See the picture. **mar lins.**

mar ried 1. See **marry.** 2. having a husband or wife: *We know lots of married people.*

mar ry 1. join as husband and wife: *The minister marries many brides and grooms.* 2. take as a husband or wife: *He will marry the girl he loves.* **mar ried, mar ry ing.**

Mar y land one of the fifty states of the United States. See page 347.

mash beat into a soft mass; crush: *I'll mash the potatoes.* **mashed, mash ing.**

mask a covering to hide or protect the face. See the picture. **masks.**

mass 1. a lump; something that sticks together: *An island is a mass of land.* 2. a large amount together: *a mass of people.* **mass es.**

Mas sa chu setts one of the fifty states of the United States. See page 348.

mas ter 1. a person who rules or commands; the one in control. 2. main: *The lights went off when I pulled the master switch.* **mas ters.**

mat a thick piece of material like a small rug. **mats.**

match[1] a short stick of wood or paper. The top catches fire as you rub it on something. **match es.**

match[2] 1. a person or thing equal to another: *He is no match for you.* 2. be equal in a contest: *Can you match that throw?* 3. go well together: *The chairs match the table.* 4. a contest: *a tennis match.* 5. find one just like: *Match the numbers.* **match es; matched, match ing.**

mate 1. a husband or wife. 2. one of a pair. 3. join in a pair: *Birds mate in the spring.* **mates; mat ed, mat ing.**

ma te ri al what a thing is made from or done with: *Rock is a hard material. He got his writing materials together.* **ma te ri als.**

mat ter 1. what things are made of: *The earth and all things on it are made of matter.* 2. business things: *She has several matters to take care of.* 3. written things: *Books, papers, and other printed matter lay on the desk.* 4. be important: *Nothing seems to matter to that girl.* **mat ters; mat tered, mat ter ing.**

mat tress a case of heavy cloth stuffed with soft material and used to sleep on. **mat tress es.**

may[1] 1. allow to: *You may have an apple.* 2. be possible that it will: *Do you think it may rain tomorrow? Our flight may be late.* **might.**

May[2] the fifth month of the year. It has 31 days. **Mays.**

may be perhaps, but not surely: *Maybe it will rain.*

may flow er[1] a plant that blooms in May. See the picture. **may flow ers.**

mayflower[1]

the *Mayflower*

meadowlark

May flow er[2] the ship on which the Pilgrims came to America in 1620. See the picture.

me the person speaking: *Give me the dog. Let me go. Come with me. Take me along.*

mead ow a piece of land used for growing grass. Cattle often graze in meadows. **mead ows.**

mead ow lark a bird about the size of a robin. It is the state bird of several states. See the picture. **mead ow larks.**

meal[1] the food eaten or served at one time. **meals.**

meal[2] grain ground to a coarse powder: *corn meal.*

mean[1] 1. have in mind; want to say: *What does that sentence mean?* 2. plan to do: *You didn't mean to break the glass.* **meant, mean ing.**

mean[2] unkind; cruel: *It is mean to tease the puppy.* **mean er, mean est.**

mean ing what is meant: *Do you know the meaning of this word?* **mean ings.**

meant See **mean**[1]. *She meant what she said. He has meant to call you.*

mean while meantime.

mea sles a disease that causes a cold, a high temperature, and small red spots on the skin: *When she had the measles, she was sick in bed.*

meas ure 1. find the size or amount of anything: *He measured the boy with a ruler.* 2. mark off: *Measure out a cup of flour.* 3. the size or amount of something: *His neck measure is fourteen inches.* **meas ured, meas ur ing; meas ures.**

meat 1. the part of an animal used for food. 2. the part of something that can be eaten: *The meat of a nut is the inside part.* **meats.**

me chan ic a person who makes and repairs machines. **me chan ics.**

med al a small piece of metal. A medal may be given as a prize or a reward. See the picture. **med als.**

med i cine something to make a sick person well. **med i cines.**

meet 1. come face to face with: *I don't want to meet another car on this narrow road.* 2. come together; join: *Two roads meet at the corner.* 3. be introduced to: *I want you to meet my sister.* 4. receive and welcome: *Who will meet us at the airport?* **met, meet ing.**

meet ing a coming together: *a club meeting.* **meet ings.**

mel on a large fruit, with lots of juice, that grows on a vine. See the picture. **mel ons.**

melt change from a hard mass to a liquid: *The ice melts in the spring.* **melt ed, melt ing.**

mem ber one who belongs to a group. **mem bers.**

Me mo ri al Day a holiday; a special day to remember those who have died. **Me mo ri al Days.**

men 1. more than one man: *Boys grow up to be men.* 2. human beings; persons: *Men, animals, and plants need food.*

men tion speak about: *Do not mention the accident again.* **men tioned, men tion ing.**

menu a list of the food served at a meal: *Look at the menu and choose your lunch.* **men us.**

me ow 1. sound made by a cat or kitten. 2. make that sound. **me owed, me ow ing; me ows.**

mer ry gay and happy. **mer ri er, mer ri est.**

mer ry-go-round wooden animals and seats on a platform that goes round and round. See the picture. **mer ry-go-rounds.**

medal

melon

merry-go-round

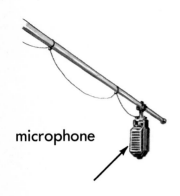

mesquite

microphone

microscope

mes quite a low tree often found in the desert. See the picture. **mes quites.**

mes sage words or ideas sent from one person to another. **mes sag es.**

mes sen ger a person who carries a message. **mes sen gers.**

met See **meet.** *They met in the park. Have you met my aunt?*

met al 1. a material such as iron, gold, or silver. 2. made of metal: *a metal cover.* **met als.**

me te or a mass of stone or metal falling toward the earth from space; a shooting star. **me te ors.**

Mex i can 1. of Mexico: *the Mexican flag, a Mexican dance.* 2. a person born or living in Mexico. **Mex i cans.**

Mex i co a country in North America, south of the United States. See the map on page 384.

Mex i co City the capital of Mexico. See page 384.

mice more than one mouse.

Mich i gan one of the fifty states of the United States. See page 349.

mi cro phone an instrument for sending sounds. See the picture. **mi cro phones.**

mi cro scope an instrument that magnifies. With it you can see things that are too small to see without it. See the picture. **mi cro scopes.**

mid dle 1. halfway between; in the center: *The middle house is ours.* 2. the place halfway between: *the middle of the street.* **mid dles.**

mid night twelve o'clock at night; the middle of the night. **mid nights.**

might[1] See **may**[1]. *Mother said we might play after dinner. He might have gone yesterday.*

might[2] great power: *Pull with all your might.*

mike a microphone. **mikes.**

mile a distance equal to 5280 feet. **miles.**

milk 1. the white liquid, from cows, which we drink. 2. a liquid produced by female mammals as food for their young. 3. draw milk from a cow, goat, or other animal. **milked, milk ing.**

milk man a person who delivers milk. **milk men.**

mill 1. a machine for grinding grain into flour or meal. 2. the building containing such a machine. See the picture. 3. a factory: *The steel mill hires many workers.* **mills.**

mil lion one thousand thousand; 1,000,000: *I wish I had a million dollars.* **mil lions.**

mil lionth one of 1,000,000 equal parts. **mil lionths.**

mind 1. the part of a person that thinks: *She has a good mind.* 2. take care of: *Please mind the baby.* 3. obey: *You must mind me while your parents are away.* 4. feel bad about: *I don't mind cold weather.* **minds; mind ed, mind ing.**

mine[1] belonging to me: *This scarf is mine.*

mine[2] a large hole dug in the earth to get out minerals: *We saw a gold mine.* **mines.**

min er a person who works in a mine. **min ers.**

min er al material dug from the earth. Anything on earth that is not a plant or an animal is a mineral. **min er als.**

min is ter a person whose work is to help the people who go to his or her church. **min is ters.**

mink a mammal that lives in water part of the time. See the picture. **minks** or **mink.**

Min ne so ta one of the fifty states of the United States. See page 350.

mint 1. a sweet-smelling plant. Its leaves are used to make candy and jelly. See the picture. 2. a piece of candy that tastes like mint. **mints.**

mill 2.

mink

mint 1.

mirror

mi nus 1. less: *7 minus 2 leaves 5.* **2.** without: *The book was returned minus its cover.* **3.** the minus sign (−). **mi nus es.**

min ute 1. one of sixty equal parts of an hour; sixty seconds. **2.** a short time: *We should be there in a minute.* **3.** an exact point of time: *The minute he calls, let me know.* **min utes.**

mir ror a glass in which you can see yourself. See the picture. **mir rors.**

mis chief conduct that causes harm or trouble, often without meaning to: *Don't get into mischief.*

mis chie vous full of mischief.

mis for tune bad luck. **mis for tunes.**

miss[1] 1. fail to hit: *He shot twice but missed.* **2.** fail to get: *Don't miss the train.* **3.** leave out or skip: *She missed a word when she read the sentence.* **4.** notice or feel bad because something is gone: *I did not miss my glove till I got home. We miss you.* **missed, miss ing.**

Miss[2] a title given to a girl or to a woman who is not married. **Miss es.**

mis sion some special work a person is sent to do. **mis sions.**

Mis sis sip pi one of the fifty states of the United States. See page 351.

Mis sou ri one of the fifty states of the United States. See page 352.

mis take 1. something that is not right or correct: *I made a mistake.* **2.** think something that is not right or true: *Don't mistake salt for sugar.* **mis takes; mis took, mis tak en, mis tak ing.**

mis tak en See **mistake.** *I have mistaken you for your sister many times.*

mis tle toe a plant that grows on trees. See the picture.

mistletoe

mis took See **mistake**. *I mistook her for someone I used to know.*

mit ten a kind of glove that covers the four fingers together and the thumb separately. **mit tens.**

mix 1. put together; stir together. 2. a material that is already mixed: *a cake mix.* 3. **Mix up** can mean confuse: *I was so mixed up I turned the wrong corner.* **mixed, mix ing; mix es.**

mix ture what has been mixed together. **mix tures.**

moat a deep, wide ditch, usually full of water, around a castle or town to protect it against enemies. See the picture. **moats.**

moc ca sin a soft shoe, often made from buckskin. See the picture. **moc ca sins.**

moc ca sin flow er another name for lady's slipper. **moc ca sin flow ers.**

mock ing bird a bird that sounds like other birds. It is the state bird of several states. See the picture. **mock ing birds.**

mod el 1. a small copy: *a ship model.* 2. make or shape: *Let's model an elephant.* **mod els; mod eled, mod el ing.**

mod ule part of a space ship: *The lunar module landed on the moon.* **mod ules.**

mo lar one of your big back teeth. **mo lars.**

mo las ses 1. a sweet, thick liquid used in cooking. 2. made of molasses: *molasses candy.*

mole a small animal that lives under the ground. See the picture. **moles.**

mom mother. **moms.**

mo ment 1. a very short space of time: *In a moment it will be dark.* 2. a certain point of time: *The phone rang the very moment there was a knock on the door.* **mo ments.**

moat

pair of moccasins

mockingbird

mole

Monday

---

mosque

mongoose

monkey

moose

mosque

Mon day the second day of the week; the day after Sunday. **Mon days.**

mon ey coins and paper bills used in buying and selling things.

mon goose a very long, slender animal that kills snakes. See the picture. **mon goos es.**

mon key a small animal that looks and acts quite human. See the picture. **mon keys.**

mon ster in stories, a creature so ugly-looking it may frighten people to death. **mon sters.**

Mon tana one of the fifty states of the United States. See page 353.

month one of the twelve parts of a year. **months.**

month ly happening every month or once a month: *a monthly magazine, a monthly meeting. The store sends us a bill monthly.*

moon a body that revolves around the earth. **moons.**

moon light 1. the light of the moon: *The moonlight came through my window.* 2. having the light of the moon: *a moonlight night.*

moose a large animal with antlers. See the picture. **moose.**

mop 1. a bundle of rags or a sponge fastened to a long handle for cleaning floors. 2. wash or wipe up: *He mopped his face. We should mop the floor.* **mops; mopped, mop ping.**

more 1. larger in size or amount: *A pound is more than an ounce. This soup needs more salt.* 2. a greater amount: *Tell me more. We need more than ten players for the team.*

morn ing the early part of the day, ending at noon. **morn ings.**

mosque a place where Moslem people go to worship. See the picture. **mosques.**

mos qui to a small, thin insect. See the picture.
mos qui toes or **mos qui tos.**

moss tiny plants that grow close together in shady
places. Moss looks like a carpet. See the picture.
moss es.

most 1. greatest or largest in amount: *Ice-skating
is the most fun of all. He had the most macaroni
on his plate.* 2. the greatest amount or number:
We gave the most of any class. 3. almost all:
Most people like music.

mo tel an inn near a highway. *Motel* comes
from the first two letters of *motor* and the last
three letters of *hotel.* **mo tels.**

moth a small flying insect that often eats holes in
clothing. See the picture. **moths.**

moth er your female parent. **moth ers.**

mo tion 1. the act of moving from one position to
another: *The motion of the ship made him sick.*
2. move your hand or head to show what you
mean: *She motioned for us to go in.* **mo tions;
mo tioned, mo tion ing.**

mo tor 1. a small engine, usually run by electricity
or gas: *an electric motor.* 2. run by a
motor: *a motor scooter.* **mo tors.**

mo tor cy cle a kind of bicycle run by a motor.
See the picture. **mo tor cy cles.**

mound a heap of earth or stones. **mounds.**

mount[1] 1. go up: *We'll mount the hill to look for
berries.* 2. get up on: *The mayor is mounting
the platform.* **mount ed, mount ing.**

mount[2] 1. a mountain; a high hill. 2. **Mount** is
the name of some mountains: *Mount Washington.*
mounts.

moun tain 1. a very high hill. 2. of a mountain:
Mountain air is fresh. **moun tains.**

mosquito

moss

moth

motorcycle

mouse

mule

mouse a small animal. See the picture. **mice.**

mouth 1. the opening through which you eat and talk. 2. an opening like a mouth: *the mouth of a cave, the mouth of a river.* **mouths.**

move 1. change the place or position of: *Move your chair to the table.* 2. change position: *She moved from one chair to another.* 3. change your place of living: *They moved to the city.* 4. put in motion: *The wind moved the branches.* 5. an action taken: *She made a fast move across the room.* **moved, mov ing; moves.**

move ment the act of moving: *The movement of the train put us to sleep.* **movements.**

mov ie a moving picture. **mov ies.**

mow[1] cut down: *It is time to mow the grass again.* **mowed, mowed** or **mown, mow ing.** (Mow[1] rhymes with so.)

mow[2] a hayloft. (Mow[2] rhymes with now.)

mow er a person or thing that mows: *a lawn mower.* **mow ers.** (Mower rhymes with slower.)

mown See **mow**[1]. (Mown rhymes with groan.)

Mr. a title put in front of a man's name.

Mrs. a title put in front of a married woman's name.

Ms. a title put in front of a woman's name. **Ms es.**

much a large amount of: *I don't have much money. You gave me too much cake.* **more, most.**

mud wet earth that is soft and sticky.

muf fler 1. a warm scarf worn around your neck. 2. part of a car that takes away noise. **muf flers.**

mule an animal which is half donkey and half horse. See the picture. **mules.**

mul ti ply take a number a certain number of times. To multiply 5 by 2 you take 5 two times, and get 10. **mul ti plied, mul ti ply ing.**

mumps a disease that puts your neck and face out of shape and makes it hard for you to swallow.

mus cle one of the parts of your body that make it move: *Can you feel the muscles in your arm?* **mus cles.**

mu se um the building or rooms in which a collection of objects is shown: *Our class saw paintings at the art museum.* **mu se ums.**

mush room a small plant, often shaped like an umbrella. Some are good to eat. See the picture. **mush rooms.**

mu sic 1. sounds arranged so they are pleasing to hear: *He studied music at school. I hear music in the next room.* 2. written or printed notes for different sounds: ♩ ♩ ♩ ♩ ♩ .

mu si cal of music; sounding like music.

mu si cal in stru ment any object that makes musical sounds, like a horn when air is blown into it or a guitar when strings are moved or a drum when it is hit. **mu si cal in stru ments.**

mu si cian a person who sings or who plays a musical instrument. **mu si cians.**

mus kel lunge a muskie. **mus kel lunge.**

mus kie a large fish. See the picture. **mus kies.**

must be forced to: *You must eat the right food. I must go now.*

mus tache the hair growing on a man's top lip. See the picture. **mus tach es.**

mus tard 1. a plant whose seeds have a sharp, hot taste. 2. a powder or paste made from these seeds. Mustard is often spread on hot dogs.

my of me; belonging to me: *I forgot my gloves. My house is around the corner.*

my self *Myself* is used instead of *me* in sentences like: *I can do it myself. I cut myself.* **our selves.**

mushroom

muskie

mustache

mys te ri ous hard to understand or explain:
She heard a mysterious noise.

mys tery a secret; something that is hidden or
not understood. **mys ter ies.**

N   n

N or **n** the fourteenth letter of the alphabet.
N's or **n's.**

nail 1. a small, pointed piece of metal that can
be hammered into pieces of wood to hold them
together. 2. fasten with a nail or nails. 3. the
hard surface at the end of a finger or toe. See
the picture. **nails; nailed, nail ing.**

name 1. the word or words by which a person,
animal, place, or thing is spoken of or to: *His
name is Jack.* 2. give a name to: *They named
the baby Helen after her aunt.* **names; named,
nam ing.**

nap a short sleep. **naps.**

nap kin a piece of cloth or paper used at meals
to protect the clothing and to wipe your lips
and fingers. **nap kins.**

nar ra tor a person who tells a story.
nar ra tors.

nar row 1. not wide; not far from one side to
the other: *a narrow street.* 2. close; with
nothing extra: *She had a narrow escape.*
nar row er, nar row est.

nar row ly closely: *He narrowly missed being
hit by the ball.*

na tion a group of people in the same country,
having the same government, and usually speaking
the same language. **na tions.**

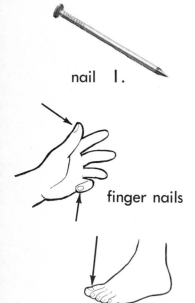

nail 1.

finger nails

toe nail

nat u ral 1. made or done by nature, not by man: *The natural color of her hair is gray, but she has colored it brown.* 2. true to life: *She doesn't look natural with curly hair.*

nat ur al ly as might be expected; of course: *She offered me an orange; naturally, I took it.*

na ture the whole world; all things except those made by man.

naugh ty not good; not doing what you ought to do. **naugh ti er, naugh ti est.**

na vy 1. all of a country's ships of war with their crews and the department that manages them. 2. The U.S. Navy is one part of the armed forces of the United States. See the picture. **na vies.**

near close to; not far from: *We live near a city. My birthday is near.* **near er, near est.**

near ly close to: *It is nearly time for dinner.*

neat 1. clean and in order: *His room was always neat.* 2. keeping things in order: *A neat child is careful with library books.* 3. clever: *a neat trick.* **neat er, neat est.**

neat ly in a neat way: *Write your name neatly.*

Ne bras ka one of the fifty states of the United States. See page 354.

nec es sary that must be done: *It is necessary to study so that you will learn.*

neck 1. the part of your body between the head and shoulders. 2. the part of a piece of clothing that fits the neck. **necks.**

neck lace a chain or string of beads, worn around the neck. See the picture. **neck lac es.**

need 1. be in want of; ought to have; not be able to do without: *We need food.* 2. whatever is needed: *Their greatest need is a place to live.* **need ed, need ing; needs.**

the seal of the U.S. Navy

necklace

sewing needle

knitting needles

compass
needle

nene

nest

nee dle 1. a thin, pointed tool for sewing. 2. a long, thin, pointed rod for knitting. 3. a pointer on a compass or dial. See the picture. 4. a sharp, hollow tool used by doctors to give shots. 5. the leaf of some evergreens. **nee dles.**

neigh 1. sound a horse makes. 2. make such a sound. **neighed, neigh ing; neighs.**

neigh bor someone who lives nearby. **neigh bors.**

neigh bor hood 1. the streets and houses surrounding the place you live. 2. of a neighborhood: *a neighborhood newspaper.* **neigh bor hoods.**

nei ther not either: *Neither you nor I should be late for school. Neither sentence is true.*

ne ne a kind of goose. See the picture. **ne nes.**

neph ew a son of your brother or your sister. **neph ews.**

nerve a part of the body that connects your brain with your muscles, eyes, and so on. **nerves.**

ner vous easily excited or upset.

nest a thing shaped like a bowl, built of sticks, straw, and other material. Birds build nests in which to lay their eggs. See the picture. **nests.**

Ne vada one of the fifty states of the United States. See page 355.

nev er not ever; at no time.

new 1. never made or used before. 2. not old or used up. **new er, new est.**

New Bruns wick one of the ten provinces of Canada. See the map on page 383.

New found land one of the ten provinces of Canada. See the map on page 383.

New Hamp shire one of the fifty states of the United States. See page 356.

New Jer sey one of the fifty states of the United States. See page 357.

new ly just done or finished: *Our house has newly painted walls.*

New Mex i co one of the fifty states of the United States. See page 358.

news the facts about something which has just happened or will soon happen.

news pa per sheets of paper printed every day or week, telling the news and useful facts. **news pa pers.**

news stand a place where newspapers and magazines are sold. **news stands.**

New Year's Day a holiday, January 1. **New Year's Days.**

New York one of the fifty states of the United States. See page 359.

next 1. nearest: *The girl next to me is taller than I am.* 2. following at once: *the next bus. The next month after March is April.*

nib ble 1. eat away with quick, small bites. 2. bite gently or lightly. **nib bled, nib bling.**

nice pleasing; good; satisfying. **nic er, nic est.**

nice ly in a polite or pleasing or clever way: *She answered the question very nicely.*

nick el 1. a metal that looks somewhat like silver. 2. a United States or Canadian coin worth five cents. See the picture. **nick els.**

niece a daughter of your brother or your sister. **niec es.**

night 1. the time between evening and morning. 2. of or for night: *night wind, night light.* **nights.**

night time the time when it is dark.

nine 1. one more than eight; 9. 2. Nine and nine make eighteen. **nines.**

nine teen nine more than ten; 19. **nine teens.**

U.S. nickel

Canadian nickel

nine teenth 1. next after the eighteenth; 19th. 2. one of 19 equal parts. **nine teenths.**

nine ti eth 1. next after the eighty-ninth; 90th. 2. one of 90 equal parts. **nine ti eths.**

nine ty nine times ten; 90. **nine ties.**

ninth 1. next after the eighth; 9th. 2. one of 9 equal parts. **ninths.**

nip 1. squeeze tight and quickly; pinch; bite: *The crab nipped my toe.* 2. a tight squeeze; a pinch; a sudden bite: *I felt a nip on my toe.* 3. give a sharp, biting feeling to: *A cold wind nipped our ears.* **nipped, nip ping; nips.**

no 1. a word used to say you can't or won't, or that something is wrong. *No* means the same as shaking your head from side to side. 2. not any: *Worms have no legs.* **noes.**

no body no one; no person. **no bod ies.**

nod 1. bow the head a little bit and raise it again quickly. 2. say yes by nodding. 3. let your head fall forward when you are sleepy or falling asleep. **nod ded, nod ding.**

noise a sound, often an unpleasant one. **nois es.**

nois i ly in a noisy way: *He chewed gum noisily.*

noisy 1. making much noise: *The noisy boy disturbed us.* 2. full of noise: *The auditorium was crowded and noisy.* **nois i er, nois i est.**

none no one; not any: *None of the cake was left.*

non sense words, ideas, or acts without meaning.

noon twelve o'clock; the middle of the day. **noons.**

nor and no: *Neither snow nor rain fell.*

north 1. the direction to which a compass needle points; the direction to your right as you face the setting sun. 2. to the north: *Drive north for six miles.* 3. coming from the north: *north wind.*

North Amer i ca a continent; one of the large masses of land on the earth. See the map on page 379.

North Car o li na one of the fifty states of the United States. See page 360.

North Da ko ta one of the fifty states of the United States. See page 361.

north east halfway between north and east.

north ern 1. toward the north: *We took the northern road.* 2. from the north: *a northern wind.*

North Pole the point farthest north on the earth.

north ward toward the north.

north west halfway between north and west.

North west Ter ri to ries one of the two territories of Canada. See the map on page 382.

nose the part of your face or head just above the mouth. **nos es.**

nose print a mark made by the tip of the nose. **nose prints.**

not a word that says "no": *Down is not up. I will not go. It is not true.*

note 1. words written down to help you remember what you have heard or read. 2. a very short letter. 3. in music, a single sound or the written sign to show the sound (♪). **notes.**

noth ing no thing: *We could see nothing. Nothing happened.*

no tice 1. attention: *Take no notice of the baby's crying.* 2. see; give attention to: *She noticed a hole in my sweater.* 3. a sign or a paper giving facts or directions: *We saw a notice of the sale.* **no tic es; no ticed, no tic ing.**

noun a part of speech. In the sentences *The boy is tall* and *John is tall,* the words *boy* and *John* are nouns. **nouns.**

No va Sco tia one of the ten provinces of
Canada. See the map on page 383.

No vem ber the eleventh month of the year. It
has 30 days. **No vem bers.**

now at this time or by this time.

no where in no place; at no place; to no place:
We got stuck in the mud and went nowhere.

num ber 1. a word that tells exactly how many.
Three, eighteen, twenty-six, are numbers.
2. the sum of a group of things or persons: *The
number of players for this game is four.*
3. give a number to: *We numbered the boxes as
we filled them.* 4. **Numbers** sometimes means
arithmetic. **num bers; num bered,
num ber ing.**

nu mer al a figure or group of figures standing
for a number. 2, 5, 12, 117, are numerals.
nu mer als.

nurse 1. a person who takes care of sick people.
2. wait on or try to cure the sick: *He nursed his
sick dog back to health.* 3. a person who cares
for other people's children. **nurs es; nursed,
nurs ing.**

nut 2.

nut 1. a dry fruit or seed with a hard shell.
2. a small metal block with a hole in the center
into which a screw fits. See the picture. **nuts.**

O o

O or **o** the fifteenth letter of the alphabet.
O's or o's.

oak a tree having hard wood and nuts called
acorns. See the picture. The oak is the state
tree of several states. **oaks.**

oak tree

oar a long pole with one flat end. To row a boat you use two oars, one on each side of the boat. You sit facing backward and pull the oars through the water. See the picture. **oars.**

oat 1. a plant and its grain. See the picture. 2. **Oats** usually means the grain of the oat plant: *Horses like to eat oats.* **oats.**

oat meal a breakfast food made of oats: *I cooked my own oatmeal this morning.*

obe di ent doing as you are told: *An obedient dog is a good pet.*

obe di ent ly in an obedient way: *The dog waited obediently at the corner.*

obey do what you are told to do: *The dog obeyed its master. We obey the rules in school and on the playground.* **obeyed, obey ing.**

ob ject 1. anything that can be seen or touched. 2. say you don't like something or are against it: *Do you object to playing this game?* **ob jects; ob ject ed, ob ject ing.**

ob serv a to ry a building with a round top that opens. Through a huge telescope scientists can study the stars. See the picture. **ob serv a to ries.**

oc ca sion 1. a certain time: *I have met your father on several occasions.* 2. a special event: *The queen wears her crown on great occasions.* **oc ca sions.**

oc ca sion al ly now and then; once in a while: *We meet occasionally.*

ocean a great body of salt water that covers almost three fourths of the earth's surface. **oceans.**

o'clock of the clock; by the clock: *Meet me at twelve o'clock.*

Oc to ber the tenth month of the year. It has 31 days. **Oc to bers.**

oars in a boat

oat

observatory

octopus

ogre

oc to pus a sea animal. It has a soft, thick body and eight arms. See the picture. **oc to pus es.**

odd 1. left over; extra: *I found an odd glove in the closet. The girl did odd jobs.* 2. leaving a remainder of one when divided by two: *Seven, nine, and eleven are odd numbers.* 3. strange or queer: *He has an odd name.* **odd er, odd est.**

odd ly strangely: *He was oddly dressed.*

odor a smell: *The odor of roses is sweet.* **odors.**

of 1. belonging to: *The members of the team went home.* 2. made from: *They built a house of bricks.* 3. named: *The state of Texas is very big.*

off 1. away from; far from: *The cat jumped off the bench.* 2. away; at a distance: *He went off by himself.* 3. not on; not connected: *The radio is off. The buckle is off his belt.* 4. stop: *The gardener turned the water off. The game was called off because of rain.* 5. **Off and on** means now and then.

of fer 1. hold out to be taken or refused: *He offered me his coat. Is she offering us her help?* 2. the act of holding out something to be taken: *Ten dollars for the bike was the best offer she had.* 3. suggest: *She may offer a few ideas if she is asked.* **of fered, of fer ing; of fers.**

of fice 1. a place where some people work. 2. a certain position: *the office of president.* **of fic es.**

of fi cer 1. a person who commands others in the army or navy. 2. a person who holds an office or position: *My father is an officer of the bank.* **of fi cers.**

of ten many times: *It often snows in January. We have been here often.* **of ten er, of ten est.**

ogre in stories, a giant or monster that is supposed to eat people. See the picture. **ogres.**

oh a word used to express surprise, joy, pain, and other feelings: *Oh, dear me! Oh! Joy!* **ohs.**

Ohio one of the fifty states of the United States. See page 362.

oil 1. a thick liquid from animal fat or vegetable fat or a liquid taken from the earth. 2. put oil on or in: *Did you oil the lawn mower?* **oils; oiled, oil ing.**

Okla ho ma one of the fifty states of the United States. See page 363.

old 1. not young or new. 2. **Old-fashioned** means liking or keeping old fashions or ways. **old er, old est.**

ole o mar ga rine margarine.

ol ive 1. a small, round fruit with a hard stone. 2. the tree it grows on. See the picture. **ol ives.**

olive

om e let eggs mixed with milk or water, fried or baked, and then folded over. **om e lets.**

on 1. held up by: *The lizard is on the rock.* 2. touching; placed around: *Put your left shoe on your left foot.* 3. against: *There is a calendar on the wall.* 4. about: *a book on rocks.* 5. **On and on** means without stopping. 6. **And so on** means and more of the same. 7. **On time** can mean not too early or too late.

once 1. one time: *Play that song once more.* 2. at some time in the past: *The plant was once a sprout.* 3. **At once** means right now. 4. **Once upon a time** means long ago. 5. **Once in a while** means not too often.

onion

one 1. the number 1. 2. a single: *one chair, one day.* 3. a single thing: *Which one do you want?* **ones.**

on ion a plant. Its bulb is eaten as a vegetable. See the picture. **on ions.**

on ly 1. by itself; no more: *an only child. This is the only road to town.* 2. just: *She had three papers but she sold only two.* 3. **If only** often means I wish: *If only I could play the piano!*

On tar io one of the ten provinces of Canada. See the map on page 383.

open 1. not shut; not closed: *an open window, an open box.* 2. make open: *Open the door.* 3. spread out: *Open the magazine to page 15.* 4. start: *Dad will open a new gas station.* **opened, open ing.**

open ing a hole or open place in something. A door is an opening in a wall. **open ings.**

open ly without trying to hide anything: *He openly confessed that he had eaten all the cake.*

op era a play in which the characters sing instead of speak. **op eras.**

op er ate 1. run: *You operate this machine by pushing a button. These buses operate all night.* 2. manage: *My sister operates a theater.* 3. try to cure a sick person by cutting into his or her body: *A doctor can operate on a patient if it is necessary.* **op er at ed, op er at ing.**

op er a tion 1. doing something or making a thing work: *The operation of a factory takes many people.* 2. the way a thing works: *The operation of this machine is not easy.* 3. something done to the body to help it: *Taking out tonsils is a common operation.* **op er a tions.**

op er a tor a person who runs something or makes something work: *He is a telephone operator.* **op er a tors.**

opos sum a small mammal that often carries its young on its back. When it is caught, it pretends to be dead. See the picture. **opos sums.**

opossum

op po site 1. placed against; face to face; back to back: *The post office is opposite the firehouse.* 2. as different as can be: *East and west are opposite directions.*

or *Or* is used when there is something to choose: *Is it hot or cold? She didn't know whether to laugh or cry. Hurry, or you will be left behind.*

or ange 1. a round, yellowish-red fruit, full of juice, that is good to eat. 2. the tree it grows on. See the picture. 3. the color of an orange. 4. having that color. **or ang es.**

or bit 1. the path of a planet around the sun; the path of a satellite around the earth. 2. travel around the earth or some other body in an orbit: *The satellite began to orbit at 6:02 a.m.* **or bits; or bit ed, or bit ing.**

or chard 1. a piece of ground on which fruit trees are grown. 2. all the trees in an orchard. **or chards.**

or ches tra 1. musicians playing together: *Her mother is a member of the orchestra.* 2. all the instruments played together by the musicians in an orchestra: *The orchestra has played beautiful music.* **or ches tras.**

or der 1. the way a group of things is placed or arranged: *Line up in order of size.* 2. a command: *His orders came from his boss.* 3. give directions: *He ordered a hamburger.* 4. tell what to do: *The police officer ordered him to stop.* **or ders; or dered, or der ing.**

Or e gon one of the fifty states of the United States. See page 364.

or gan 1. a musical instrument that looks like a piano. See the picture. 2. a part of your body, such as the heart, that does a special job. **or gans.**

opposite

organ

orange

girl playing an organ

185

oriole

ostrich

otter

or gan ize 1. put into working order; put into order or arrange: _Please organize your work._ 2. join in a company, club, or other group: _We organized a music club at school._ **or gan ized, or gan iz ing.**

ori ole a bird with yellowish-red and black feathers. See the picture. **ori oles.**

os trich a large, long-legged bird that can run fast but cannot fly. See the picture. **os trich es.**

oth er 1. what is remaining or the rest: _One baby cried, but the others went to sleep._ 2. different: _some other time. I have no other clothes._ 3. the rest of the people or things: _Here are two books; where are the others?_ **oth ers.**

Ot ta wa the capital of Canada. See the map on page 383.

ot ter a mammal that lives in water part of the time. See the picture. **ot ters.**

ouch an exclamation expressing sudden pain.

ought be expected: _You ought to wash the dishes. At your age you ought to know the alphabet._

ounce 1. a measure for dry material. Sixteen ounces equal one pound. 2. a measure for liquids. Sixteen ounces equal one pint. **ounc es.**

our belonging to us: _We sold our house._

ours the one belonging to us: _This house is ours._

our selves _Ourselves_ is used in sentences like: _We ourselves got the tickets for you. We wiggled ourselves free from the ropes._

out 1. away; forth: _The horses ran out the gate._ 2. not at home; away: _I called the doctor but he was out._ 3. in baseball, no longer at bat or on base. 4. not burning; no longer lighted: _The candle is out._

out doors out of or outside a building.

out fit 1. all the things necessary for an event: *a camping outfit.* 2. get together everything necessary for an event: *His parents outfitted him for the camping trip.* **out fits; out fit ted, out fit ting.**

out side 1. the side or surface that is not in: *The outside of my coat is worn.* 2. on the outside: *outside leaves of the cabbage.* 3. to the outside: *Run outside and get the paper.* 4. out of; beyond: *Keep the dog outside while I wash the kitchen floor.*

ov en 1. a space in a stove for baking food. 2. a furnace for heating or drying. **ov ens.**

over 1. above: *the roof over our heads.* 2. on or to the other side of; across: *The stream was so narrow we could jump over it.* 3. down from the edge of: *The wild horse nearly fell over the edge of the cliff.* 4. more than: *My bank has over three dollars in it.* 5. **Over and over** means again and again.

o ver flow 1. flow over; cover; flood. 2. be very abundant. **o ver flowed, o ver flow ing.**

over throw take away the power: *The knights will overthrow the king.* **over threw, over thrown.**

over thrown See **overthrow.** *Her Majesty's government has been overthrown.*

owe have to pay: *I owe the butcher a dollar for the meat.* **owed, ow ing.**

owl a bird with big eyes and a short, curved bill. See the picture. **owls.**

own 1. have; keep because you bought it or because someone gave it to you: *I own a football.* 2. belonging to oneself or itself: *This is my own football helmet. I make my own bed.* 3. **Own up** means confess. **owned, own ing.**

outfit

own

owl

ox

---

page

oxen

oyster

burro carrying a pack

paddles in a canoe

ox a kind of cattle that is fitted and trained for farm work. See the picture. **ox en.**

ox en more than one ox.

oys ter a sea animal with a shell. The shell may contain a pearl. See the picture. **oys ters.**

P   p

P or **p** the sixteenth letter of the alphabet. **P's** or **p's.**

pace 1. a step: *three paces to the right.* 2. walk with even steps: *He paced the floor.* 3. measure by paces: *We paced off the distance for the race.* 4. **Keep pace with** means keep up with; go as fast as. **pac es; paced, pac ing.**

Pa cif ic the great ocean west of the Americas.

pack 1. a bundle of things tied together. 2. put together in a box or bag. 3. a case to be carried on the back. See the picture. **packs; packed, pack ing.**

pack age things packed or wrapped together and tied or fastened; a parcel. **pack ag es.**

pad 1. a mass of soft material used for protection or as a cushion: *The baby's crib has a pad made to fit it.* 2. fill with something soft: *We padded the box with cotton.* 3. a tablet of writing paper. **pads; pad ded, pad ding.**

pad dle[1] 1. a short oar used to move a canoe. See the picture. 2. move a canoe by pulling a paddle through the water: *She paddled up the river.* **pad dles; pad dled, pad dling.**

pad dle[2] move your hands and feet around in the water. **pad dled, pad dling.**

page one side of a leaf or sheet of paper: *A page in this book is torn.* **pag es.**

paid See **pay.** *I paid ten cents for this comic book. He has paid for his book.*

pail a deep, round container, with a handle, for carrying liquids. **pails.**

pain 1. a sharp feeling that hurts: *She has a pain in her stomach.* 2. **Take pains** means be careful. **pains.**

paint 1. a thick liquid that you put on a surface to color and protect it. 2. cover with paint. 3. draw a picture in colors: *The artist will paint a picture.* **paints; paint ed, paint ing.**

paint er 1. a person who paints pictures; an artist. 2. a person who paints houses. **paint ers.**

pair 1. a set of two; two things that go together: *a pair of shoes.* 2. a thing with two parts that can't be used separately: *a pair of scissors.* **pairs.**

pa ja mas clothes to sleep in, with a coat or shirt and loose trousers.

pal ace a grand house for a king or a queen to live in. **pal ac es.**

pale 1. without much color: *When you are ill, your face is often pale.* 2. not bright; dim.

palm[1] the inside of the hand between the wrist and the fingers. **palms.**

palm[2] a tree that grows in warm places. A palm has a tall trunk and a bunch of large leaves at the top. See the picture. **palms.**

pal met to a kind of palm with fan-shaped leaves. See the picture. **pal met tos** or **pal met toes.**

pal o ver de a tree that grows in dry places. See the picture. **pal o ver des.**

pan a dish for cooking, usually made of metal, sometimes with a handle. **pans.**

pan cake a small, flat cake that is fried. **pan cakes.**

palm tree

palmetto tree

paloverde tree

pansy

papaya

parachute

parakeet

pane a sheet of glass in a window: *The hail broke several panes.* **panes.**

pan pipe an early musical instrument made of reeds or tubes. **pan pipes.**

pan sy a flower somewhat like a violet, but larger and with several colors in it. See the picture. **pan sies.**

pants a common name for trousers.

pa pa father; dad. **pa pas.**

pa pa ya 1. a fruit, yellowish and like a melon. 2. the tree it grows on. See the picture. **pa pa yas.**

pa per 1. material used as a surface for writing, printing, or drawing, and also used for wrapping packages and covering walls. 2. a piece of paper with writing or printing on it: *Important papers should be kept in a safe place.* 3. a newspaper. 4. made of paper: *a paper cup.* **pa pers.**

pa poose or **pap poose** a North American Indian baby sometimes carried on his mother's back. **pa poos es** or **pap poos es.**

par a chute a huge piece of cloth like a big umbrella, used to bring a person or object down safely through the air. See the picture. **par a chutes.**

pa rade a march for some special event: *Clowns were in the circus parade.* **pa rades.**

par a graph a group of sentences about one main idea. **par a graphs.**

par a keet a kind of small parrot with a long tail. See the picture. **par a keets.**

par cel a bundle of things wrapped or packed together: *I brought a parcel from the post office.* **par cels.**

par don 1. being excused from blame for doing something: *I beg your pardon for bumping you.* 2. excuse: *Grandmother pardons us when we are naughty.* 3. set free from being punished: *The governor pardoned the man who was in jail.* 4. being free from being punished: *After two years in jail the man got a pardon.* **par dons; par doned, par don ing.**

par ent a person's father or mother. **par ents.**

park 1. land used for the pleasure of the people: *Many families go to parks for picnics.* 2. leave a vehicle in a certain place: *Park your bicycle here.* **parks; parked, park ing.**

park ing lot a piece of ground used for parking vehicles. **park ing lots.**

par lor a room where people sit and talk or receive guests. **par lors.**

par rot a brightly colored bird. It can be taught to say words. See the picture. **par rots.**

part 1. less than the whole; not all: *He ate only part of his dinner.* 2. a thing that helps make up something: *A string is one part of a guitar.* 3. a line you make when you comb your hair. 4. divide or force apart: *The policewomen parted the crowd so the parade could pass.* 5. leave; separate: *The two friends parted after the movie.* **parts; part ed, part ing.**

part ly not all; not completely: *She's partly right.*

part ner one who works or plays with you: *She was my tennis partner. Who was your partner at the dance?* **part ners.**

par ty 1. a group of people having a good time. 2. a group of people doing something together: *A party of soldiers explored the woods.* 3. of or for a party: *a party dress.* **par ties.**

parrot

pasqueflower

patch 1.

pasque flow er a flower that blooms in early spring. See the picture. **pasque flow ers.**

pass 1. go by; move beyond: *The truck passed two cars. The days pass slowly.* 2. hand from one to another: *Please pass the meat.* 3. succeed in a test: *She passed arithmetic.* 4. a free ticket: *He gave me a pass to the movies.* 5. a way through: *The guide looked for a pass through the mountains.* **passed, pass ing; pass es.**

pas sen ger one who rides in a vehicle and usually one who pays a fare. **pas sen gers.**

Pass o ver a yearly Jewish holiday. It comes in the spring. **Pass o vers.**

past 1. gone by; ended: *Winter is past.* 2. just gone by: *The past week was rainy.* 3. beyond: *It is half-past two. I ran past the house.*

paste 1. a mixture that sticks paper together. 2. stick together. **pastes; past ed, past ing.**

pas time pleasant way of passing time. **pas times.**

pat 1. strike or tap lightly with something flat: *Watch her pat the mud into a mud pie.* 2. tap gently with the hand: *He patted the dog.* **pat ted, pat ting.**

patch 1. a piece put on to mend a hole or a tear. See the picture. 2. a piece of cloth or tape put over a wound. 3. anything like a patch: *There is a patch of sun light on the lawn.* 4. put patches on; mend: *I patched my bicycle tire.* **patch es; patched, patch ing.**

patch work pieces of cloth of various colors or shapes sewed together.

path a road made by people or animals walking, usually too narrow for automobiles. **paths.**

pa tience waiting quietly for something you want very much or that you want to happen.

pa tient 1. having patience: *She was very patient as she stood in line.* 2. a person who is being treated by a doctor: *The doctor took care of three patients that afternoon.* **pa tients.**

pa tient ly in a patient way: *She waited patiently for the late bus.*

pat io a small yard that may be closed in by walls but is open to the sky. **pat i os.**

pat ter make rapid taps: *The rain pattered on our car as we rode.* **pat tered, pat ter ing.**

pause 1. stop for a time; wait: *The dog paused in its barking when it heard me.* 2. a short stop: *There was a pause in the talking as he came into the room.* **paused, paus ing; paus es.**

paw the foot of an animal that has claws. See the picture. **paws.**

pay 1. give money for things or for work done: *Pay for the groceries.* 2. the money given for things or for work: *She works hard, but her pay is small.* 3. give or offer: *He always pays attention to the teacher.* **paid, pay ing.**

pea 1. a small, round, green seed used as a vegetable. 2. the plant it grows on. See the picture. **peas.**

peace 1. being free from war of any kind. 2. a quiet or calm; being still: *Can you feel the peace of the country?*

peach 1. a yellowish-red fruit, full of juice and with a pit in the center. 2. the tree it grows on. See the picture. **peach es.**

pea cock a large bird with beautiful green, blue, and gold feathers, and a splendid tail. See the picture. **pea cocks** or **pea cock.**

peak 1. the pointed top of a mountain. 2. a mountain that stands alone: *Pike's Peak.* **peaks.**

animal's paw

peas

peach

peacock

peanut

pear

pecan

pea nut 1. a seed, like a nut, that is good to eat when it is roasted. 2. the plant it grows on. See the picture. **pea nuts.**

pea nut but ter food made of ground peanuts.

pear 1. a sweet fruit rounded at one end. 2. the tree it grows on. See the picture. **pears.**

pearl 1. a white or nearly white jewel that has a soft shine like satin: *Sometimes pearls are found inside the shells of oysters.* 2. like or of pearl: *She wore a pearl necklace.* **pearls.**

pe can 1. a nut shaped like an olive and with a smooth shell. 2. the tree it grows on. See the picture. **pe cans.**

ped al 1. a lever worked by the foot: *Pushing the pedals of a bicycle makes it go.* 2. move by the pedals: *Sara pedaled her bicycle to the store.* **ped als; ped aled, ped al ing.**

ped dle travel about with things to sell: *We peddled magazines from house to house.* **ped dled, ped dling.**

peek look quickly and slyly; peep: *Close your eyes and do not peek.* **peeked, peek ing.**

peel 1. the outside covering of fruit: *orange peel.* 2. strip the skin, bark, or other covering from: *He peeled the banana.* 3. come off: *The paint on the barn is peeling.* **peels; peeled, peel ing.**

peep[1] 1. look through a hole or crack; take a little look: *He peeped over the fence.* 2. a look through a small hole or crack; a little look: *He took a peep in the oven to see the cake.* **peeped, peep ing; peeps.**

peep[2] 1. the cry of a young bird or chicken; a sound like a squeak: *I didn't hear a peep out of the children.* 2. make such a sound: *The baby birds peeped loudly.* **peeps; peeped, peep ing.**

pel i can a large sea bird with a pouch under its bill for storing fish for food. See the picture. **pel i cans.**

pen¹ a tool used in writing with ink. **pens.**

pen² 1. a small, closed place to keep babies or animals: *We put the baby in the play pen.*
2. shut in a pen: *She pens her dog in the back yard.* **pens; penned, pen ning.**

pen cil a pointed tool to write or draw with. **pen cils.**

pen guin a sea bird that swims but does not fly. Penguins live near the South Pole. See the picture. **pen guins.**

Penn syl va nia one of the fifty states of the United States. See page 365.

pen ny a cent; a copper coin of the United States and Canada. One hundred pennies are equal to one dollar. See the picture. **pen nies.**

pe o ny a garden plant with large red, pink, or white flowers. See the picture. **pe o nies.**

peo ple 1. men, women, and children; persons: *There were only three people at the meeting.*
2. family or relatives: *His people live in Iowa.*

pep per 1. a spice; a coarse powder with a hot taste, used to season food. 2. a hollow red or green vegetable. See the picture. **pep pers.**

perch¹ 1. a bar or branch on which a bird can light. 2. come and rest; sit: *A bluebird perched on our roof.* **perch es; perched, perch ing.**

perch² a small fresh-water fish. See the picture. **perch es** or **perch.**

per fect 1. having no faults or mistakes; not at all spoiled: *He turned in a perfect test.* 2. having all its parts; complete: *The set of dishes was perfect; nothing was broken.*

pelican

---

perfect

pelican

penguin

U.S. penny

Canadian penny

peony

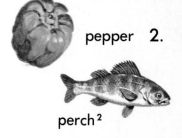
pepper 2.

perch²

per fect ly completely; in a perfect way: *She was perfectly right. The dress fitted perfectly.*

per form 1. do: *The machine performed very well in the test.* 2. act, play, sing, or do tricks in public. **per formed, per form ing.**

per form ance 1. the carrying out; doing: *She was careful in the performance of her work.* 2. the thing performed: *The evening performance is over.* **per form anc es.**

per fume 1. a sweet smell: *The perfume of the lilacs filled the room.* 2. a liquid having the sweet smell of flowers. **per fumes.**

per haps able to happen but not sure to happen: *Perhaps a package will come in the mail today.*

pe ri od 1. a length of time. 2. a dot (.) marking the end of most sentences or of an abbreviation. **pe ri ods.**

per ma nent 1. meant to last: *The dentist put a permanent filling in my tooth.* 2. curls or waves put into the hair to stay a long time: *Her new permanent is very pretty.* **per ma nents.**

per mis sion the act of permitting someone to do something: *Have you your teacher's permission to leave class?* **per mis sions.**

per mit 1. let; not stop from doing something: *Our parents permit us to stay up late on Friday night.* 2. a written notice giving permission to do something: *Dad got a permit to build a garage.* **per mit ted, per mit ting; per mits.**

per son a man, woman, or child. **per sons.**

pest an animal or person that causes trouble: *Moths and flies are pests.* **pests.**

pet 1. a favorite animal kept and treated with love. 2. pat gently: *Pet the kitten.* 3. treated as a pet: *a pet rabbit.* **pets; pet ted, pet ting.**

pheas ant a bird with a long tail. See the picture. **pheas ants** or **pheas ant.**

phone a telephone. **phones.**

pho to a photograph. **pho tos.**

pho to graph a picture made with a camera. **pho to graphs.**

pho tog ra pher a person who takes photographs. **pho tog ra phers.**

pi ano a large musical instrument. A piano is played by striking keys with the fingers. See the picture. **pi an os.**

pick 1. choose: *I picked the brown shoes.* 2. pull away with the fingers: *We pick flowers.* 3. a pointed tool for breaking hard material. See the picture. 4. **pick up** can mean get and take with you: *I picked up a pizza on the way home.* **picked, pick ing; picks.**

pick et 1. a stake driven into the ground to make a fence or tie a horse to. 2. tie to a picket: *Picket your dog at this fence.* 3. a person guarding a place: *Pickets around the camp watched for the enemy.* 4. a person who tries to keep people from going into a building. **pick ets; pick et ed, pick et ing.**

pick le 1. salt water, vinegar, or other liquid in which food can be kept from spoiling. 2. food kept in salt water, vinegar, and spices. **pick les.**

pic nic a party with a meal outdoors. **pic nics.**

pic ture 1. a drawing or painting made to look like someone or something; a photograph of someone or something. 2. a scene: *The house on the hill makes a lovely picture.* **pic tures.**

pie any food served in a baked crust made of flour, water, and oil: *chicken pie, apple pie, sweet-potato pie.* **pies.**

pheasant

boy playing a piano

pick 3.

pig

pigeon

pike

pillow

piece one of the parts into which a thing is divided or broken; a bit or scrap; a single thing: *Put a piece of wood on the fire. I lost one piece from my puzzle.* **piec es.**

pig a hog; an animal raised for its meat. See the picture. Bacon, ham, and pork come from a pig. **pigs.**

pi geon a bird with a plump body and short legs; a kind of dove. See the picture. **pi geons.**

pike a large fresh-water fish with a long, narrow, pointed head. See the picture. **pike.**

pile 1. a lot of things lying one upon another: *a pile of logs.* 2. a mass: *a pile of dirt.* 3. make into a pile: *Ask the boys to pile the blankets in the closet.* 4. a large amount: *I have a pile of laundry to do.* **piles; piled, pil ing.**

Pil grim one of the English settlers who came to Plymouth, Massachusetts, in 1620. **Pil grims.**

pill medicine made into a tiny ball to be swallowed without being chewed. **pills.**

pil low a bag or case filled with feathers or other soft material, usually to put under your head. See the picture. **pil lows.**

pi lot 1. a person whose business is to steer a ship or an airplane. 2. act as a pilot of; steer: *She piloted the ship up the river.* **pi lots; pi lot ed, pi lot ing.**

pin 1. a short, thin piece of wire with one sharp end to stick through things and fasten them together. 2. a small sign or a piece of jewelry fastened on to clothing by a pin: *a class pin, a diamond pin.* 3. fasten with a pin: *Pin his mittens to his coat.* 4. hold fast in one position: *A log fell on his leg and pinned it to the ground.* **pins; pinned, pin ning.**

pinch 1. squeeze with your thumb and finger. 2. press; squeeze: *Don't let the baby pinch his finger in the door.* 3. a sharp pressure that hurts: *a pinch.* **pinched, pinch ing; pinch es.**

pine a tree with evergreen leaves shaped like needles. See the picture. A pine tree is the state tree of several states. **pines.**

pine ap ple a large fruit, looking like a big pine cone. See the picture. **pine ap ples.**

pink 1. light red; the color made by mixing red with white. 2. having this color. **pinks; pink er, pink est.**

pi ñon a kind of small pine tree. See the picture. **pi ñons.**

pint a measure specially used for liquids. Two cups are equal to one pint. **pints.**

pi o neer 1. a person who settles in a part of the country where very few people have lived before. 2. a person who goes first or does something first and so prepares a way for others: *He was a pioneer in space.* **pi o neers.**

pipe 1. a tube through which liquid or gas flows. 2. a tube with a bowl at one end, for smoking. 3. a musical instrument. **pipes.**

pi rate a person who robs ships at sea. **pi rates.**

pit[1] 1. a hole in the ground. 2. a hole, dent, or hollow in any surface: *The old table had many pits and scratches on it.* 3. mark with small holes. **pits; pit ted, pit ting.**

pit[2] 1. the stone in a cherry, peach, plum, and some other fruits. 2. take the pits from fruit: *Everyone helped pit cherries for a pie.* **pits; pit ted, pit ting.**

pitch er[1] a container for liquids. It has a handle and a place for pouring. **pitch ers.**

pine tree

pineapple

piñon tree

pitchfork

pizza

plaid

plane² 1.

pitch er² in baseball, the player who throws the ball for the batter to hit. **pitch ers.**

pitch fork a large fork for lifting hay, grass, and so on. See the picture. **pitch forks.**

piz za a kind of pie made of tomatoes, cheese, meat, and spices. See the picture. **piz zas.**

place 1. the part of space a person or thing is in. 2. a city, town, village, island, and so on. 3. a building: *A theater is a place where movies are shown.* 4. a spot: *I have a sore place on my foot.* 5. a position: *He won second place.* 6. a space: *Find a place and sit down.* 7. put in a position: *Place the books on the table.* 8. **In place of** means instead of. 9. **Take place** means happen. **plac es; placed, plac ing.**

plaid 1. any cloth with crossed stripes. See the picture. 2. having crossed stripes: *She wore a plaid jacket.* **plaids.**

plain 1. clear; easy to understand; easily seen or heard: *The meaning of this sentence is plain.* 2. without any trimming: *He wore a plain shirt.* **plain er, plain est.**

plan 1. something you have thought out and will do: *Have you a plan for earning money?* 2. think out how something is to be made or done: *We are planning the class party.* 3. a drawing to show how something is arranged: *She drew a plan of the house.* **plans; planned, plan ning.**

plane¹ an airplane. **planes.**

plane² 1. a carpenter's tool for making wood or metal smooth. See the picture. 2. shave the edges of wood or metal with a plane to smooth them. **planes; planed, plan ing.**

plan et one of the bodies, like the earth, that move around the sun. **plan ets.**

plank a long, flat piece of sawed wood, thicker than a board: *We walked on a plank to get across the stream.* See the picture. **planks.**

plant 1. any living thing that is not an animal. 2. any living thing with leaves, roots, and a soft stem that is smaller than a tree or bush. 3. put in the ground to grow: *Plant these seeds in the spring.* **plants; plant ed, plant ing.**

plas tic 1. a material that can be shaped when it is hot and will become hard when it cools: *Many dishes, toys, and containers are made of plastic.* 2. made of a plastic: *a plastic boat, a plastic spoon, plastic flowers.* **plas tics.**

plate 1. a dish, usually round, that is almost flat. 2. something like a plate. 3. in baseball, the home base. **plates.**

plat form a raised, level surface: *The mayor and the governor will sit on the platform.* See the picture. **plat forms.**

plat ter a flat dish that is longer than it is wide, used for serving food. **plat ters.**

play 1. fun; something done to amuse yourself: *There will be time for play after school.* 2. have fun; do something in a sport: *Let's play ball. Our team played the third-grade team.* 3. a story acted on the stage: *We saw a play about witches.* 4. act a part: *My sister played a witch.* 5. make believe: *Let's play that this closet is a store.* 6. perform on a musical instrument: *Can you play the piano?* **plays; played, play ing.**

play er one who plays. **play ers.**

play ground a place to play. See the picture. **play grounds.**

play mate a person who plays with you. **play mates.**

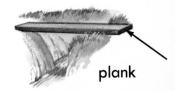
plank

platform

playground

pleasant

plum

snow plow

plum

pleas ant 1. giving pleasure: *We had a pleasant swim on a hot day.* 2. friendly: *He had a pleasant manner.* 3. fair; without a storm: *After the rain it was pleasant and sunny.* **pleas ant er, pleas ant est.**

pleas ant ly in a pleasant way: *The child smiled pleasantly. The breeze blew pleasantly.*

please 1. give pleasure to: *Reading aloud to children pleases them.* 2. be happy or delighted: *Sam was pleased with the flowers.* 3. **Please** is a polite way of asking something. 4. **If you please** means if you like or if you will allow it. **pleased, pleas ing.**

pleas ure 1. the feeling of being made happy; delight; joy: *You could see her pleasure as she opened her present.* 2. something that pleases; a cause of delight: *Seeing a friend is a pleasure. It's a pleasure to help you.* **pleas ures.**

plen ty enough; all that you need: *I had plenty of sleep last night.*

plot 1. a secret plan, usually to do something bad: *Two men hatched a plot to steal the money.* 2. plan secretly to do something bad: *They plotted against the king.* 3. the plan of a play, book, or story: *The plot of this book is exciting.* 4. a small piece of ground: *In the back yard we have a garden plot.* **plots; plot ted, plot ting.**

plow 1. a farm machine that cuts and turns up soil. 2. turn up soil. 3. a machine that moves snow. See the picture. **plows; plowed, plow ing.**

pluck 1. pick; pull off: *The man plucked feathers from the chicken.* 2. pull at: *She plucked the strings of her guitar.* **plucked, pluck ing.**

plum 1. a sweet fruit with lots of juice. 2. the tree it grows on. See the picture. **plums.**

plumb er a person whose work is putting in and repairing water pipes. **plumb ers.**

plunge 1. throw into something with force: *Why did the little boy plunge his hand into the cake?* 2. rush or throw yourself into: *She plunged into the water.* **plunged, plung ing.**

plu ral the form of a word that shows it means more than one. **plu rals.**

plus 1. added to: *1 plus 4 equals 5.* 2. and also: *A spy needs brains plus courage.* 3. and more: *Her mark was C plus.* 4. the plus sign (+). **plus es.**

Plym outh a town settled by the Pilgrims in 1620.

pneu mo nia a disease of the lungs: *They took the boy to the hospital when he got pneumonia.*

pock et 1. a small bag sewed into clothing for carrying things. See the picture. 2. carried in a pocket: *a pocket watch.* **pock ets.**

pocket

po em an idea expressed in words of great beauty, usually with accents repeated in each line and sometimes with words that rhyme. **po ems.**

po et person who writes poems. **po ets.**

po et ry poems.

point 1. a sharp end: *Don't hurt yourself on the point of this needle.* 2. a place or position: *Find the middle point of the line.* 3. the main idea or purpose: *I didn't get the point of his story.* 4. turn or face toward: *Don't point the hose this way!* 5. show with the finger. 6. a narrow piece of land sticking out into the water. 7. an amount in scoring: *Our team won by three points.* 8. **Point out** means call attention to. 9. **Point of view** means the way you think about something. **points; point ed, point ing.**

point ed having a point or points: *a pointed roof.*

point er a hunting dog. See the picture. **point ers.**

pointer

pool

police dog

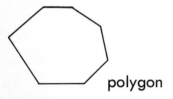

polygon

pond

pony

poodle

poke 1. push against with something pointed: *Poke the fire. He poked me in the ribs.* 2. push: *She pokes her nose into other people's business.* 3. **Poke fun at** means laugh at. 4. a poking; a push: *She gave me a poke.* 5. a bag or sack. 6. go slowly: *Don't poke on your way to school or you'll be late.* **poked, pok ing; pokes.**

pole[1] a long, thin piece of wood. **poles.**

pole[2] either end of the earth: *the North Pole, the South Pole.* **poles.**

po lice 1. the people who protect us and catch those who break the law. 2. of the police: *a police car, a police station, the police department.*

po lice dog a large dog that looks like a wolf. See the picture. **po lice dogs.**

po lice man a police officer. **po lice men.**

po lice of fi cer a member of a police department. **po lice of fi cers.**

po lice wom an a police officer. **po lice wom en.**

po lite behaving correctly; having good manners: *A polite boy held the door.* **po lit er, po lit est.**

po lite ly in a polite way.

pol lute make dirty: *Smoke pollutes the air.* **pol lut ed, pol lut ing.**

pol lu tion the act of polluting: *Some factories cause pollution of the water.*

pol y gon a shape that has three or more straight sides. See the picture. **pol y gons.**

pond a body of still water, smaller than a lake. See the picture. **ponds.**

po ny a small horse. See the picture. **po nies.**

poo dle a dog with thick, curly hair. See the picture. **poo dles.**

pool[1] 1. a small pond: *a wading pool.* 2. a place, indoors or outdoors, to swim. **pools.**

pool² a game played on a special table.

poor 1. having just a few things or nothing: *That family was very poor.* 2. not good: *This is very poor soil.* 3. needing help: *This poor child is lost.* **poor er, poor est.**

poor ly not enough; not well: *He did poorly at first, but he got better. The toy was poorly made.*

pop 1. make a short, quick, bursting sound: *The fire popped, and sparks flew out.* 2. burst open: *The bag popped.* **popped, pop ping.**

pop corn a kind of corn that bursts open and puffs out when heated: *Popcorn is good to eat.*

pop lar a tree that grows rapidly. See the picture. **pop lars.**

pop py a plant having many red, yellow, or white flowers. See the picture. **pop pies.**

pop u lar 1. liked by most people: *a popular song.* 2. common: *a popular belief.*

porch a covered entrance or platform on the outside of a building. See the picture. **porch es.**

por cu pine an animal covered with stiff, sharp quills. See the picture. **por cu pines.**

pork the meat of a hog used for food.

po si tion 1. the place where a thing or person is: *The ship reported its position.* 2. a way of being placed: *The table is in its position against the wall.* 3. a job: *He held a high position in the bank.* **po si tions.**

pos si ble 1. that can be; that can be done; that can happen: *Be early if possible. It is possible to finish on time.* 2. that can be true: *It is possible that I have seen her before.*

pos si bly no matter what happens: *I can't possibly agree with her. I can't possibly win the race.*

pos sum an opossum. **pos sums.**

poplar tree

poppy

porch

porcupine

poster

potato

post 1. a piece of timber or iron set firmly into the ground to hold up something: *a sign post.* 2. put up a sign or notice where everyone can see it: *She posted the names of the winners on the bulletin board.* **posts; post ed, post ing.**

post er a large printed sheet or notice put up for everyone to see. See the picture. **post ers.**

post man a mail carrier. **post men.**

post of fice the place where mail is taken care of and sent to the right address. **post of fic es.**

pos ture the way you stand. You have good posture when you stand straight. **pos tures.**

pot 1. a kind of deep dish or bowl: *Don't spill that big pot of soup.* 2. put into a pot to grow: *We must pot these bulbs before winter.* **pots; pot ted, pot ting.**

po ta to a plant. Part of it grows under the ground and is eaten as a vegetable. See the picture. **po ta toes.**

pouch 1. a bag or sack: *The mail carrier's pouch was full of letters.* 2. a fold of skin that is like a bag: *Kangaroos and koalas carry their young in pouches.* **pouch es.**

poul try birds that are raised for meat, such as chickens, turkeys, geese, and ducks.

pound[1] a measure of weight. Sixteen ounces are equal to a pound. **pounds.**

pound[2] strike or beat something heavily again and again. **pound ed, pound ing.**

pour 1. cause to flow in a steady stream: *Pour some milk on your cereal.* 2. flow in a steady stream: *People poured out of the theater. The rain poured down for hours.* **poured, pour ing.**

pow der material turned to dust by pounding or grinding it. Powder feels soft. **pow ders.**

pow er 1. how strong someone or something is; how much someone or something can do: *A horse has the power to pull a wagon. The witch had power over the elves.* 2. a force that can work: *Electric power runs many machines.* **pow ers.**

pow er shov el a machine that can dig and move dirt. See the picture. **pow er shov els.**

prac tice 1. something done many times to get skill: *They spent an hour a day on football practice.* 2. do something again and again: *He practices on the piano at least an hour every day.* **prac tic es; prac ticed, prac tic ing.**

prai rie a large piece of almost level land, with grass but not many trees. **prai ries.**

prai rie dog an animal like a woodchuck. See the picture. **prai rie dogs.**

praise 1. saying that a thing or person is good; words that tell how good a thing or person is: *words of praise. Everyone likes praise.* 2. speak well of: *Everyone praised the athlete.* **prais es; praised, prais ing.**

prance spring about on the hind legs: *Horses prance in a parade.* **pranced, pranc ing.**

pray give thanks; worship; ask sincerely: *She knelt to pray.* **prayed, pray ing.**

prayer 1. the act of praying; words to be used in praying: *He learned a prayer.* 2. the thing prayed for: *Our prayers were answered.* **prayers.**

preach er a minister. **preach ers.**

pre fix a syllable, syllables, or word put at the beginning of a word to change its meaning or to make another word. *Unkind* is made by adding the prefix *un* to *kind.* **pre fix es.**

pre pare make ready; get ready: *Prepare for a test.* **pre pared, pre par ing.**

power shovel

prairie dog

printing press

cider press

pre sent[1] 1. give: *They are going to present a gift to their teacher.* 2. something presented: *I received a present.* 3. introduce; make known: *She was presented to the queen.* **pre sent ed, pre sent ing; pre sents.**

pres ent[2] 1. being here; not absent: *Three people are present.* 2. **At present** means now.

pres i dent the chief officer of a country, company, club, or other group. **pres i dents.**

press 1. use force or weight against; move away from you; push with steady force: *Press this button to open the box.* 2. squeeze; squeeze out: *You press the juice from apples to make cider.* 3. a machine that presses: *a printing press, a cider press.* See the picture. 4. make smooth and flat: *I will press my shirt in the morning.* **pressed, press ing; press es.**

pres sure a steady pushing of a weight or force. **pres sures.**

pre tend act as if something is true: *Let's pretend we are astronauts.* **pre tend ed, pre tend ing.**

pret ty pleasing; sweet; charming: *She wore a pretty coat.* **pret ti er, pret ti est.**

pre vi ous earlier: *He did better in the previous lesson.*

prey hunt and kill for food: *Cats prey upon mice and birds.* **preyed, prey ing.**

price the amount for which a thing is sold or bought; the cost to the one who buys. **pric es.**

pride 1. a feeling of being pleased or satisfied with yourself or anything that you have: *He took pride in his fine garden.* 2. too high an idea of yourself: *His pride may get him into trouble.*

priest a minister in certain Christian churches. **priests.**

pri ma ry first in time; first in order: *We start school in the primary grades.*

prim rose a plant with flowers of many different colors. See the picture. **prim ros es.**

prince 1. the son of a king or queen. 2. a ruler of a small country. **princ es.**

Prince Ed ward Is land one of the ten provinces of Canada. See the map on page 383.

prin cess 1. the daughter of a king or queen. 2. the wife of a prince. **prin cess es.**

prin ci pal 1. most important; chief; main: *The principal character in this story is a dog.* 2. the head of a school. **prin ci pals.**

print 1. press words on paper to make books and newspapers. 2. words pressed on paper: *Buy a book with big print.* 3. make letters: *Print your name on this paper.* 4. a mark made on something by pressing or stamping: *I made a print of my hand in clay.* **print ed, print ing; prints.**

print er a person whose work is printing books, newspapers, magazines, and so on. **print ers.**

pri vate 1. not for everyone; not public. 2. secret. 3. **In private** means secretly.

prize 1. a reward in a contest: *The prize goes to the winner.* 2. worth a prize: *He grows prize vegetables in his garden.* **priz es.**

prob a ble expected to be true or to happen: *A rainbow is probable after a shower.*

prob a bly more nearly true than not: *We probably should wait for her.*

prob lem a hard question or matter to be thought about and worked out. **prob lems.**

proc ess doing or making something by following each step in order: *There are many steps in the process of making cheese.* **proc ess es.**

primrose

pro duce 1. make; cause; bring into being: *This factory produces machines. Cows produce milk.* 2. bring out; show: *Our class produced a newspaper.* **pro duced, pro duc ing.**

prod uct 1. the thing produced. 2. the number you get from multiplying numbers. **prod ucts.**

pro duc tion 1. the act of producing: *Production of a newspaper takes work.* 2. what is produced: *Our class play was a big production.* **pro duc tions.**

prof it in business, the money you have left after all your bills are paid. **prof its.**

pro gram 1. a list of events or performers: *I dropped my program. She was next on the program. We had a Thanksgiving program.* 2. a plan of what is to be done: *Her program for the week was very full.* **pro grams.**

proj ect 1. a plan for doing something: *Have you decided on your science project?* 2. **A project** sometimes means a group of buildings where many people live. **proj ects.**

prom ise 1. words said or written to say you will or won't do something: *He always keeps a promise.* 2. give your word; make a promise: *She promised to stay till six o'clock.* **prom is es; prom ised, prom is ing.**

proof the way of showing that something is true: *Do you have proof that he took it?* **proofs.**

pro pel ler revolving blades that make some boats and airplanes move. See the picture. **pro pel lers.**

prop er ty 1. the thing or things someone owns: *This car is the property of our family.* 2. a piece of land: *My uncle owns property in the country.* **prop er ties.**

airplane propeller

pro tect shelter or guard; keep from harm or danger: *A raincoat protects you from the rain.* **pro tect ed, pro tect ing.**

proud thinking well of yourself or of something: *He was a proud man. He was proud of his children.* **proud er, proud est.**

proud ly in a proud manner: *She looked proudly at what she had drawn.*

prove 1. show that a thing is true or right: *Prove these arithmetic answers.* 2. turn out to be: *The book proved to be very dull.* **proved, prov ing.**

pro vide 1. see that someone has what he needs: *Farmers provide us with food.* 2. arrange for the future: *She saved money to provide for her family.* **pro vid ed, pro vid ing.**

prov ince a big division of a country: *Canada is divided into provinces and territories.* **prov inc es.**

ptar mi gan a kind of bird found in mountains and cold lands. See the picture. **ptar mi gans.**

pub lic 1. having something to do with the people; belonging to the people: *Public libraries and public schools are open to all the people.*
2. **In public** means openly; not secret.

pud ding a soft food. Pudding is often eaten as a dessert. See the picture. **pud dings.**

pud dle 1. a small pool of water: *a puddle of rain.* 2. a small pool of any liquid: *a puddle of ink.* **pud dles.**

Puer to Ri co an island off the coast of Florida. It is protected by the United States.

puff 1. let out short, quick breaths of air: *She puffed as she skated across the pond.* 2. a short, quick breath of air: *A puff of wind blew my hat off.* 3. become full of air: *His cheeks puffed out as he blew the horn.* **puffed, puff ing; puffs.**

ptarmigan

pudding

pulley

water pump

girl's pump

pumpkin

puppet

pull 1. move toward yourself. 2. move with force: *The dentist will pull your tooth.* 3. a motion toward you: *I gave one pull at the rope.* **pulled, pull ing; pulls.**

pul ley a wheel with a hollow edge in which a rope can move to lift or lower weights. See the picture. **pul leys.**

pulse the beat of the heart. You can feel your pulse in your wrist. **puls es.**

pump[1] 1. a machine for forcing liquids, air, or gas into or out of things: *A pump brings water up from a well.* See the picture. 2. move liquids, air, or gas: *We pumped air into the bicycle tires.* **pumps; pumped, pump ing.**

pump[2] a shoe having no laces, straps, or buttons. See the picture. **pumps.**

pump kin a large fruit that grows on a vine. See the picture. **pump kins.**

punc tu a tion the use of periods, commas, and other marks in writing. Punctuation helps make the meaning of sentences clear when we read.

pun ish cause pain to someone who did wrong: *Our parents punish us when we are naughty.* **pun ished, pun ish ing.**

pu pil[1] a person who is learning in school or is being taught by someone. **pu pils.**

pu pil[2] the black center of the eye. **pu pils.**

pup pet a small doll moved by someone's hands. See the picture. **pup pets.**

pup py a young dog. **pup pies.**

pure 1. not mixed with anything else: *pure gold.* 2. perfectly clean: *pure water.* **pur er, pur est.**

pur ple 1. a dark color made by mixing red and blue. 2. having this color. **pur ples; pur pler, pur plest.**

purr 1. a low sound such as a cat makes when pleased. 2. to make this sound. **purred, pur ring.**

push 1. press against something to make it move away from you. 2. go by force: *We tried to push through the crowd.* 3. the act of pushing: *Give the gate a push.* **pushed, push ing; push es.**

pussy wil low a small tree with soft, gray flowers that look like cat's fur. See the picture. **pussy wil lows.**

put 1. place; lay; set: *I put lemon in my tea. Did you put your toys on the shelf?* 2. cause to be in position: *Have you put your room in order? I put away my books.* 3. **Put off** means make something wait: *She put off her work until later.* 4. **Put out** means make an end to: *Put out the fire.* 5. **Put up with** means bear: *He will not put up with her rude manner.* **put, put ting.**

puz zle 1. a hard problem. 2. a problem or task to be done for fun: *He was working a puzzle.* 3. be unable to understand something: *How the mouse got in puzzled us. They puzzled over the game.* **puz zles; puz zled, puz zling.**

pussy willow

Q   q

Q or **q** the seventeenth letter of the alphabet. **Q's** or **q's.**

quack 1. the sound a duck makes. 2. make such a sound. **quacks; quacked, quack ing.**

quail a small bird. See the picture. **quail.**

quar rel 1. an angry talk with someone who does not agree with you. 2. speak angrily to each other about something. **quar rels; quar reled, quar rel ing.**

quail

quill pen

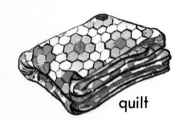

quilt

quart a measure specially for liquids. Four quarts are equal to one gallon. **quarts.**

quar ter 1. one of four equal parts; one fourth: *Each of the four boys ate a quarter of the apple. I'll meet you in a quarter of an hour.* 2. a coin of the United States and Canada worth 25 cents. **quar ters.**

quar ter-size one/fourth as large as normal: *The clown wore a small, quarter-size hat.*

Que bec one of the ten provinces of Canada. See the map on page 383.

queen 1. the wife of a king. 2. a woman ruler. 3. a woman chosen as the most beautiful: *The May Queen rode in the parade.* **queens.**

ques tion a thing asked to find out something: *A teacher asks questions.* **ques tions.**

quick fast and sudden; swift: *We made a quick trip to the store.* **quick er, quick est.**

quick ly fast; in a quick way: *The girls quickly arranged for the party.*

qui et 1. making no sound; with little or no noise: *It was a quiet night.* 2. not moving; still: *We sat by a quiet pond.* **qui et er, qui et est.**

qui et ly in a quiet way: *The girls talked quietly.*

quill 1. a large, stiff feather. 2. a pen made from a feather. See the picture. 3. a stiff, sharp hair like the end of a feather: *The porcupine's quills stood straight out.* **quills.**

quilt a covering for a bed, usually made from two pieces of cloth sewed together with soft material between them. See the picture. **quilts.**

quit 1. stop: *The workers always quit at five. Yesterday Beth quit early.* 2. leave: *Bob is quitting his job tomorrow. He had quit once before.* **quit, quit ting.**

quite 1. completely: *I am quite alone.* 2. really; truly: *There was quite a change in the weather.* 3. very; rather: *It is quite cold today.*

quo ta tion 1. someone's exact words stated by someone else; something repeated from a book or speech: *From what book does this quotation come?* 2. **Quotation marks** (" ") are put at the beginning and end of any quotation: *"Thank you very much," she said.* **quo ta tions.**

R   r

R or **r** the eighteenth letter of the alphabet. **R's** or **r's.**

rab bi As a minister or priest is head of a Christian church, so a rabbi is head of a Jewish temple. **rab bis.**

rab bit an animal with soft fur and long ears. See the picture. **rab bits.**

rabbit

rac coon a small animal that roams around at night. See the picture. **rac coons.**

race 1. a contest to see who can do something fastest. 2. run to get ahead: *She raced me to the house.* 3. run; move fast: *Race to the doctor for help.* **rac es; raced, rac ing.**

raccoon

ra dio 1. a way of sending and receiving sounds through the air: *The pilot talked to us by radio.* 2. an instrument for hearing these sounds: *He got a radio for his birthday.* 3. of radio: *a radio station, a radio program.* **ra di os** (for 2.).

rad ish a small plant. Its root is eaten as a vegetable. See the picture. **rad ish es.**

radish

rag 1. a torn or worn piece of cloth. 2. made of rags: *a rag doll.* **rags.**

215

rage

---

rapid

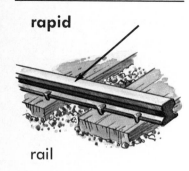
rail

rainbow

raincoat

raisins

rage the state of being very angry: *She flew into a rage when her bicycle was stolen.* **rag es.**

rail a bar of wood or metal: *Railroad trains run on steel rails.* See the picture. **rails.**

rail road 1. a road or track on which trains go. 2. the tracks, stations, trains, and the people who manage them: *Which railroad goes through this town?* **rail roads.**

rain 1. water falling in drops from the clouds: *The rain lasted all night.* 2. fall in drops: *It rained all night.* **rains; rained, rain ing.**

rain bow part of a circle of colors seen sometimes in the sky when the sun shines during a rain. See the picture. **rain bows.**

rain coat a coat that water will not go through. See the picture. **rain coats.**

rainy 1. having a lot of rain: *a rainy day.* 2. wet with rain: *rainy streets.* **rain i er, rain i est.**

raise 1. lift up: *Raise your hand.* 2. cause to rise: *The horses raised a cloud of dust.* 3. make grow: *The farmer raises poultry.* **raised, rais ing.**

rai sin 1. a sweet dried grape. See the picture. 2. made with raisins: *I like raisin pie.* **rai sins.**

rake 1. a tool with a long handle. You gather leaves with a rake. 2. make clean or smooth with a rake. **rakes; raked, rak ing.**

ran See **run.** *He ran home.*

ranch a large farm and its buildings. **ranch es.**

rang See **ring.** *Who rang the bell?*

rang er 1. a person who guards a forest against fires. 2. a kind of police officer. **rang ers.**

rap 1. a quick, light blow: *I heard a rap on the door.* 2. knock sharply: *Did you rap on the door?* **raps; rapped, rap ping.**

rap id very quick; swift: *He is a rapid talker.*

rap id ly quickly: *He ran rapidly toward home.*

rare¹ 1. not often found; few: *A talking bird is rare.* 2. not happening often: *Snow is rare in Louisiana.* **rar er, rar est.**

rare² not cooked much. **rar er, rar est.**

rare ly not often: *He rarely comes to meetings.*

rasp ber ry a small fruit that grows on a bush. See the picture. **rasp ber ries.**

rat a long-tailed gnawing animal like a mouse, but larger. See the picture. **rats.**

rath er 1. be more willing to: *I would rather play than work.* 2. quite: *He was rather angry.*

rat tle 1. make short, sharp sounds: *The door rattled.* 2. short, sharp sounds: *the rattle of dishes.* 3. a baby's toy that makes a noise. See the picture. **rat tled, rat tling; rat tles.**

raw 1. not cooked. 2. damp and cold: *A raw wind was blowing.* 3. sore: *His hands were raw from pulling on the rope.* **raw er, raw est.**

ra zor a tool with a sharp blade for shaving. See the picture. **ra zors.**

reach 1. get to; come to: *Your letter reached me today.* 2. stretch: *She reached for the milk.* 3. touch: *I can reach the lowest branch of the tree.* **reached, reach ing.**

read¹ 1. understand what writing or print means: *Have you learned to read?* 2. speak out loud the words of writing or print: *Read this story.* **read, read ing.** (Read¹ rhymes with seed.)

read² See **read¹**. *She read that book in school. Have you read it?* (Read² rhymes with head.)

read er 1. a person who reads. 2. a book for learning and practicing reading. **read ers.**

ready be prepared for use or for action: *Lunch is ready. She will be ready to go in a minute.*

raspberry

rat

rattle 3.

razor

horse rearing

recess **2.**

re al 1. not made up; true; not pretended: *The party was a real surprise to me.* 2. not copied: *This is a real pearl.*

re al ize understand clearly: *Your mother realizes that you want a bike.* **re al ized, re al iz ing.**

re al ly 1. truly; in fact: *He is really a good friend.* 2. an exclamation of surprise: *Oh, really?*

rear[1] 1. the back part; the back: *The rear of the house has not been painted, but the front is done.* 2. at the back: *Look out the rear window. Leave by the rear door.* 3. behind; in back of: *The garage is at the rear of the house.* **rears.**

rear[2] 1. make grow; help to grow; bring up: *They reared their children well.* 2. of an animal, rise on the hind legs: *The horse reared and then ran away.* See the picture. **reared, rear ing.**

rea son a cause; whatever causes something to happen or someone to do something: *Tell me your reason for not going. She had a good reason for being absent; she was sick.* **rea sons.**

re ceive get or be given something: *How many presents did you receive? He received a birthday card in the mail.* **re ceived, re ceiv ing.**

re cess 1. the time during which work stops: *We'll talk about our project at recess.* 2. a part in a wall, set back from the rest: *Our refrigerator fits in a recess.* See the picture. **re cess es.**

rec i pe a set of directions for preparing something, usually something to eat. **rec i pes.**

rec og nize know again; remember from knowing before: *I didn't recognize my old friend. Do you recognize this song?* **rec og nized, rec og niz ing.**

re cord 1. write down in order to remember: *Great events are recorded in books. Photographers record history in pictures.* 2. facts written down: *We kept a record of the money we spent.* 3. a round, flat object that gives off sounds when its top surface is touched by a needle: *We played some records.* 4. put sounds on a record: *We are going to record our school song.* 5. the facts about what someone has done: *My teacher said I have a fine record at school.* 6. **Break a record** can mean do something better than anyone has ever done it before. **re cord ed, re cord ing; re cords.**

re cord play er a machine that plays records. See the picture. **re cord play ers.**

re cov er 1. get back: *Did you recover the stolen money?* 2. get well: *I hope he will recover soon.* **re cov ered, re cov er ing.**

re cov ery 1. a getting back: *The recovery of the lost ring made her happy.* 2. getting well: *She made a rapid recovery from the measles.* **re cov er ies.**

re cy cle to treat or process something so that it may be used again. **re cy cled, re cy cling.**

red 1. the color of blood. 2. having that color. **reds; red der, red dest.**

red bud a tree with heart-shaped leaves and dark pink flowers. See the picture. **red buds.**

red wood a very tall evergreen tree. See the picture. **red woods.**

reel 1. a spool to hold things like thread, yarn, film, rope, or hose: *Our hose is wound on a reel.* See the picture. 2. something wound on a reel: *Here is a reel of film.* **reels.**

ref er ee a judge in some games. **ref er ees.**

record

referee

record player

redbud tree

redwood tree

hose on a reel

refrigerator

reindeer

re flect throw back light, heat, or sound. A calm lake reflects the blue of the sky. The sun is reflected from a shiny surface. A mirror reflects what is in front of it. **re flect ed, re flect ing.**

re fresh ment 1. refreshing; being refreshed. 2. food and drink. **re fresh ments.**

re frig er a tor a large container that keeps things cool and keeps food from spoiling. See the picture. **re frig er a tors.**

ref u gee a person who escapes from his home or country during dangerous times. **ref u gees.**

re fuse say no to: *They refused to go without me.* **re fused, re fus ing.**

reg u lar 1. usual: *He bought the regular size.* 2. coming again and again at the same time.

rein deer a kind of large deer. See the picture. **rein deer.**

rel a tive a person who belongs to the same family as another. **rel a tives.**

re lease 1. let go: *Release the door and it will shut by itself.* 2. let loose; set free: *She released the rabbit from its cage.* **re leased, re leas ing.**

re main 1. stay in a place: *We'll remain here until spring.* 2. continue; last: *The house remains the same year after year.* 3. be left: *A few leaves remain on the tree. If you take 10 from 20, 10 remains.* **re mained, re main ing.**

re mark 1. say; speak: *Dad remarked that the grass needed to be cut.* 2. something said. **re marked, re mark ing; re marks.**

re mark a ble worth noticing; not common; unusual: *It is remarkable that he came at all.*

re mem ber 1. call to mind: *Can you remember my name?* 2. keep in mind; take care not to forget. **re mem bered, re mem ber ing.**

rent[1] 1. money paid for the use of property: *She pays her rent every week.* 2. pay to use: *We rent the house from my uncle.* 3. receive pay for the use of property: *My uncle rents the house to us.* **rents; rent ed, rent ing.**

rent[2] a tear; a torn place. See the picture. **rents.**

re o pen open again. **re o pened, re o pen ing.**

re pair 1. put in good shape again: *Will you repair my torn coat?* 2. the act or work of repairing: *Repairs on the car cost a lot.* **re paired, re pair ing; re pairs.**

re peat 1. do again: *Don't repeat your mistakes.* 2. say again: *Please repeat that word.* 3. say after someone else: *Repeat the words after me.* 4. tell anyone else: *Did you repeat what he said?* **re peat ed, re peat ing.**

re ply 1. an answer: *What is your reply to them?* 2. answer someone or something: *Please reply to her question.* **re plies; re plied, re ply ing.**

re port 1. an account of something: *Her report of the trip was interesting.* 2. make a report: *Dad reported the fire.* 3. repeat what you have heard or seen; describe; tell: *The ranger reported bad storms.* **re ports; re port ed, re port ing.**

re port er a person who finds and reports news for a newspaper. **re port ers.**

rep tile a kind of animal with cold blood. Snakes, lizards, and alligators are reptiles. **rep tiles.**

re quest 1. ask or ask for: *He requested us to stop talking.* 2. what is asked for: *The queen granted their request at once.* **re quest ed, re quest ing; re quests.**

re quire 1. need: *We require lots of food for our party.* 2. demand; command: *Learning to skate requires practice.* **re quired, re quir ing.**

rent[2]

rescue

---

rhinoceros

reservoir 1.

retriever

rhinoceros

res cue 1. save from harm: *The prince rescued the princess.* 2. the act of rescuing: *He came to my rescue.* **res cued, res cu ing; res cues.**

res er voir 1. a place where water is held and stored for use. See the picture. 2. anything to hold a liquid. **res er voirs.**

re spect 1. show special attention to and thought for: *We respect a kind person.* 2. the act of respecting: *This teacher has the respect of his class.* **re spect ed, re spect ing.**

rest[1] 1. be still: *Rest for a while.* 2. a pause after hard work: *Take a rest for a few minutes.* 3. be held up by: *The roof rests on beams.* **rests; rest ed, rest ing.**

rest[2] what is left; the remainder: *He ate half the apple and threw away the rest.*

res tau rant a place to eat. **res tau rants.**

re sult what happens because of something: *The result of her fall was a broken arm.* **re sults.**

re triev er a dog that is trained to help a hunter. See the picture. **re triev ers.**

re turn 1. go back; come back: *She will return in a moment.* 2. the going or coming back: *We look forward to the return of spring.* 3. bring back; pay back: *Did you return the books to the library?* **re turned, re turn ing; re turns.**

re volve move in a circle; turn around a center: *The earth revolves around the sun. A record on a record player revolves.* **re volved, re volv ing.**

re ward 1. something given for something done. 2. give a reward to: *She rewarded me for finding her cat.* **re wards; re ward ed, re ward ing.**

rhi noc er os a large, wild animal. It has thick skin and one or two horns above its mouth. See the picture. **rhi noc er os es** or **rhi noc er os.**

222

Rhode Is land one of the fifty states of the United States. See page 366.

rho do den dron an evergreen bush somewhat like an azalea, but with larger blossoms. See the picture. **rho do den drons.**

rhyme 1. a sound at the end of a word or words that matches a sound at the end of another word or words. *Kitten* is a rhyme for *mitten*. *Moon* and *June* are rhymes. 2. make a rhyme. *True* and *blue* are words that rhyme. 3. a short poem having many lines ending in words that rhyme. **rhymes; rhymed, rhym ing.**

rhythm movement with a regular beat. **rhythms.**

rib one of the bones that curve round your chest. See the picture. **ribs.**

rib bon 1. a long strip or band of cloth. Ribbons are often silk or velvet. 2. anything like a ribbon: *a typewriter ribbon.* **rib bons.**

rice 1. the grain of a plant used for food. 2. the plant itself. See the picture.

rich 1. having a lot of money. 2. having plenty of what is needed: *This dessert is very rich with butter.* **rich er, rich est.**

rid 1. make free: *Can you rid this house of flies? He rid the room of smoke by opening a window. The wind has rid the sky of clouds.* 2. **Get rid of** means get free from or do away with. **rid** or **rid ded, rid ding.**

rid dle a puzzling question or problem with a surprise answer. **rid dles.**

ride 1. sit on something and make it go: *Some people ride camels.* 2. be carried along: *We ride in a bus to school.* 3. a trip on an animal or a vehicle: *We took a ride on our bikes.* **rode, rid den, rid ing; rides.**

Rhode Island

ride

rhododendron

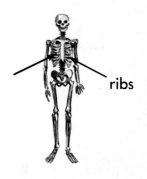
ribs

rice

circus ring

road runner

right 1. good; just: *The right thing to do is tell the truth.* 2. something that a person should have or should be allowed to do: *Each citizen has a right to vote. He has no right to block that street.* 3. correct; true: *the right answer.* 4. correctly; truly: *I guessed right.* 5. opposite of left: *the right hand. Make a right turn.* **rights.**

rim the edge or border around anything. **rims.**

ring[1] 1. a circle: *The dancers formed a ring.* 2. a thin circle of metal or other material: *a gold ring.* 3. a closed space: *The horses pranced around the circus ring.* See the picture. **rings.**

ring[2] 1. give out a sound like a bell: *Did the phone ring?* 2. the sound of a bell: *I heard a ring during the night.* 3. make something ring: *Did you ring the bell?* **rang, rung, ring ing; rings.**

rip 1. cut or pull off; tear off: *Rip the cover off this box.* 2. cut or pull out threads in sewing. 3. a torn place: *Aunt Jane sewed up the rip in my sleeve.* **ripped, rip ping; rips.**

ripe grown and ready to be gathered; not green: *The ripe apples were picked.* **rip er, rip est.**

rise 1. get up from a lying, sitting, or kneeling position: *Please rise when your name is called.* 2. get up from bed: *I must rise early tomorrow.* 3. go up; come up: *What time will the sun rise tomorrow?* 4. go higher: *The price of food is rising.* **rose, ris en, ris ing.**

ris en See **rise.** *He has risen early this morning.*

riv er a large stream of running water. Most big rivers flow into an ocean. **riv ers.**

road a way on which to go from one place to another: *Take this road to the city.* **roads.**

road run ner a bird that can run very fast. See the picture. **road run ners.**

roar 1. make a loud, deep sound: *The crowd roared when he caught the ball.* 2. a loud, deep sound: *The roar of the wind woke me.* **roared, roar ing; roars.**

roast 1. cook by dry heat in an oven; bake: *We roasted a chicken.* 2. a piece of meat baked or to be baked: *Father cooked a roast.* 3. cooked in the oven: *roast beef.* **roast ed, roast ing; roasts.**

rob take away from by force; steal: *The bank was robbed.* **robbed, rob bing.**

rob ber person who robs; thief. **rob bers.**

robe a long piece of clothing like a loose coat. Kings and judges wear robes. See the picture. **robes.**

rob in a large American thrush. See the picture. **rob ins.**

ro bot machine that does work in response to commands: *The robot opened the door for us.* **ro bots.**

rock[1] 1. the large masses of hard material found in the earth. 2. a large stone. **rocks.**

rock[2] move back and forth or from side to side; sway: *I rocked the baby.* **rocked, rock ing.**

rock et a long tube filled with fuel. When the fuel burns, it pushes the rocket upward or forward. See the picture. **rock ets.**

rocky[1] full of rocks or made of rock: *The road was very rocky.* **rock i er, rock i est.**

rocky[2] shaky; not steady; rocking back and forth: *I felt a little rocky after a fall.* **rock i er, rock i est.**

rode See **ride.** *I rode my bicycle to school.*

ro deo a contest or a show in which cowboys rope cattle and ride wild horses. **ro de os.**

king wearing a robe

robin

rocket

lawn roller

rooster

rope 1.

rose¹

roll 1. move along by turning over and over: *The pencil rolled under the desk.* 2. turn around itself or on something; wrap: *Grandmother rolled yarn into a ball. He rolled himself up in a quilt.* 3. something rolled up: *a roll of film.* 4. a kind of bread: *a sweet roll.* **rolled, roll ing; rolls.**

roll er something that rolls: *Dad used a roller to make the lawn smooth.* See the picture. **roll ers.**

roof 1. the top of a building. 2. something like a roof: *the roof of your mouth.* **roofs.**

room 1. a part of a house or building. 2. space: *I haven't enough room to turn around. There is room in this box for another book.* **rooms** (for 1.).

roost 1. a perch on which birds sleep. 2. sit as birds do on a roost: *Turkeys were roosting in the tree.* 3. a shed for birds to roost in. **roosts; roost ed, roost ing.**

roost er a male chicken. See the picture. **roost ers.**

root 1. the part of a plant that grows under the ground. 2. something like a root: *the root of a tooth.* 3. a word or syllable from which other words are made. **roots.**

root word a word or part of a word that is used as a base for forming other words: ***New** is the root of **renew**. **Beauty** is the root of **beautiful**.* **root words.**

rope 1. hemp stalks twisted together in bundles to make a strong, sturdy material for tying things. See the picture. 2. catch a horse or calf with a looped rope. **ropes; roped, rop ing.**

rose¹ a flower that grows on a bush. Some roses have thorns. See the picture. The rose is the state flower of several states. **ros es.**

rose² See **rise.** *They rose when the judge entered.*

rosy rose-red. **ros i er, ros i est.**

ro tor on a machine, a part that rotates. Rotors
make a helicopter fly. See the picture. **ro tors.**

rot ten 1. no longer good; spoiled: *a rotten egg,
a rotten banana.* 2. not strong; weak; ready to
break: *The rotten wood in the floor gave way.*
rot ten er, rot ten est.

round 1. shaped like a ball or a circle or a tree
trunk. The earth is round. A wheel is round.
A telephone pole is round. 2. on all sides of;
around: *She walked round the block.* 3. in a
circle: *The hands of a clock go round.*
4. **Round up** means gather cattle into a herd.
round er, round est.

row[1] a line of people or things: *Cars were parked
in a row. I climbed over a row of people to get
to my seat.* **rows.**

row[2] move a boat by pulling oars through the
water. **rowed, row ing.**

roy al of or about kings and queens: *The knight
received a royal command to go to the castle.*

rub move one thing back and forth against another.
rubbed, rub bing.

rub ber 1. a material made from the juice of
certain trees. Rubber can stretch and bounce and
will not let air or water through it. 2. **Rubbers**
are coverings for your shoes. Rubbers keep
your feet dry. 3. made of rubber: *Wear rubber
gloves when you clean the stove.*

rude having bad manners. **rud er, rud est.**

rude ly in a rude way: *He laughed rudely.*

ruf fle a strip of cloth, ribbon, or lace gathered
along one edge and used for trimming things.
See the picture. **ruf fles.**

ruf fled having ruffles: *a ruffled shirt.*

rug a heavy floor covering. **rugs.**

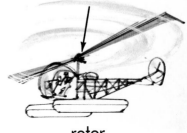

rotor

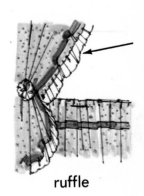

ruffle

ruler **2.**

rung[1]

rule 1. something that tells what to do and what not to do: *playground rules.* 2. decide which is right or which to do; make a rule: *The referee ruled that the game should stop. The judges ruled that no one could win two prizes.* 3. control: *The king ruled his kingdom well.* 4. mark with lines: *She ruled the paper with a ruler.* 5. **As a rule** means usually. **rules; ruled, rul ing.**

rul er 1. a king, queen, or anyone who controls a government. 2. a straight strip of wood or metal used to measure. See the picture. **rul ers.**

run 1. go faster than walking: *Have you ever run a mile?* 2. go in a hurry: *Run to the store.* 3. go; move; work: *Why won't my watch run?* 4. cause to go or work: *Mom runs a machine.* 5. the act of running: *He came down the street on the run.* 6. **Run down** means stop going or working. 7. **Run out** means come to an end. **ran, run, run ning.**

rung[1] a rod or bar used as a step of a ladder. See the picture. **rungs.**

rung[2] See **ring**[2]. *The church bell has rung all day.*

run ner a person, animal, or thing that runs. **run ners.**

ru ral of the country: *Rural life is not like city life.*

rush 1. move with speed, force, or haste: *The stream rushed down the hill.* 2. a hurry: *Why are you in a rush?* **rushed, rush ing; rush es.**

rust 1. the red-brown covering that sometimes forms on iron or steel. 2. become covered with this: *Don't let your tools rust.* **rust ed, rust ing.**

rus tle 1. a light, soft sound of things gently rubbing together. 2. make or cause to make this sound: *Leaves rustled in the breeze.* **rus tled, rus tling.**

S   s

S or **s** the nineteenth letter of the alphabet.
  S's or **s's.**

Sab bath a day of the week saved for rest and
  worship. **Sab baths.**

sack a bag made of paper or coarse cloth. **sacks.**

sad not happy. **sad der, sad dest.**

sad dle 1. a seat for a rider. See the picture.
  2. put a saddle on: *Saddle the horses, and
  we'll ride.* **sad dles; sad dled, sad dling.**

sad ly in a sad or unhappy way: *The little child
  picked up the broken doll sadly.*

safe 1. free from harm or danger: *Find a safe
  place to swim.* 2. a place or container for
  keeping things safe. See the picture. **saf er,
  saf est; safes.**

safe ly in a safe way: *The plane landed safely
  in a field.*

safe ty 1. being out of danger: *Safety is
  important to everyone.* 2. keeping from danger:
  A safety belt can save your life.

sage brush a kind of bushy plant that grows in
  dry country. See the picture.

said See **say.** *He said it was true. He has said so.*

sail 1. a piece of canvas that catches the wind
  to move a boat. 2. a trip on a sailboat: *We
  had a sail down the river.* 3. run a sailboat:
  The girls are sailing in the race today. **sails;
  sailed, sail ing.**

sail or 1. a member of a ship's crew; one who
  sails. 2. a member of the United States Navy.
  sail ors.

saddle 1.

safe 2.

sagebrush

salmon

sampan

pair of sandals

sal ad 1. vegetables or other food usually served raw and cold with a dressing. 2. for a salad: *salad dressing, a salad plate.* **sal ads.**

sale 1. the act of selling; giving something in return for receiving money: *That house is for sale.* 2. selling for a low price: *The bakery is having a sale on doughnuts.* **sales.**

sales man a salesperson. **sales men.**

sales per son somebody whose business is selling things: *The salesperson was showing TV sets to a customer.* **sales per sons.**

sales wom an a salesperson. **sales wom en.**

salm on a large salt-water fish, good to eat. See the picture. **salm ons** or **salm on.**

salt a white material found in the earth and in sea water. Salt makes food taste better.

salty tasting of salt: *This popcorn tastes too salty.* **salt i er, salt i est.**

same 1. not another: *We ate lunch at the same restaurant every day.* 2. just alike; not different: *She has the same name I have.*

sam pan a kind of small sailboat used in some countries of Asia. See the picture. **sam pans.**

sand tiny grains of worn-down rock: *The beach is covered with sand.* **sands.**

san dal a kind of shoe fastened to the foot by straps. See the picture. **san dals.**

sand box a large box filled with sand for little children to play in. **sand box es.**

sand wich slices of bread with meat, jelly, or some other food between them. **sand wich es.**

sandy containing or covered with sand: *We found a sandy beach. The floor is sandy since we came from the beach.* **sand i er, sand i est.**

sang See **sing.** *My aunt sang in the choir.*

sank See **sink.** *The toy boat sank before I could reach out and grab it.*

San ta Claus *Santa Claus is pictured as a jolly old man. He wears a red suit with fur trimming.*

Sa skatch e wan one of the ten provinces of Canada. See the map on page 382.

sat See **sit.** *She sat down for a minute to rest. Grandmother has sat by the window all day.*

sat el lite 1. something that revolves around a planet. The moon is a satellite of the earth. 2. an object shot into space to revolve in an orbit. See the picture. **sat el lites.**

sat in 1. cloth with one very smooth, shiny side. 2. like or of satin: *The queen wore satin robes.*

sat is fy give enough to; fill a need completely: *Will a peanut-butter sandwich satisfy your hunger?* **sat is fied, sat is fy ing.**

Sat ur day the seventh day of the week; the day after Friday. **Sat ur days.**

sauce a thick or thin liquid, served with or on food. Some sauces are sweet. **sauc es.**

sauce pan a container for cooking. See the picture. **sauce pans.**

sau cer a small, flat dish with its edge curved up. A saucer is used to hold a cup. **sau cers.**

sau sage meat that has been chopped, seasoned, and usually stuffed into a thin case: *Sausages taste good with pancakes.* **sau sag es.**

save 1. make safe from harm or danger: *The safety belt saved my life.* 2. collect; keep: *He saves old coins.* **saved, sav ing.**

saw[1] 1. a tool for cutting. See the picture. 2. cut with a saw: *Dad sawed the board in two.* **saws; sawed, sawed** or **sawn, saw ing.**

saw[2] See **see**[1]. *I saw a bluebird in that tree.*

sank

---

saw

satellite 2.

saucepan

saw[1] 1.

sawdust

---

scary

girl playing a saxophone

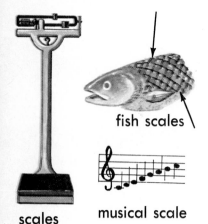

scales   fish scales

musical scale

scarecrow

saw dust the tiny bits of wood that fall as the wood is sawed: *Sawdust covered the floor.*

sawn See **saw**[1].

sax o phone a musical instrument that you play by blowing into it and pressing keys. See the picture. **sax o phones.**

say speak; put into words. **said, say ing.**

scale[1] an instrument for measuring weight. It is usually called **scales.** See the picture. **scales.**

scale[2] 1. one of the thin, hard pieces that form the outside covering of fish and snakes. See the picture. 2. a thin layer: *Scales of paint were peeling off the old barn.* **scales.**

scale[3] 1. a set of numbers used to measure some things. The scale on a thermometer measures the heat. 2. in music, a group of notes that go up or down like steps. See the picture. **scales.**

scalp 1. the skin and hair on the top of your head. 2. cut or tear the scalp from. **scalps; scalped, scalp ing.**

scam per run quickly: *The squirrel scampered up the tree.* **scam pered, scam per ing.**

scare 1. frighten: *Storms scare me.* 2. being frightened: *We had a scare when the tree blew down.* **scared, scar ing; scares.**

scare crow a figure of a person dressed in old clothes. A scarecrow is set up in a field to frighten birds away from growing crops. See the picture. **scare crows.**

scarf a piece of cloth worn on the head or around the neck and shoulders. **scarfs** or **scarves.**

scar let very bright red.

scarves more than one scarf.

scary able to scare; making one afraid: *We saw a scary movie on TV.* **scar i er, scar i est.**

232

scat ter 1. throw around here and there: *It's my job to scatter corn for the chickens. Please scatter some sand on that icy walk before someone falls.* 2. separate and go in different directions: *The crowd scattered when the rain began.* **scat tered, scat ter ing.**

scene 1. one time and place of a play or story: *The first scene is a city street.* 2. a sight: *When I looked out the window, I saw a beautiful country scene.* **scenes.**

scent a smell: *The scent of blossoms came in my window. This perfume has a strong scent. It is not my favorite scent.* **scents.**

school 1. a place for teaching and learning: *My uncle goes to night school.* 2. the pupils and teachers of a school: *Our whole school visited the zoo.* **schools.**

school room a room in which pupils are taught. **school rooms.**

sci ence a careful study of facts about the earth or anything on it. There are many different kinds of science. **sci enc es.**

sci en tist a person who studies a science. There are many different kinds of scientist. **sci en tists.**

scis sors a tool for cutting, with two sharp blades that move toward each other.

scold speak to angrily: *Will Mother scold us for being late?* **scold ed, scold ing.**

scoop 1. a tool like a shovel. 2. a large, deep spoon to dip out things. See the picture. 3. take up or out with a scoop, or as a scoop does. **scoops; scooped, scoop ing.**

scoot er a vehicle with two wheels, moved by pushing one foot against the ground. Some scooters have motors. See the picture. **scoot ers.**

ice-cream scoop

motor scooter

Scotch terrier

screen 1.

screen 2.

scorch burn a little bit: *I scorched this sleeve when I ironed it.* **scorched, scorch ing.**

score 1. the points won in a game or test: *The score was 73 to 61.* 2. make points: *Our team scored first.* **scores; scored, scor ing.**

Scotch ter ri er a small dog with short legs. See the picture. **Scotch ter ri ers.**

Scot ty a Scotch terrier. **Scot ties.**

scout lead er a person in charge of a group of Girl Scouts. **scout lead ers.**

scout mas ter a person in charge of a group of Boy Scouts. **scout mas ters.**

scowl 1. look angry; frown. 2. an angry look; a frown. **scowled, scowl ing; scowls.**

scram ble 1. go by climbing and crawling: *Billy scrambled up the hill.* 2. struggle with others for something: *Both teams scrambled for the ball.* 3. mix together: *Father scrambled eggs.* **scram bled, scram bling.**

scrap a small piece; a small part left over: *There were scraps of paper on the floor.* **scraps.**

scrape 1. rub with something sharp to make clean: *Scrape your shoes to get the mud off.* 2. rub off with something sharp: *Scrape the mud off your shoes.* **scraped, scrap ing.**

scratch 1. rub or scrape with something sharp: *The pin scratched my arm.* 2. a mark made by scratching: *The scratch on my leg hurts.* **scratched, scratch ing; scratch es.**

scream 1. make a loud, sharp cry: *She screamed when she saw the ghost.* 2. a loud, sharp cry: *I heard a scream!* **screamed, scream ing; screams.**

screen 1. a covered frame that hides something: *Behind that screen is the kitchen.* 2. a surface of woven wire. See the picture. **screens.**

screw a piece of metal shaped somewhat like a nail. It is twisted, not pounded, into wood. See the picture. **screws.**

scrub rub hard; wash or clean by rubbing. **scrubbed, scrub bing.**

sculp tor a person who sculptures. **sculp tors.**

sculp ture 1. the making of statues or figures from stone or wood or other material. 2. the figure made: *the sculpture of a horse.* 3. cut from stone or other material or model from clay: *My mom sculptured a statue for the city.* **sculp tures; sculp tured, sculp tur ing.**

scur ry run quickly. **scur ried, scur ry ing.**

sea 1. a great body of water, smaller than an ocean. Oceans and seas are filled with salt water. Rivers and lakes are filled with fresh water. 2. of the sea: *The sea breeze was cool.* 3. **At sea** can mean confused or puzzled about something. **seas.**

sea horse a small fish that has a head like a horse. See the picture. **sea hors es.**

seal[1] 1. a picture stamped on something. The seal of the United States has an eagle on it. See the picture. 2. a tool for stamping things. 3. close very tightly; fasten: *He sealed the envelope and mailed it. Mother sealed the jars of jelly with wax.* **seals; sealed, seal ing.**

seal[2] a sea animal with thick fur. Seals usually live in cold places. See the picture. **seals** or **seal.**

search 1. try to find by looking: *We searched everywhere for that book.* 2. go over carefully: *The police searched the house.* 3. the act of searching: *Everybody joined in the search for eggs.* **searched, search ing; search es.**

screw

seahorse

the seal
of the United States

seal[2]

sea son 1. one of the four parts of a year; spring, summer, fall, or winter. 2. improve the taste of: *The soup was seasoned with pepper.* **sea sons; sea soned, sea son ing.**

seat 1. something to sit on. 2. a place to sit: *Our seats are in the first row.* 3. the part of a chair you sit on: *Put a cushion on the seat of that chair.* 4. put into a seat: *He seated himself in the chair. I was seated next to the president.* **seats; seat ed, seat ing.**

sec ond[1] next after the first: *She won second prize at the art show.*

sec ond[2] the smallest measure of time. Sixty seconds equal one minute. **sec onds.**

se cret 1. something that you don't tell anyone. 2. not known to everyone: *The club had a secret code.* **se crets.**

sec tion part; slice: *Cut the pie into eight equal sections.* **sec tions.**

see 1. look at: *See the falling star!* 2. understand: *I can see why the baby is crying.* 3. find out: *Let's see what's wrong.* 4. visit: *Last summer we went to see Grandmother and Grandfather on the farm.* **saw, seen, see ing.**

seed 1. the thing from which a plant grows. See the picture. 2. scatter seed over: *Dad seeded our lawn.* **seeds; seed ed, seed ing.**

seek try to get; try to find; search. **sought, seek ing.**

seem give the feeling of being: *The baby seemed hungry, but she wouldn't eat. The cat seems to like that toy. Does this radio seem too loud to you? I've drunk three glasses of water, but I still seem to be thirsty.* **seemed, seem ing.**

seen See **see.** *I have seen him twice today.*

package of seeds

seg ment a piece cut off; a part. You can divide an orange into segments. See the picture. **seg ments.**

se lect choose: *Did you select your own birthday present?* **se lect ed, se lect ing.**

se lec tion the thing chosen. **se lec tions.**

self one's own person: *Your self is you. My self is I.* **selves.**

self ish caring too much for yourself and not enough for other people: *A selfish child doesn't like to share toys with anyone.*

self ish ly in a selfish way: *He selfishly ate all the candy on the plate.*

sell trade a thing for money: *I am going to sell my bike.* **sold, sell ing.**

selves more than one self.

send cause to go: *Mother often sends Frank to the store.* **sent, send ing.**

sense 1. the power to think clearly and act wisely: *The captain of a team must have good sense.* 2. **The five senses** are sight, hearing, touch, taste, smell. **sens es.**

sen si tive 1. receiving impressions readily: *The eye is sensitive to light.* 2. easily affected or influenced.

sent See **send.** *He sent us to look for water. Two of the children have been sent to the library.*

sen tence a group of words that is complete in itself. A sentence usually ends with a period or a question mark. **sen tenc es.**

sep a rate 1. be between: *A wall separates these rooms.* 2. put or come apart: *Please separate the pencils from the pens.* 3. away from each other: *We sat at separate tables in the cafeteria.* **sep a rat ed, sep a rat ing.**

segment

separate

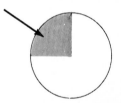

segment of a circle

segments of an orange

sep a rate ly alone; by itself: *We wrapped the two books separately.*

Sep tem ber the ninth month. It has 30 days. **Sep tem bers.**

se ri ous 1. thoughtful; not joking: *Dad had a serious look on his face.* 2. important: *A mistake in counting money could be serious.*

serv ant a person hired to work for someone. **serv ants.**

serve 1. work for: *Soldiers serve their country. This old car has served us well.* 2. put food on the table: *The waitress served the salad.* 3. have or be enough for: *This meat will serve six persons.* **served, serv ing.**

serv ice 1. being useful or helpful to others: *May I be of service? The waiter gave us good service.* 2. **The service** can mean the army, navy, air force, marines, or the Coast Guard: *Dad was in the service for two years.* **serv ic es.**

serv ing the amount of food served to one person; a helping. **serv ings.**

set 1. put in some place: *Set the table and chair in this corner.* 2. arrange; put in order: *Have you set the table?* 3. show for others to follow: *She set a good example.* 4. go down: *When the sun sets, we must go home.* 5. a group of things that go together: *a set of books, a set of numbers.* **set, set ting; sets.**

set ter a hunting dog with long hair. See the picture. **set ters.**

setter

set tle 1. agree upon: *Let's settle the question of what we're going to do.* 2. go to live somewhere: *The Pilgrims settled in Plymouth.* 3. be or put in a pleasant position: *The lost girl settled down in the big chair.* **set tled, set tling.**

set tle ment a group of buildings and the people living in them: *Pioneers lived in early settlements.* See the picture. **set tle ments.**

set tler a person who settles in a new country: *The early settlers built log cabins.* **set tlers.**

sev en one more than six; 7. *Seven and seven are fourteen.* **sev ens.**

sev en teen seven more than ten; 17. **sev en teens.**

sev en teenth 1. next after the sixteenth; 17th. 2. one of 17 equal parts. **sev en teenths.**

sev enth 1. next after the sixth; 7th. 2. one of 7 equal parts. **sev enths.**

sev en ti eth 1. next after the sixty-ninth; 70th. 2. one of 70 equal parts. **se ven ti eths.**

sev en ty seven times ten; 70. **sev en ties.**

sev er al more than two or three but not many: *There were several cars on the road.*

sew 1. work on cloth with a needle and thread: *Judy likes to sew.* 2. fasten or close by sewing. **sewed, sew ing.** (Sew rhymes with go.)

sew er a drain under the ground to carry off waste. **sew ers.** (Sewer rhymes with newer.)

sew ing ma chine a machine for sewing. See the picture. **sew ing ma chines.**

shade 1. a place not in the bright sun: *It is quite cool in the shade.* 2. something that shuts out light: *Pull down the shade if you want to sleep late in the morning.* See the picture. **shades.**

shad ow the shade made by a person or object in a bright light: *Sometimes my shadow is very long.* **shad ows.**

shad owy 1. having much shadow: *Shadowy woods are scary.* 2. like a shadow: *I saw a shadowy shape.* **shad ow i er, shad ow i est.**

settlement

sewing machine

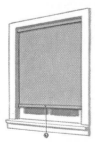

shade 2.

shady 1. in the shade: *We found a shady spot.*
2. giving shade: *We ate under a shady tree.*
shad i er, shad i est.

shag gy covered with a thick mass of hair or fur:
He has a shaggy dog. **shag gi er, shag gi est.**

shake move quickly back and forth, up and down,
or from side to side: *Shake your head. The wet
dog shook itself. Shake some salt on the meat.*
shook, shak en, shak ing.

shak en See **shake.** *Have you shaken the rugs?*

shaky 1. not firm or steady: *He spoke in a shaky
voice.* 2. not strong; weak: *There was a shaky
porch on the old house.* **shak i er, shak i est.**

shall *Shall* is used when something will happen
or must happen: *I shall be there soon. Shall
we go? You shall go to bed right now.* **should.**

shame 1. a feeling that you have done something
wrong or silly: *He turned red with shame.*
2. cause to feel you have done something wrong
or silly: *My mistake shamed me.* 3. something
to feel sorry about: *It's a shame we can't go.*
shamed, sham ing.

shan't shall not.

shape 1. the way something looks on all sides:
*The shape of the vase is square. An apple is
different in shape from a banana.* 2. give a
shape to: *The children shape clay to look like
animals.* **shapes; shaped, shap ing.**

share 1. the part belonging to one person: *She
did more than her share of the work.* 2. use or
have together: *My brothers share a room.*
3. separate into parts for sharing: *She shared
her lunch with me.* **shares; shared, shar ing.**

shark any of a group of large, fierce fishes.
See the picture. **sharks.**

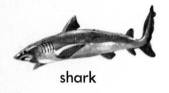

shark

sharp 1. having a thin edge to cut with or a fine point: *a sharp knife, a sharp needle.* 2. noticing things quickly: *Detectives must have sharp eyes.* 3. in music, a tone one-half step above; the sign (#). **sharp er, sharp est; sharps.**

sharp ly in a sharp or unfriendly manner: *"Stop that!" he said sharply.*

shave 1. cut hair off very close to the skin, usually with a razor: *Grandfather shaves every day.* 2. the cutting off of hair: *Dad got a shave at the barber shop.* 3. cut off in thin slices: *She shaved the edge of the door so it would fit.* See the picture. **shaved, shav ing; shaves.**

shawl a square or long piece of cloth worn about the shoulders or head. See the picture. **shawls.**

she any girl, woman, or female animal spoken about before: *My sister says she will hurry home. She has many books.*

shed a building used for shelter or storing things: *We keep garden tools in a shed.* **sheds.**

she'd 1. she had: *She'd taken the early bus home.* 2. she would: *Did she say she'd wait for us?*

sheep an animal raised for its wool and its meat. See the picture. **sheep.**

sheep dog a dog trained to help take care of sheep. See the picture. **sheep dogs.**

sheep ish shamed and timid: *He gave a sheepish smile when he saw that he had walked into the wrong class.*

sheet 1. a large piece of cloth used to sleep on or under. 2. a broad, thin piece of anything: *a sheet of ice, a sheet of paper.* **sheets.**

shelf 1. a flat piece of wood or metal to hold things: *a book shelf.* 2. anything like a shelf: *A shelf of rock hung over the cliff.* **shelves.**

sharp

---

shelf

shave 1.

shave 3.

woman wearing a shawl

sheep

sheep dog

sea shell

nut shell

egg shell

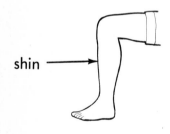

shelter 1.

shin

shirt

shell 1. the hard covering of some animals. Snails, oysters, crabs, turtles, have shells. 2. the hard covering of a nut or egg. See the picture. 3. take out of a shell: *I'll shell peas.* **shells; shelled, shell ing.**

she'll 1. she will. 2. she shall.

shel ter 1. something that covers or protects: *We looked for a shelter from the freezing wind.* See the picture. 2. cover or protect: *The old oak tree sheltered us from the rain.* **shel ters; shel tered, shel ter ing.**

shelves more than one shelf.

sher iff a county police officer: *My favorite TV show is about a sheriff.* **sher iffs.**

she's 1. she is: *She's going to the opera.* 2. she has: *She's dropped her purse.*

shin the front part of the leg from the knee to the ankle. See the picture. **shins.**

shine 1. send out light; glow: *The sun is going to shine today. It shone brightly yesterday.* 2. make bright: *Shine your shoes with this old cloth. We shined the silver.* 3. the glow or light: *The silver has a bright shine.* **shone** or **shined, shin ing; shines.**

shiny bright; shining: *Our town has a shiny new fire truck.* **shin i er, shin i est.**

ship 1. a large boat. 2. send or carry by ship, train, truck, or plane: *Will you ship the package to me?* **ships; shipped, ship ping.**

shirt a piece of clothing for the upper part of the body. See the picture. **shirts.**

shiv er 1. shake with cold or fear: *The scary noise made us shiver.* 2. the act of shivering: *I had the shivers after I came out of the pool.* **shiv ered, shiv er ing; shiv ers.**

shock[1] 1. a sudden hard shake, blow, or crash: *She felt the shock of the tree falling.* 2. something that upsets you suddenly: *The news is a shock to us.* 3. the feeling caused by an electric current going through the body: *She got a shock from the toaster.* 4. cause to feel shock: *His bad manners shock me.* **shocks; shocked, shock ing.**

shock[2] stalks of corn or bundles of grain set up on end. See the picture. **shocks.**

shoe a covering for a person's foot. **shoes.**

shoe lace a cord for fastening a shoe. **shoe lac es.**

shone See **shine.** *The sun shone yesterday. It has shone every day this week.*

shook See **shake.** *She shook her head. His hands shook when he picked up the cup.*

shoot 1. hit with a bullet or arrow: *Did he ever shoot a pheasant?* 2. send from a gun or other weapon: *The girls shot at the wooden ducks.* 3. move suddenly: *Flames shoot up when you poke a fire.* 4. grow: *Is the corn shooting up in this hot weather?* 5. a new part growing out: *The shoots on that bush are bright green.* See the picture. **shot, shoot ing; shoots.**

shop 1. a place where things are sold; a store. 2. visit stores to buy things: *We shopped all day.* 3. a place where things are made or repaired: *a repair shop.* **shops; shopped, shop ping.**

shop keep er person who owns or manages a shop or store. **shop keep ers.**

shop ping cen ter a group of stores with a large parking lot. **shop ping cen ters.**

shore land at the edge of a sea or lake. **shores.**

short 1. not tall: *The short children sit in the front seats.* 2. not long: *Summer seems short.* **short er, short est.**

shock[2]

shoot 5.

shot[1] 1. the sound of shooting: *We heard a shot across the field.* 2. act of shooting: *You only get one shot at the rock.* 3. medicine given to a patient by needle. **shots.**

shot[2] See **shoot.** *The hunter shot a lion. He had shot an elephant too.*

should 1. *Should* is used to mean ought to: *She should be here by now. We should have known better.* 2. *Should* can mean something may or may not happen: *If it should rain, we won't go.*

shoul der the part of your body to which an arm is joined. **shoul ders.**

should n't should not.

shout 1. call loudly: *He shouted, but I didn't hear him.* 2. a loud call: *I heard a shout of joy.* 3. talk or laugh loudly: *Don't shout!* **shout ed, shout ing; shouts.**

shove 1. push; move along by force from behind: *He shoved the chair across the floor.* 2. push against: *The people shoved to get into the hall.* 3. a push: *She gave the boat a shove into the water.* **shoved, shov ing; shoves.**

shov el 1. a tool used to lift and throw dirt or snow or other loose material. See the picture. 2. lift and throw with a shovel: *The young man shoveled snow from the walk.* **shov els; shov eled, shov el ing.**

show 1. bring or put in sight: *My aunt showed us her new car.* 2. be in sight: *Does the hole in my sock show?* 3. make clear to: *The salesperson showed me how to do the puzzle.* 4. special things being shown: *the flower show, the automobile show.* 5. a play, movie, TV program: *We saw a good show.* **showed, shown** or **showed, show ing; shows.**

coal shovel

snow shovel

show er 1. a short rain: *We had a shower this evening.* 2. anything like rain: *A shower of sparks fell from the log.* 3. a bath in which water pours down in small jets. See the picture. **show ers.**

shrimp a small sea creature with a long tail. *Shrimp is good to eat.* See the picture. **shrimps** or **shrimp.**

shrink 1. back away from; move backward: *Our dog shrinks at the crash of thunder.* 2. get smaller: *Will the blanket shrink in hot water?* 3. make smaller: *Hot water shrinks wool.* **shrank** or **shrunk, shrunk** or **shrunk en, shrink ing.**

shrug 1. raise the shoulders to show doubt: *He shrugged when we asked for directions.* 2. raising the shoulders in this way: *She replied with a shrug.* **shrugged, shrug ging.**

shrunk en See **shrink.**

shud der 1. tremble with fear or cold: *I shudder at the sight of snakes.* 2. trembling: *He gave a shudder at the sight of the snake.* **shud dered, shud der ing.**

shut 1. cover by pushing or pulling some part into place. *You can shut a gate, a window, or a trunk.* 2. close by bringing parts together: *Shut your eyes. She shut the book.* **shut, shut ting.**

shy 1. uneasy in company or with people: *He is shy and doesn't say much.* 2. easy to scare; timid: *Deer are shy animals.* **shi er, shi est.**

shy ly do something in a shy way: *The deer looked at us shyly from the bushes.*

sick 1. not well; having a disease: *Is he sick?* 2. throwing up food from the stomach or feeling like it. **sick er, sick est.**

shower 3.

shrimp

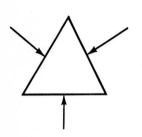

sides of a triangle

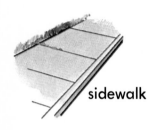

sidewalk

signs

sick ness a disease; feeling sick; having poor health: *I hope you are over your sickness by this time.* **sick ness es.**

side 1. a surface or a line around a shape: *a side of a box, a side of a triangle.* See the picture. 2. one surface of an object that is not the front or back: *There is a dent on this side of the car. I will draw a picture on both sides of the paper.* 3. either the right or the left part of the body of a person or an animal. 4. **Take sides** in a quarrel means agree with one person or one group against another. **sides.**

side walk a place to walk at the side of a street. See the picture. **side walks.**

sift separate large pieces from small pieces by shaking through a kind of screen: *Sift the sand.* **sift ed, sift ing.**

sigh 1. let out a long, deep breath. 2. the sound of sighing: *She gave a loud sigh.* **sighed, sigh ing; sighs.**

sight 1. the power or sense of seeing: *The old woman's sight is very good.* 2. the act of seeing: *At first sight, I thought it was you.* 3. something worth seeing: *A rainbow is a lovely sight.* **sights.**

sign 1. any mark or thing used to tell something or stand for something: *Read the sign on the door. Those clouds are a sign of rain. An arrow is used as a sign that cars must turn.* See the picture. 2. put your name on: *Did you sign the letter?* **signs; signed, sign ing.**

sig nal 1. a sign: *They sent smoke signals to each other. A flashing red light is a signal of danger.* 2. make a signal: *He signaled the driver to go ahead by waving his arms.* **sig nals; sig naled, sig nal ing.**

si lent 1. quiet; still; without noise: *a silent house.* 2. not speaking; saying little or nothing: *Please be silent during the movie.* 3. not spoken; not said out loud: *a silent prayer.*

si lent ly without any sound: *The cat crept silently through the grass.*

silk 1. a fine, soft thread spun by a certain kind of worm. 2. cloth made from it. 3. of or like silk: *She used silk thread.*

silky like silk. **silk i er, silk i est.**

sill a piece of wood or other hard material at the bottom of a door or window: *Your book is on the window sill.* See the picture. **sills.**

sil ly without good sense; without making any sense: *Those kids are acting silly. This is a silly joke.* **sil li er, sil li est.**

si lo a round building for storing feed for cattle. See the picture. **si los.**

sil ver 1. a shiny white metal of great value: *Much jewelry is made from silver.* 2. tools such as knives, forks, and spoons for eating: *Please put the silver on the table.* 3. made of silver or looking like it: *a silver bowl, silver hair.*

sim ple 1. easy to do or understand: *She learned to play a simple song on the piano. That's a simple problem.* 2. not fancy; without anything extra: *a simple lunch.* **sim pler, sim plest.**

since 1. from before until now: *I have been up since dawn.* 2. after: *She has worked very hard since school began.*

sin cere honest; meaning what you say or do; not fooling: *He had a sincere desire to help me.* **sin cer er, sin cer est.**

sin cere ly in a sincere manner: *He said he was sincerely sorry that he couldn't go.*

window sill

silo

sink   3.

sing 1. make music with the voice: *He sings well.*
2. make pleasant sounds: *Meadowlarks sing.*
sang or **sung, sung, sing ing.**

sing er one who sings. **sing ers.**

sin gle 1. only one: *What do you do with a single sock? This button is hanging by a single thread.* 2. not married: *He is a single man.*

sink 1. go down slowly; go lower and lower: *The sun sinks in the sky.* 2. go under: *The ship is sinking.* 3. a small tub with a drain: *The girls washed their hands in the sink.* See the picture.
sank or **sunk, sunk, sink ing; sinks.**

sip 1. drink a little bit at a time: *Grandmother began to sip her tea.* 2. a small drink: *She drank it sip by sip.* **sipped, sip ping; sips.**

sir a title that shows respect to a man. **sirs.**

si ren a warning whistle. A siren makes a loud, shrill high-and-low sound. **si rens.**

sis ter a girl with the same parents as another. **sis ters.**

sit 1. rest on the lower part of the body. 2. be placed: *The clock should sit on top of that corner cupboard.* **sat, sit ting.**

site a place; location: *Is this a good site for the new building?* **sites.**

six one more than five; 6. *Six and six are twelve.* **six es.**

six teen six more than ten; 16. **six teens.**

six teenth 1. next after the fifteenth; 16th. 2. one of 16 equal parts. **six teenths.**

sixth 1. next after the fifth; 6th. 2. one of 6 equal parts. **sixths.**

six ti eth 1. next after the fifty-ninth; 60th. 2. one of 60 equal parts. **six ti eths.**

six ty six times ten; 60. **six ties.**

size 1. the amount of surface or space a thing takes up: *The size of this rug is just right for this room.* 2. one of several amounts in measuring something: *She wears size ten even though she is only eight years old.* **siz es.**

skate 1. a sharp blade fastened to a shoe so you can slide over ice. 2. a shoe or a metal piece shaped like your foot. It has rollers or wheels instead of a blade so you can roll over a smooth surface. See the picture. 3. slide or move along on skates. **skates; skat ed, skat ing.**

skat ing rink 1. a sheet of ice for ice-skating. 2. a smooth floor or surface for roller-skating. **skat ing rinks.**

skel e ton the bones of a body put together. See the picture. **skel e tons.**

ski 1. one of a pair of long, narrow boards on which a person can stand and slide over snow. See the picture. 2. slide on skis. **skis; skied, ski ing.**

skid slip or slide to one side: *The truck skidded on the ice.* **skid ded, skid ding.**

skill being able to do something well after practicing for a long time: *It takes skill to play the piano.* **skills.**

skim 1. take from the top of something: *She skims the cream off the milk.* 2. read hastily. **skimmed, skim ming.**

skin 1. the covering of any body or plant: *a banana skin.* 2. take the skin off: *I skinned my elbow. The hunter skinned the rabbit.* **skins; skinned, skin ning.**

skip 1. leap lightly; jump: *Some kids like to skip rope.* 2. pass over: *Skip the hard words and read the rest.* **skipped, skip ping.**

ice skates

roller skates

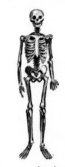
dinosaur skeleton

human skeleton

pair of skis

skirt 2.

skunk

sled

skirt 1. the lower part of a dress. 2. a piece of clothing for women and girls. See the picture. **skirts.**

skunk a small black animal with a bushy tail and white stripes along its back. See the picture. **skunks.**

sky space high above, that seems to cover the earth; the air above us. **skies.**

Sky lab a space station orbiting the earth.

sky scrap er a tall building, usually in a large city. **sky scrap ers.**

slacks loose trousers.

slam 1. shut noisily: *Don't slam the door!* 2. hit hard and noisily: *She slammed her book down on the desk.* **slammed, slam ming.**

slant be higher on one end or side than the other; not be straight up and down: *Most roofs slant. The pole slants to the right since a truck ran into it.* **slant ed, slant ing.**

slap 1. a blow given with the open hand: *Give that noisy dog a slap.* 2. strike with a hand or with something flat: *The man slapped his brother on the back. Dad slapped his newspaper against his leg as he walked.* **slaps; slapped, slap ping.**

sled a vehicle without wheels for sliding over ice and snow and down hills. See the picture. **sleds.**

sleep 1. rest your body and mind: *It's easy to sleep when it's quiet.* 2. a rest of body and mind: *I felt better after my long sleep.* **slept, sleep ing; sleeps.**

sleep i ly in a sleepy way: *She yawned sleepily and closed her eyes.*

sleepy 1. ready to go to sleep: *This cat is always sleepy.* 2. quiet: *It was a sleepy little town.* **sleep i er, sleep i est.**

sleeve the part of a shirt, coat, dress, or sweater that covers your arm. See the picture. **sleeves.**

sleigh a vehicle without wheels, sometimes pulled by horses, for travel on snow or ice. See the picture. **sleighs.**

slept See **sleep.** *I slept in a big bed. I have slept in a tent.*

slice 1. a thin, flat, broad piece: *Please have a slice of meat.* 2. cut into thin, flat pieces: *She sliced the bread.* **slic es; sliced, slic ing.**

slick smooth; easy to slide on: *The icy walk was slick.* **slick er, slick est.**

slid See **slide.** *She slid across the ice. Her brother had slid down the hill.*

slide 1. move smoothly. 2. the act of sliding: *Take a slide down the hill.* 3. a smooth surface that slants from the top of a ladder to the ground: *There is a slide on the playground.* 4. a picture shown on a screen. See the picture. **slid, slid ing; slides.**

slim thin; narrow: *He's a slim boy.* **slim mer, slim mest.**

sling 1. a loop of cloth around the neck to hold a hurt arm. See the picture. 2. hang in a sling or hang loosely: *Can you sling this sack of flour over your shoulder?* **slings; slung, sling ing.**

slip¹ 1. move smoothly, quietly, or quickly: *She slipped out of the room.* 2. slide suddenly without wanting to: *He will slip on the ice.* 3. the act of slipping: *A slip on a banana peel can be dangerous.* 4. a piece of clothing worn by a woman or girl under a dress. **slipped, slip ping; slips.**

slip² a narrow strip of paper: *The clerk gave me a sales slip when I bought a tablet.* **slips.**

sleeve

slip

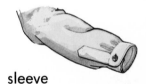

sleeve

sleigh

slide 3.

slide 4.

sling 1.

house slipper

slope 2.

slip per a light, soft shoe: *house slippers, dancing slippers.* See the picture. **slip pers.**

slope 1. slant: *The land slopes toward the road. The roof slopes.* 2. any surface that slants: *We couldn't see the top of that long slope.* See the picture. **sloped, slop ing; slopes.**

slow 1. taking a long time; not fast or quick: *a slow trip, a slow driver.* 2. showing time earlier than the correct time: *I was late because the clock was slow.* 3. make slow or slower: *The driver slowed down the bus.* 4. go slower: *Slow up or you will drop something.* 5. in a slow manner: *Walk slow and I will catch up with you.* **slow er, slow est.**

slow ly in a slow manner: *The police car moved slowly down the street.*

slung See **sling.** *He slung the bag of books over his back. She had slung her sweater over her shoulders.*

sly able to do things without letting others know: *The sly cat took the meat while my back was turned.* **sly er, sly est.**

sly ly in a sly manner; secretly.

smack 1. make a sound by opening the lips quickly: *He smacked his lips when he saw food.* 2. the sound of smacking. 3. kiss loudly. 4. a slap. **smacked, smack ing; smacks.**

small 1. not large: *a small dog.* 2. not much: *a small serving of food, a small piece of land.* 3. not important: *a small problem.* **small er, small est.**

smart 1. feel or cause sharp pain: *Her eyes smart from the pollution in the air. The cut on my finger smarts.* 2. clever; bright: *a smart child.* **smart ed, smart ing; smart er, smart est.**

smash 1. break into pieces: *He smashed the lamp.*
2. hit something hard: *The boat smashed into the dock.* **smashed, smash ing.**

smell 1. recognize or notice by breathing in through the nose: *Can you smell the bacon cooking?* 2. the sense of smelling. 3. something you breathe in and recognize: *The smell of the turkey cooking made me hungry.* **smelled, smell ing; smells.**

smile 1. look happy by turning up the corners of your mouth: *The baby smiled.* 2. the act of curving up the corners of the mouth to show you are pleased: *He has a nice smile.* See the picture. **smiled, smil ing; smiles.**

smog smoke and fog in the air: *Smog often hangs over a large city.*

smoke 1. gases that rise in a cloud from anything that is hot or burning. See the picture. 2. give off smoke: *The stove smokes.* 3. draw into the mouth and blow out smoke: *Grandfather smokes a pipe.* **smoked, smok ing.**

smoky full of smoke; like smoke: *His clothes smell smoky. The air in the room was smoky.* **smok i er, smok i est.**

smooth 1. having an even surface without lumps: *a smooth stone, a smooth lake, a smooth road.* 2. make even and flat; take out wrinkles and lumps: *She smoothed the towels.* **smooth er, smooth est; smoothed, smooth ing.**

smooth ly in a smooth, even manner: *The engine ran smoothly.*

smoth er keep air from; kill by keeping air from: *Smother the fire with sand. I had so many blankets on my bed, I almost smothered.* **smoth ered, smoth er ing.**

smile 1.

smoke 1.

snail

snake

snorkel 1.

snorkel 2.

smudge 1. a dirty mark: *There's a smudge on your clean dress.* 2. make a smudge on: *Don't smudge your picture.* **smudg es; smudged, smudg ing.**

snack something to eat, usually between meals. **snacks.**

snail a small animal that crawls slowly. See the picture. **snails.**

snake a long, thin, crawling reptile without legs. See the picture. **snakes.**

snap 1. make a sudden, sharp sound: *Dry wood snaps as it breaks.* 2. a quick, sharp sound: *The lid of the box fell with a snap.* 3. break suddenly: *The rope snapped when I pulled too hard on it.* 4. something that fastens: *This snap on your dress is loose and needs to be sewed.* **snapped, snap ping; snaps.**

snap per something that snaps. **snap pers.**

sneak ers light canvas shoes with rubber soles.

sneeze 1. suddenly blow air through the nose and mouth: *Dust in the air makes her sneeze.* 2. a sudden blowing of air through the nose and mouth: *They heard a loud sneeze in the next room.* **sneezed, sneez ing; sneez es.**

sniff 1. take in air through the nose in short, quick breaths that can be heard: *The little boy finally stopped crying, but he sniffed loudly so we'd feel sorry for him.* 2. smell with sniffs: *The dog sniffed at the kitten.* 3. a breath: *She took one sniff of the rose and sneezed four times.* **sniffed, sniff ing; sniffs.**

snor kel 1. a tube for taking in air or breathing under water. 2. a moving platform on a fire truck used by firefighters to get near a fire. See the picture. **snor kels.**

snort 1. force the breath through the nose with a loud, harsh sound: *The horse snorted.* 2. make a sound like this. **snort ed, snort ing.**

snow 1. water frozen in white flakes: *Snow falls in winter.* 2. fall as snow: *It snowed all day.* **snows; snowed, snow ing.**

snow mo bile a vehicle with a motor and skis to travel over snow. Snowmobiles can go fast. See the picture. **snow mo biles.**

snug 1. warm; safe: *It is snug sitting by the fire.* 2. fitting closely: *That jacket is a little too snug on him.* **snug ger, snug gest.**

snug ly in a snug way: *Ice skates must fit snugly.*

so 1. in that way: *Don't eat so fast.* 2. of such a size: *The fire was so big the firemen couldn't put it out.* 3. for this reason: *The wind felt cold, so we went in.* 4. very: *This tastes so good.*

soap a material used for washing. Soap can be in the form of a bar or a powder or a liquid. **soaps.**

soar fly very high or fly upward: *Birds can soar without moving their wings.* **soared, soar ing.**

sob 1. cry with short breaths: *The baby sobbed until I picked her up.* 2. a catching of short breaths when you are crying: *Her sobs could be heard for blocks.* **sobbed, sob bing; sobs.**

so cial 1. having something to do with friends and being with other people: *Our social club meets today.* 2. a kind of party: *We are having an ice-cream social next Friday.* **so cials.**

so ci e ty 1. a group of people joined together; a club. 2. all the people living in a community: *Fighting pollution will help society.* **so ci e ties.**

sock a short knitted covering for the foot and leg. See the picture. **socks.**

snowmobile

socks

girl and boy turning
somersaults

soft 1. not hard; not stiff; giving way easily to a touch: *This pillow feels very soft.* 2. pleasant to touch: *A kitten has soft fur.* 3. gentle: *She has a soft voice.* **soft er, soft est.**

soft ly in a soft, quiet, or gentle way: *The mother sang softly to her child.*

soil¹ earth; dirt: *Our garden has such rich soil that anything will grow in it.* **soils.**

soil² make or become dirty: *The dust soiled my white gloves.* **soiled, soil ing.**

sold See **sell.** *The clerk sold me a green skirt. She could have sold me a red one too.*

sol dier 1. one who serves in an army. 2. a member of the United States Army. **sol diers.**

so lu tion 1. explanation; the solving of a problem: *The police are seeking a solution to the crime.* 2. liquid or mixture formed by dissolving: *We made a solution of sugar and water.* **so lu tions.**

solve find the answer to: *The detective solved the mystery.* **solved, solv ing.**

sol ver person who solves something. **sol vers.**

some 1. not all: *Some people like to swim; some don't.* 2. an amount of: *Drink some more water.* 3. any: *Aren't there some chocolate doughnuts left over from the party?*

some body some person. **some bod ies.**

some day at some future time.

some how in a way not known; in one way or another.

some one some person; somebody.

som er sault a roll or jump, head over heels. See the picture. **som er saults.**

some time at one time or another.

some what not exactly; in some way.

some where in or to some place.

son the male child of his parents: *John is the son of Bob and Mary Johnson.* *My parents have two sons and three daughters.* **sons.**

song 1. something to sing: *We learned a new song today.* 2. singing: *He was so happy he sang a song.* **songs.**

soon 1. in a short time; before long: *Will I see you again soon?* 2. early: *The end of the show came too soon.* 3. quickly: *Come to my house as soon as you can.* **soon er, soon est.**

sor ry feeling sad: *I am sorry I was late.* *We are sorry to hear about his fall.* **sor ri er, sor ri est.**

sort 1. kind; class: *What sort of work do you do? I like this sort of house best.* 2. arrange in order: *Sort these cards according to their colors.* 3. separate from others. **sort ed, sort ing; sorts.**

sound¹ 1. what can be heard: *We heard the sound of music.* 2. make a sound: *The wind sounds like a whistle blowing.* *A policeman sounded the alarm.* **sounds; sound ed, sound ing.**

sound² 1. healthy; not having any disease: *An athlete knows the value of a sound body.* 2. not weak or rotten; strong: *The walls of the old house are sound.* **sound er, sound est.**

soup a liquid food made by cooking meat, grains, vegetables, and other foods in water. See the picture. **soups.**

sour having a taste like vinegar or lemon juice: *These pickles are sour.* **sour er, sour est.**

south 1. the direction to your right as you face the rising sun. 2. to the south: *Drive south for seven miles.* 3. coming from the south: *a south wind.* 4. **The South** means the southern part of the United States.

bowl of alphabet soup

South America

soybean

spade 1.

South Amer i ca a continent; one of the large masses of land on the earth. See the picture.

South Car o li na one of the fifty states of the United States. See page 367.

South Da ko ta one of the fifty states of the United States. See page 368.

south east halfway between south and east.

south ern 1. toward the south: *The southern road is closed.* 2. from the south: *A southern breeze blew softly.*

South Pole the point farthest south on the earth.

south ward toward the south.

south west halfway between south and west.

sow scatter seed on the ground; plant seed: *The farmer sows wheat and oats.* **sowed, sow ing.** (Sow rhymes with go.)

soy bean 1. a kind of bean. Soybeans are used in making foods, oil, and other things. 2. the plant it grows on. See the picture. **soy beans.**

space 1. empty air in all directions: *The module moved through space.* 2. a certain amount of empty air: *Is there space in the trunk for my books? This desk will fill a space in my room.* **spac es.**

space hel met a helmet worn by an astronaut while traveling in space. **space hel mets.**

space ship a vehicle for traveling through space to other planets. **space ships.**

space suit a suit that protects a traveler in space. **space suits.**

spade 1. a tool for digging; a kind of shovel. See the picture. 2. dig with a spade. **spades; spad ed, spad ing.**

spa ghet ti a food made of flour and water rolled into long, thin sticks or strings.

spare 1. keep from killing or harming: *Frost killed some flowers but spared others.* 2. get along without: *Father could spare the car, so he let my sister take it.* 3. extra: *Have you a spare tire?* **spared, spar ing.**

spark a small bit of fire: *Sparks flew from the broken wire.* **sparks.**

spar kle 1. send out little sparks; shine brightly: *A diamond sparkles.* 2. a shine; a flash: *She has a sparkle in her eyes.* **spar kled, spar kling; spar kles.**

spar row a small, brown-gray bird. See the picture. **spar rows.**

sparrow

speak 1. say words; talk: *Speak louder, please.* 2. make a speech: *She spoke to our class about swimming.* **spoke, spo ken, speak ing.**

spear 1. a long pole with a sharp point. See the picture. 2. poke with a spear: *The boy speared a fish.* **spears; speared, spear ing.**

spear 1.

spe cial of a kind different from all others: *a special day, a special friend, a special place.*

spe cial ist one who studies one branch of business or science. *Some doctors are ear specialists; some are bone specialists.* **spe cial ists.**

spec ta cles glasses. *Some people must wear spectacles in order to read.*

sped See **speed**. *He sped down the street on his bike. He would have sped farther if he hadn't fallen off.*

speech 1. the act of speaking; manner of speaking: *His speech was slow.* 2. a public talk: *We heard her speech on the radio.* **speech es.**

speed 1. the act of moving fast: *The speed made the ride exciting.* 2. go fast: *The boat speeds over the water.* **speeds; sped, speed ing.**

spider

spike 1.

spikes on a golf shoe

spell[1] write or say the letters of a word in order: *I had to spell "cat" for my little sister.* **spelled, spell ing.**

spell[2] a group of words supposed to have magic power: *The witch's spell turned the girls into frogs.* **spells.**

spell[3] a period of time: *We had a spell of rainy weather in April.* **spells.**

spell er 1. someone who spells. 2. a book for teaching spelling. **spell ers.**

spell ing writing or saying the letters of a word in order: *Spend more time on your spelling.*

spend 1. pay money: *He will spend ten dollars for his boots.* 2. use up: *Don't spend more than an hour playing outside.* **spent, spend ing.**

spent See **spend.** *I spent five dollars for a fishing license. Grandfather has spent many years fishing.*

spice parts of certain plants used for seasoning food. *Pepper is a spice.* **spic es.**

spi der a small animal with eight legs and no wings. *See the picture.* **spi ders.**

spike 1. a large, strong nail. 2. a pointed piece of metal: *Some athletes have spikes on their shoes to keep from slipping. See the picture.* **spikes.**

spill 1. let something fall and run out: *Don't spill the honey.* 2. fall or flow out: *The milk spilled from the pail.* **spilled** or **spilt, spill ing.**

spilt See **spill.**

spin 1. turn around rapidly or make something turn around rapidly: *A top spins. Can you spin a nickel on the table?* 2. pull out and twist: *Early settlers had to spin their thread from cotton or wool.* **spun, spin ning.**

spire the top part of a tower or steeple. See the picture. **spires.**

spite 1. a feeling of wanting to annoy someone: *She picked her neighbor's flowers out of spite.* 2. **In spite of** means not being stopped by: *We'll have our picnic in spite of bad weather.*

splash 1. cause liquid to fly about. 2. get wet or soil: *The car splashed me.* 3. the sound of liquid hitting a hard surface: *We heard a loud splash.* **splashed, splash ing; splash es.**

splen did bright and beautiful; excellent: *It was a splendid parade.*

split 1. break or cut from end to end or in layers: *Can he split a log with his ax? She split a banana and put ice cream on it.* 2. separate into parts; divide: *The money has been split up among us.* 3. a break or crack: *Hitting a hole in the road caused a split in the tire.* **split, split ting; splits.**

spoil 1. hurt; make something no good: *I spoiled the first picture I drew.* 2. be hurt by getting what you want: *That child has been spoiled by his parents.* 3. become bad: *The meat spoiled because we didn't put it in the refrigerator.* **spoiled** or **spoilt, spoil ing.**

spoilt See **spoil.**

spoke[1] See **speak.** *I spoke with him yesterday.*

spoke[2] one of the rods from the center of a wheel to the outside edge. See the picture. **spokes.**

spo ken 1. See **speak.** *They have spoken to me often.* 2. said aloud: *My dog obeys spoken commands.*

sponge 1. a kind of sea animal. See the picture. 2. material like a sponge that holds lots of water: *We washed the car with a sponge.* **spong es.**

spire

spoke[2]

sponge 1.

spool of thread

teaspoon

serving spoon

spool a round piece of wood or metal on which thread or wire is wound. See the picture. **spools.**

spoon a small tool for lifting liquids and soft foods. See the picture. **spoons.**

sport a kind of game or amusement often done outdoors. Baseball and fishing are outdoor sports. Sports give you exercise. **sports.**

spot 1. a mark: *She has an ink spot on her sleeve.* 2. a part different from the rest: *Peter's new necktie is red with white spots.* 3. a place: *From this one spot on the hill you can see the whole valley.* 4. make a spot: *Big drops of rain are beginning to spot the sidewalk.* **spots; spot ted, spot ting.**

sprain 1. twist a joint or muscle: *He sprained his ankle.* 2. the hurt caused by twisting: *The sprain was beginning to ache.* **sprained, sprain ing; sprains.**

sprang See **spring.** *Paco sprang out of bed when the phone rang.*

spray 1. liquid moving through the air in small drops: *Spray from the fountain made her hair wet.* 2. something that sends a liquid out as spray: *Please bring a can of hair spray from the drugstore.* 3. sprinkle; scatter spray on: *She sprayed yellow paint on the fence.* **sprays; sprayed, spray ing.**

spread 1. cover a large space; open out: *Spread a blanket on the ground. The eagle spread its wings and flew away.* 2. scatter: *Please don't spread the news.* 3. cover with a thin layer: *He spread butter on his bread.* 4. a covering for a bed or table: *a bed spread.* **spread, spread ing; spreads.**

spring 1. jump; rise or move suddenly: *Watch this dancer spring into the air.* 2. a jump. 3. something, usually made of metal, that will return to the same shape after it is pulled out of shape: *a watch spring.* See the picture. 4. the season of the year when plants begin to grow. 5. a small stream of water coming from the earth. 6. grow: *These plants will spring up if we have a lot of sun.* **sprang** or **sprung, sprung, spring ing; springs.**

sprin kle 1. scatter in drops or tiny bits: *She sprinkled salt on the icy walk.* 2. rain a little bit: *It's beginning to sprinkle.* **sprin kled, sprin kling.**

sprin kler a thing that sprinkles. See the picture. **sprin klers.**

sprout 1. start growing: *The buds are sprouting on that blackberry bush.* 2. a young plant or a new part of an old plant. **sprout ed, sprout ing; sprouts.**

spruce a kind of evergreen tree. See the picture. Different kinds of spruce are state trees of several states. **spruc es.**

sprung See **spring.** *The vegetables have sprung up in the garden.*

spun See **spin.** *The wheels spun on the wet street. One car has spun completely around.*

spur 1. a pointed object worn on the heel. See the picture. 2. poke with a spur; push forward: *He spurred his horse. Her shout spurred me on to run faster.* **spurs; spurred, spur ring.**

spy 1. a person who secretly watches what others are doing. 2. keep a secret watch: *The other team spied on us and found out our secret play.* **spies; spied, spy ing.**

springs 3.

lawn sprinkler

spruce tree

spur 1.

square 1.

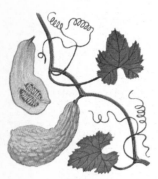

squash²

squirrel

horse stable

square 1. a figure with four equal sides and four equal corners. See the picture. 2. anything having this shape: *The town square has a courthouse.* 3. having this shape: *I need a square piece of paper.* **squares; squar er, squar est.**

squash¹ squeeze flat: *Don't squash that bug. Be careful not to squash this package.* **squashed, squash ing.**

squash² a vegetable that grows on a vine. See the picture. **squash** or **squash es.**

squeak 1. make a short, sharp, shrill sound: *This chair squeaks when you sit on it.* 2. the sound of squeaking: *There was a faint squeak in the corner.* **squeaked, squeak ing; squeaks.**

squeeze 1. push hard against. You push an orange hard against a surface to squeeze out its juice. 2. a steady pressure: *She gave my hand a squeeze.* 3. hug: *She squeezed her pet.* 4. force by a steady pressure: *I can't squeeze these books into my drawer.* 5. force a path: *Can you squeeze through the crowd?* **squeezed, squeez ing; squeez es.**

squint 1. look with the eyes partly closed: *I squinted at the bright sun.* 2. a look with the eyes partly closed: *He looked at me with a squint.* **squint ed, squint ing; squints.**

squir rel a small animal with a bushy tail. Squirrels live in trees and eat nuts. See the picture. **squir rels.**

squish 1. squash something: *I squished the mud with my toes.* 2. the sound of something being squashed: *She stepped into the puddle with a squish.* **squished, squish ing.**

sta ble a building where horses or cattle are kept. See the picture. **sta bles.**

stack 1. a pile of objects: *a stack of papers.* 2. pile or arrange in a stack: *Stack the wood here.* **stacks; stacked, stack ing.**

stage the raised platform in a theater: *No one was on the stage.* See the picture. **stag es.**

stage coach a vehicle, drawn by horses, used before railroads were built to carry passengers and baggage. See the picture. **stage coach es.**

stair one of a group of steps for going from one level or floor to another: *He went up the stairs fast.* **stairs.**

stake 1. a pointed stick driven into the ground. 2. fasten to a stake. 3. mark with stakes: *We staked out a garden.* **stakes; staked, stak ing.**

stalk¹ the stem of a plant. **stalks.**

stalk² 1. follow without being seen: *The hunter stalked the lion.* 2. walk with slow, stiff steps: *She stalked across the room.* **stalked, stalk ing.**

stall 1. a place in a stable for one animal: *Each horse has a stall.* 2. a small place for selling things: *a book stall.* See the picture. 3. lose power and stop: *Our car stalled on the hill.* **stalls; stalled, stall ing.**

stamp 1. a small piece of paper with glue on the back. 2. put a stamp on. 3. bring down your foot with force. 4. put a mark on: *Please stamp this bill "Paid."* 5. a tool that puts a mark on something. See the picture. **stamps; stamped, stamp ing.**

stand 1. be on your feet. 2. rise to your feet: *The people stood in line for the movie. Those who are ready to go, please stand.* 3. bear: *This plant cannot stand cold weather.* 4. a place for a small business: *a newspaper stand, a vegetable stand.* **stood, stand ing; stands.**

stage

stagecoach

book stall

 40-cent stamp

rubber stamp

265

5-pointed star

 6-pointed star

starfish

starling

statue

star 1. one of the bright points seen in the sky at night. 2. a figure with five or six points. See the picture. 3. something with this shape. 4. a very famous person: *a movie star.* **stars.**

stare 1. look long with the eyes wide open: *It's rude to stare at someone.* 2. a long look. **stared, star ing; stares.**

star fish a sea animal shaped like a star. See the picture. **star fish es** or **star fish.**

star ling a bird that often lives in the city. Starlings fly in large flocks. See the picture. **star lings.**

start 1. make the first move to do something or go somewhere: *The car started to roll.* 2. the first move to do or go: *an early start.* 3. move suddenly in surprise: *The cat started when I dropped a book.* **start ed, start ing; starts.**

starve suffer and die with hunger: *Birds starve if we don't feed them in winter.* **starved, starv ing.**

state 1. how you feel or are getting along: *What is the state of his health?* 2. one of the fifty governments and pieces of land that make up the United States. 3. say: *State your name and address.* **states; stat ed, stat ing.**

sta tion 1. a place for sending out or receiving programs: *a TV station.* 2. a place used for a special thing: *a gas station.* **sta tions.**

sta tion ery writing paper, cards, and envelopes.

stat ue a figure sculptured from stone or wood made to look like a person or animal. See the picture. **stat ues.**

stay continue to be in a place: *Stay in this chair.* **stayed, stay ing.**

stead i ly in a steady manner: *The soldiers marched steadily forward.*

steady 1. firm; not swaying or shaking: *This beam is steady as a rock. Hold the rope steady.* 2. make steady; keep steady: *Steady this ladder, and I'll paint the ceiling.* **stead i er, stead i est; stead ied, stead y ing.**

steak a slice of meat, specially beef: *They had steak for dinner.* **steaks.**

steal take something that does not belong to you and keep it. **stole, sto len, steal ing.**

steam 1. hot water in the form of gas or a very fine spray. *Steam can cause a burn.* 2. run by steam: *a steam engine.*

steel 1. iron made very hard and strong. *Most hammers are made from steel.* 2. made of steel: *An engine has many steel parts.*

steep having a sharp slant; almost straight up and down: *This hill is steep.* **steep er, steep est.**

stee ple a high, slim tower on a building. See the picture. **stee ples.**

steer[1] guide; control: *She steered her bike well.* **steered, steer ing.**

steer[2] one of a herd of beef cattle raised for food. **steers.**

stem 1. the main part of a plant above the ground. *The stem of a tree is its trunk.* 2. the part of a flower, fruit, or leaf that joins it to the plant. See the picture. **stems.**

step 1. a motion by lifting the foot and putting it down in a new position: *Take three steps.* 2. move the legs as in walking: *Step to the front of the line.* 3. a place for the foot in going up or down: *cellar steps.* See the picture. **steps; stepped, step ping.**

ster i lize make free from germs: *They boiled the water to sterilize it.* **ster i lized, ster i liz ing.**

steeple

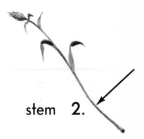

stem 2.

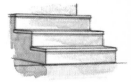

cellar steps

stethoscope

girl walking on stilts

steth o scope an instrument doctors use to listen to your heart. See the picture. **steth o scopes.**

stew 1. cook by slow boiling. 2. food cooked by slow boiling: *Betty made lamb stew.* **stewed, stew ing; stews.**

stick[1] 1. a long, thin piece of wood. 2. something shaped like a stick: *a stick of candy.* **sticks.**

stick[2] 1. push into with a pointed tool: *Stick the turnip with a fork to see if it is cooked enough.* 2. put; place: *Stick this handkerchief in your pocket.* 3. fasten: *He stuck a tag on this present.* 4. become fastened: *It was about to stick in the mud.* **stuck, stick ing.**

sticky made of something or covered with something that sticks: *I put my name on with sticky tape. Her hands are sticky from the candy.* **stick i er, stick i est.**

stiff 1. not easily bent: *New boots are always stiff.* 2. hard to move: *The old hinges on this trunk are stiff.* 3. firm: *The frosting is stiff enough to spread.* **stiff er, stiff est.**

stiff ly in a stiff way: *The old man walked stiffly.*

still 1. not moving; without noise; quiet: *The noisy child was told to sit still. The sea was quite still.* 2. even now; yet: *Was the library still open?*

stilt one of a pair of poles used to walk on: *Dad made me a pair of stilts.* See the picture. **stilts.**

sting 1. poke with a small point: *Some insects sting. A wasp stung her on the arm.* 2. a small wound made by stinging: *Her wasp sting began to hurt.* **stung, sting ing; stings.**

stir 1. move: *The breeze hardly stirs the leaves.* 2. move about: *Everyone began to stir in the house.* 3. mix by moving around: *Stir the soup.* **stirred, stir ring.**

stock 1. things for sale: *This shop keeps a large stock of shoes.* 2. cattle or other farm animals: *The farmer was watering his stock.* 3. put away things to be used later: *We stocked the shelf with food.* **stocks; stocked, stock ing.**

stock ade a high, strong fence: *A stockade around the cabins protected the settlers.* See the picture. **stock ades.**

stole[1] a wrap like a shawl. See the picture. **stoles.**

stole[2] See **steal**. *She stole the money years ago.*

sto len See **steal**. *Someone has stolen my scarf.*

stom ach the part of the body that receives the food we swallow. **stom achs.**

stone 1. hard material of the earth; rock. 2. a small piece of rock. 3. made of stone: *a stone wall.* **stones.**

stood See **stand**. *We stood in line for an hour. Some people have stood even longer.*

stool a seat without a back and without arms. See the picture. **stools.**

stoop bend forward: *She stooped to pick up the money.* **stooped, stoop ing.**

stop 1. keep from moving, working, doing, or being: *The red light stopped traffic. He stopped talking and sat down. Can't you stop here for a minute?* 2. come to an end: *The snow finally stopped.* 3. the act of stopping: *Put a stop to this noise.* **stopped, stop ping; stops.**

stop sign a signal for vehicles to stop before moving ahead. See the picture. **stop signs.**

store 1. a place where things are kept for sale. 2. put away for use later: *She stored her winter coat.* 3. something put away for use later: *We keep our store of canned fruit in the pantry.* **stores; stored, stor ing.**

stock

---

store

stockade

stole[1]

stool

stop sign

stork

doll house
with two stories

gas stove

stork a large, long-legged bird with a long neck. See the picture. **storks.**

storm a strong wind, usually with rain, snow, or hail. A storm in the desert blows sand. A storm at sea blows water. **storms.**

sto ry[1] an account, true or make-believe, of some things that have happened: *I hope he tells us the story of his life. I like detective stories.* **sto ries.**

sto ry[2] the set of rooms on the same level or floor of a building: *My doll house has two stories.* See the picture. **sto ries.**

stove an appliance for cooking and for heating: *Grandmother had a big stove. We have a gas stove.* See the picture. **stoves.**

straight 1. without a bend or curve: *a straight line.* 2. in a line: *Sit up straight. She went straight to the store and came straight back.* **straight er, straight est.**

straight en 1. make straight: *He straightened the bent pin.* 2. put in proper order: *Straighten up your room.* **straight ened, straight en ing.**

strange 1. not common; unusual; queer: *I heard a strange noise in the other room.* 2. not known, seen, or heard before: *A strange dog sat on our porch.* **strang er, strang est.**

strange ly in a strange or queer or odd way: *She was strangely dressed for a party.*

stran ger a person not known; someone never seen before: *Who is that stranger?* **stran gers.**

strap a narrow strip of leather or other material: *He put a strap around his skis.* **straps.**

straw 1. the dry stalks left after the grain has been taken out. 2. a hollow stalk or something like it: *We drank sodas through straws.* 3. made of straw: *She wore a straw beach hat.* **straws.**

straw ber ry 1. a small red fruit that is good to eat. 2. the plant it grows on. See the picture. **straw ber ries.**

stray 1. lose your way; wander: *Our dog strayed from the yard.* 2. lost: *Don't bring any stray cats home.* **strayed, stray ing.**

streak 1. a long, thin mark or line: *His boot left a black streak of mud on the floor.* See the picture. 2. make long, thin marks or lines on: *Rain streaked the window.* **streaks; streaked, streak ing.**

stream 1. running water: *Most streams become rivers.* 2. a steady flow of something: *A stream of light came from the window.* **streams.**

street a road in a city or town. A city street often has sidewalks on each side. **streets.**

street clean er a person or machine that cleans the streets. **street clean ers.**

stretch 1. draw the body or limbs out to full length: *The dog stood up and stretched.* 2. reach out; hold out: *She stretched out her hand for the book.* 3. become longer or wider without breaking: *The rubber band stretched.* **stretched, stretch ing.**

strid den See **stride**. *The man had stridden angrily down the street.*

stride walk with long steps: *Our mailman strides down the street.* **strode, strid den, strid ing.**

strike 1. hit: *The ship might strike a rock in this storm. Don't strike anyone smaller than yourself.* 2. make a sound: *The clock strikes every hour.* 3. stop work to get better pay: *The workers struck when the company refused their demands.* 4. a stopping of work: *The strike lasted six weeks.* 5. in baseball, **strike out** means fail to hit after three tries. **struck, strik ing; strikes.**

strawberry

streak of mud

stripe

string 1. a very thin rope. 2. a special cord for musical instruments: *My guitar has six strings.* 3. put on a string: *The child is stringing popcorn.* **strings; strung, string ing.**

strip[1] take off or take away the covering: *The man stripped bark from the birch tree.* **stripped, strip ping.**

strip[2] a long, narrow, flat piece of cloth or paper: *Tie this strip of cloth on your arm.* **strips.**

stripe a long, narrow band of color: *Stripes can be woven in cloth.* See the picture. **stripes.**

striped having stripes; marked with stripes: *John's dad likes striped shirts.*

strode See **stride**. *She knew she was late as she strode into class.*

strong having much power and force: *A strong wind blew down the tree.* **strong er, strong est.**

strong ly in a strong way or manner: *I strongly object to what you are doing.*

struck See **strike**. *The tennis ball struck me on the leg. The clock has struck one.*

strug gle 1. try hard; work hard: *The swimmer struggled through the waves. She struggled to keep her balance.* 2. hard work: *It was a great struggle to finish my lesson.* **strug gled, strug gling; strug gles.**

strung See **string**. *The class strung beads. Some Scouts have strung berries instead of beads.*

stub born firm; not giving in to what someone else wants: *The stubborn boy refused to eat.* **stub born er, stub born est.**

stub born ly in a stubborn way: *He stubbornly refused help.*

stuck See **stick**[2]. *She stuck her finger with a needle. He has stuck some candy in his pocket.*

stu dio 1. the room where an artist works. See the picture. 2. a place where movies are made. **stu di os.**

study 1. learn by reading and thinking: *He studies hard in school.* 2. the thing studied: *Arithmetic is my favorite study.* 3. examine carefully: *They studied the footprints for a long time.* 4. a small room for reading and studying; a den. **stud ied, stud y ing; stud ies.**

stuff 1. material: *Mother bought some stuff to cover pillows.* 2. things that are not used or needed: *I wish you would get rid of all your old stuff.* 3. fill; pack tightly: *She stuffed food in her mouth.* **stuffed, stuff ing.**

stum ble almost fall by hitting your foot against something: *The baby stumbled over his toy.* **stum bled, stum bling.**

stump the lower end of a tree or plant left after the main part is cut off. See the picture. **stumps.**

stung See **sting.** *The burn stung for a little while. I have been stung by a bee.*

stunt an act; a performance: *The clowns did a very funny stunt.* **stunts.**

stu pid not smart: *a stupid mistake, a stupid thing to say.* **stu pid er, stu pid est.**

stu pid ly in a stupid way: *He looked up stupidly when I opened the door.*

stur dy strong; stout: *The baby has sturdy little legs. Find a sturdy pole for the flag.* **stur di er, stur di est.**

stut ter repeat the beginning sound of a word when you speak. **stut tered, stut ter ing.**

sub ject something thought about or talked about or studied: *I study reading and other subjects. The subject of his speech was books.* **sub jects.**

studio 1.

tree stump

sub tract take away: *Subtract 3 from 12 and you have 9.* **sub tract ed, sub tract ing.**

sub trac tion process of subtracting one number from another.

suc ceed do what you planned to do; turn out well; have success: *The class succeeded in putting on two plays. You will succeed if you try hard enough.* **suc ceed ed, suc ceed ing.**

suc cess the wished-for ending; good fortune: *Success usually comes from hard work. The play was a great success.* **suc cess es.**

such 1. so great or so bad: *Dad had such a cold that he was in bed.* 2. of the same kind: *The cafeteria has such drinks as milk and orange juice.*

sud den 1. not expected: *The sudden noise made me jump.* 2. quick; rapid: *Don't make a sudden move or the bird will fly away.* 3. **All of a sudden** means quickly.

sud den ly in a sudden way; without warning: *Suddenly she screamed.*

suf fer have pain: *Does she suffer when she gets a cold?* **suf fered, suf fer ing.**

suf fix a syllable put at the end of a word to change its meaning. The suffix *ly* changes *bad* to *badly.* **suf fix es.**

sug ar a sweet material made from a certain kind of cane or from a certain kind of beet.

sug ar less having no sugar.

sug gest bring a thought or plan to your mind: *He suggested a hike, and we agreed. Hot weather suggests swimming.* **sug gest ed, sug gest ing.**

suit 1. a set of clothes: *My father's new suit has a coat, a pair of trousers, and a vest.* See the picture. 2. satisfy: *Does this picture suit you?* **suits; suit ed, suit ing.**

suit 1.

suit case a case or bag to hold or carry clothes. See the picture. **suit cas es.**

sum 1. all or a certain number of things put together: *I saved the sum of ten dollars.* 2. two or more numbers or things added together: *The sum of 7 and 12 and 2 is 21.* **sums.**

sum mer 1. the season of the year between spring and autumn or fall. 2. of summer; for summer: *summer days, summer clothes.* **sum mers.**

sun 1. the source of heat and light that the earth revolves around. 2. the light and heat of the sun: *I sat in the sun.* **suns.**

sun dae a dish of ice cream with some kind of sauce on top. See the picture. **sun daes.**

Sun day the first day of the week. **Sun days.**

sun flow er a tall plant with large yellow flowers. See the picture. **sun flow ers.**

sung See **sing.** *We have sung three songs.*

sunk See **sink.** *The boat has sunk to the bottom of the ocean.*

sun ny 1. having much sun: *a sunny afternoon.* 2. lighted or warmed by the sun: *It's too sunny by the window.* **sun ni er, sun ni est.**

sun rise the coming up of the sun; the time when the sun appears in the morning. **sun ris es.**

sun set the going down of the sun; the time when the sun is last seen in the evening. **sun sets.**

su per excellent; more than normal: *The monster had super powers.*

su per in tend ent a person who directs or manages: *a superintendent of schools.* **su per in tend ents.**

su per mar ket a large grocery store. You pick out what you want and pay the checker on your way out. **su per mar kets.**

suitcase

supermarket

suitcase

ice-cream sundae

sunflower

su per vi sor a person in charge of something: *My dad is supervisor of shipping.* **su per vi sors.**

sup per the evening meal: *We had supper as soon as we got home.* **sup pers.**

sup pose 1. think something could have happened: *Suppose Millie and Irene missed the plane.* 2. believe; imagine: *I suppose they will come for dinner on time.* **sup posed, sup pos ing.**

su preme highest; above all.

sure 1. never failing: *Clouds like that are a sure sign of rain.* 2. know without any doubt: *Are you sure you turned off the oven?* **sur er, sur est.**

sure ly without doubt: *Surely he will come. By now she is surely taller than her sister.*

sur face a side or face of something; the outside: *The surface of the road is rough. The lake had a smooth surface.* **sur fac es.**

sur prise 1. something not expected: *The news was a surprise.* 2. cause surprise: *He surprised us when he laughed.* 3. coming as a surprise: *They planned a surprise party.* **sur pris es; sur prised, sur pris ing.**

sur round shut in on all sides; be around: *A fence surrounds the school playground.* **sur round ed, sur round ing.**

sus pect 1. imagine to be so: *The bear suspected danger when he saw the trap.* 2. believe someone or something to be bad: *We suspected the woman of lying.* **sus pect ed, sus pect ing.**

swal low[1] take into your stomach through your mouth. **swal lowed, swal low ing.**

swallow[2]

swal low[2] a small bird that can fly very fast. See the picture. **swal lows.**

swam See **swim.** *Most of us swam a mile.*

swamp

swamp wet, soft land. See the picture. **swamps.**

swampy like a swamp; soft and wet: *Some trees grow best in swampy land.* **swamp i er, swamp i est.**

swan a large bird with a long, thin, curving neck. See the picture. **swans.**

sway swing back and forth or from side to side: *The trees are swaying in the wind.* **swayed, sway ing.**

sweat 1. water coming through the skin: *His face was covered with sweat.* 2. give out water through the skin: *We sweat from working hard. Everyone sweat yesterday. Have you sweat too?* **sweat** or **sweat ed, sweat ing.**

sweat er a knit piece of clothing. Some sweaters have sleeves. See the picture. **sweat ers.**

sweep clean or clear away dust and dirt with a broom or brush. **swept, sweep ing.**

sweep er a person or thing that sweeps. See the picture. **sweep ers.**

sweet 1. having a taste like sugar or honey: *These grapes are sweet.* 2. pleasant: *That little child has a sweet smile.* 3. fresh; not sour or salty: *This milk is still sweet.* **sweet er, sweet est.**

sweet heart a person who is loved: *He sent a valentine to his sweetheart.* **sweet hearts.**

sweet ly in a sweet or pleasant way: *She sang sweetly to the baby.*

swept See **sweep.** *I swept the stairs. I had swept them once today.*

swift able to move very fast. **swift er, swift est.**

swift ly in a swift or fast manner: *She threw the ball swiftly to first base.*

swim 1. move in water by moving fins or arms and legs. 2. the act of swimming: *a swim in the pool.* **swam, swum, swim ming; swims.**

swan

sweater

street sweeper

carpet sweeper

swimming pool

swings

light switch

synagogue

swim mer a person or an animal that swims. **swim mers.**

swim ming pool a large tank of water to swim in. See the picture. **swim ming pools.**

swing 1. move back and forth with a steady motion: *The rope swings from the tree.* 2. a seat in which you can move back and forth. See the picture. **swung, swing ing; swings.**

swish 1. move making a sound like the word: *The arrow swished through the air.* 2. cause to swish: *The cow swished her tail and hit me.* 3. a swishing sound: *The swish of waves on the shore made me sleepy.* **swished, swish ing; swish es.**

switch 1. a thin stick. 2. hit with a switch: *He switched the bad dog.* 3. a button or lever that controls a machine or electric current: *a light switch.* See the picture. 4. use a switch: *Switch on the light.* 5. change: *The wind switched to the northeast.* **switch es; switched, switch ing.**

swoop come down rapidly; plunge down upon something: *The kite swooped and hit a wire.* **swooped, swoop ing.**

swum See **swim.** *They told us they had swum all day.*

swung See **swing.** *The butcher swung the side of meat over one shoulder. I have swung on this swing for half an hour.*

syl la ble a unit of pronunciation. Words are divided into syllables. *Word has one syllable. Sentence has two syllables. Paragraph has three syllables.* **syl la bles.**

sym bol something that stands for something else: *The eagle is a symbol of America.* **sym bols.**

syn a gogue a building in which some people worship. See the picture. **syn a gogues.**

sy rin ga a bush with sweet-smelling white flowers. See the picture. **sy rin gas.**

T t

T or **t** the twentieth letter of the alphabet. **T's** or **t's.**

ta ble 1. a piece of furniture with a flat top on legs. 2. a list of facts or figures: *a table of contents.* **ta bles.**

tab let 1. sheets of paper fastened together at one edge. 2. a flat sheet of wood or stone with writing on it. See the picture. **tab lets.**

tack 1. a short nail with a broad, flat head. See the picture. 2. fasten with tacks. 3. sail in a zigzag course against the wind. **tacks; tacked, tack ing.**

ta co a tortilla filled with meat, cheese, and other things. **ta cos.**

tad pole a very young frog or toad, when it has a tail. See the picture. **tad poles.**

tag[1] 1. a small card fastened to something: *a price tag, a name tag.* 2. put on a tag or tags. 3. follow closely: *Her little sister tagged along.* **tags; tagged, tag ging.**

tag[2] 1. a children's game. 2. tap with the hand: *She tagged me out.* **tags; tagged, tag ging.**

tail 1. the part of an animal's body farthest from its head. See the picture. 2. anything like a tail: *a kite tail.* **tails.**

take 1. lay hold of: *Take my hand to cross the street.* 2. receive; get: *Take some cake.* 3. need: *It takes time to learn arithmetic.* 4. subtract: *If you take 10 from 20, you have 10.* 5. carry: *Take this with you.* **took, tak en, tak ing.**

syringa

take

syringa

tablet 1.

tablet 2.

tack 1.

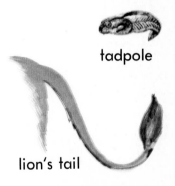

tadpole

lion's tail

girl playing a tambourine

tank 1.

tank 2.

tak en See **take.** *Have you taken a vacation yet?*

tale 1. a story; a fairy tale. 2. a lie. 3. **Tell tales** often means tell something you shouldn't. **tales.**

talk 1. use words; speak. 2. the use of words in speaking: *We had a talk.* 3. a short speech: *She gave a talk about birds.* **talked, talk ing; talks.**

tall 1. high: *a tall building.* 2. hard to believe: *a tall story.* **tall er, tall est.**

tal low hard fat from sheep and cows. Some soap is made from tallow.

tam bou rine a kind of small drum with metal plates around it. You shake it or hit it to make a sound. See the picture. **tam bou rines.**

tame 1. no longer wild; obedient: *The boy has a tame raccoon.* 2. gentle; without fear: *The deer are so tame they come into the yard.* 3. make tame: *That man tames lions for the circus.* **tam er, tam est; tamed, tam ing.**

tan 1. a light yellow-brown. 2. having that color. 3. become brown by being in the sun: *She got tanned last summer.* 4. make a hide into leather. **tans; tan ner, tan nest; tanned, tan ning.**

tank 1. a large container for liquid or gas: *a gas tank, a water tank.* 2. a vehicle made of steel and with a gun. See the picture. **tanks.**

tan nery a place where hides are tanned. **tan ner ies.**

tap 1. strike lightly: *He tapped on the table.* 2. a light blow: *There was a tap at the window.* **tapped, tap ping; taps.**

tape 1. a strip of cloth or paper or plastic: *Mend the pages with tape.* 2. fasten or wrap with tape: *Some athletes tape their ankles.* 3. make a record on tape: *The teacher taped our class program.* **tapes; taped, tap ing.**

tar a black, sticky material taken from wood or coal: *The men are patching our street with tar.*

tar dy behind time; late. **tar di er, tar di est.**

tar pon a large ocean fish. See the picture. **tar pon** or **tar pons.**

task work to be done; a piece of work; a duty: *Cleaning my room is my hardest task.* **tasks.**

tas sel a bunch of cords, fastened at one end. See the picture. **tas sels.**

taste 1. what makes something special when you put it in your mouth. The taste of sugar is sweet. 2. the one of your five senses that tells the difference between things when you put them in your mouth. 3. knowing what is excellent: *She has very good taste in books.* 4. try by taking a little into the mouth: *Taste this orange sauce.* **tastes; tast ed, tast ing.**

taste buds tiny bumps on your tongue that let you taste.

taught See **teach.** *He taught me how to roller-skate. He has taught his brothers to skate too.*

tax 1. money paid by the people to run a government: *We pay a tax on money we earn.* 2. put a tax on: *The government taxed all jewelry.* **tax es; taxed, tax ing.**

taxi cab an automobile you can hire. See the picture. **taxi cabs.**

tea 1. a drink made by pouring boiling water over a certain kind of dried leaves. 2. a meal in the afternoon: *We are invited for tea.* 3. for tea: *a tea bag, a tea cup.* **teas** (for 2.).

teach help learn; show how to do; make understand; give lessons: *She taught her dog to shake hands.* **taught, teach ing.**

teach er a person who teaches. **teach ers.**

tar

_____

teacher

tarpon

tassel on a cap

taxicab

team of horses

teeth I.

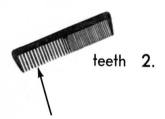

teeth 2.

telescope

team I. a group of people working or acting together. 2. two or more horses or other animals hitched together. See the picture. **teams.**

tear[1] I. pull apart by force: *Don't tear the page.* 2. become pulled apart: *Lace tears easily.* 3. a place that has been pulled apart: *She has a tear in her dress.* **tore, torn, tear ing; tears.** (Tear[1] rhymes with bear.)

tear[2] a drop of salty water coming from the eye. **tears.** (Tear[2] rhymes with ear.)

teeth I. more than one tooth. 2. anything like teeth: *teeth of a comb.* See the picture.

tel e gram a message sent over wires. **tel e grams.**

tel e graph I. a way of sending coded messages over wires by means of electricity. 2. device used for sending these messages. **tel e graphed, tel e graph ing; tel e graphs.**

tel e phone I. an instrument for talking over a distance. 2. talk by telephone. **tel e phones; tel e phoned, tel e phon ing.**

tel e scope an instrument to make distant objects appear nearer. See the picture. **tel e scopes.**

tel e vi sion I. a way of sending pictures through the air so that people far away can see them. 2. an instrument to see these pictures. **tel e vi sions** (for **2.**).

tell I. put in words; say: *Tell us a story.* 2. know: *I can't tell who it is.* 3. order; command: *I told you what to do.* 4. **Tell time** means know what time it is by the clock. **told, tell ing.**

tem per a ture I. the amount of heat or cold in something: *The temperature today is ninety.* 2. more heat in your body than usual: *He has a very high temperature.* **tem per a tures.**

tem ple a building used by some people for worship. **tem ples.**

ten one more than nine; 10. Ten and ten make twenty. **tens.**

ten der 1. not hard; soft: *Tender meat is easy to chew.* 2. kind; loving: *Her voice was tender as she spoke.* **ten der er, ten der est.**

Ten nes see one of the fifty states of the United States. See page 369.

ten nis a game played on a special court indoors or outdoors. Two or four players hit a ball back and forth over a net. See the picture.

ten sion 1. a stretching: *When you pull the bow string, the bow has tension.* 2. being worried and uneasy: *Parents feel tension when their child is late coming home.* **ten sions.**

tent a shelter made of canvas or skins, held up by poles. See the picture. **tents.**

tenth 1. next after the ninth; 10th. 2. one of 10 equal parts. **tenths.**

ter mi nal 1. the end part: *A railroad terminal is a station at the end of the line.* 2. one part of a battery. See the picture. **ter mi nals.**

ter ri ble causing great fear.

ter ri bly in a terrible way: *He was terribly burned.*

ter ri er a small dog with a loud bark. A terrier makes a good watch dog. **ter ri ers.**

ter rif ic very good; excellent: *"That's a terrific idea!"*

ter ri fy frighten very much: *The sight of the bear will terrify him. He was terrified at the noise.* **ter ri fied, ter ri fy ing.**

ter ri to ry land belonging to a government. *Alaska was a territory before it became a state.* **ter ri to ries.**

two players
playing tennis

tent

terminals on a battery

thatch

movie theater

test 1. a way to find out what you know or can do: *We had a test in arithmetic.* 2. try out; give a test to: *We can test the rope by pulling it. The doctor tested her eyes.* **tests; test ed, test ing.**

Tex as one of the fifty states of the United States. See page 370.

than compared to: *Our house is bigger than yours.*

thank say that you are pleased about something given to you or done for you: *We thanked Uncle Bob for the ride.* **thanked, thank ing.**

Thanks giv ing a holiday in November when we give thanks for the good things we have received. The Pilgrims celebrated the first Thanksgiving. **Thanks giv ings.**

that 1. *That* is used to point out some thing. We use *this* for the thing nearer us, and *that* for the thing farther away from us: *Shall we take this ball or that one?* 2. *That* is also used to connect groups of words: *I know that 5 and 3 are 8.*

thatch straw or grass, used as a roof. See the picture. **thatch es.**

that's that is.

thaw 1. a time of melting: *There was a thaw in January.* 2. melt ice, snow, or anything frozen: *Mother thawed the frozen dinners so we could eat.* **thaws; thawed, thaw ing.**

the a certain one: *The dog I saw had no tail. The boy on the horse is Al. You are the one to go.*

the a ter a place where plays are acted or movies are shown. See the picture. **the a ters.**

their of them; belonging to them: *They raised their heads as we passed. They like their new sister.*

them the persons, animals, or things spoken about: *Call the girls and ask them to come along. These skates are new; take care of them.*

them selves used instead of *they* or *them*: *The girls themselves got lost. They saw themselves on TV.*

then 1. at that time: *I wore a cap in winter. It was colder then.* 2. soon after: *The noise stopped and then began again.* 3. next in time or place: *First comes summer, then fall.* 4. in that case: *If he broke the dish, then he should clean it up.*

there 1. at that place: *Sit there. There is my hat.* 2. *There* is also used in sentences such as: *There are three houses on our street. Is there a store near here? There, that's better.*

there's there is.

ther mom e ter an instrument for measuring the temperature of something. See the picture.
ther mom e ters.

these *These* is used to point out persons, things, or ideas: *These children are small. These two books are hard to read. These are my brothers.*

they the persons, animals, things, or ideas spoken about: *I had three letters. Do you know where they are? They are on the table.*

they'd 1. they had: *They'd gone when we got there.* 2. they would: *They promised they'd wait.*

they'll 1. they will. 2. they shall.

they're they are.

they've they have.

thick 1. far from one side to the opposite side; not thin: *This is a thick stone wall.* 2. measuring from one side to the other: *This brick is two inches thick.* 3. close together: *She has thick hair.* 4. like glue; not like water. **thick er, thick est.**

thick ly in a thick way: *Weeds grow thickly in the rich soil.*

thigh the part of the leg between the hip and the knee. See the picture. **thighs.**

themselves

---

thigh

weather thermometer

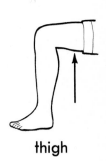

thigh

thin 1. not far from one side to the opposite side; not thick: *This paper is too thin to write on.* 2. not having much fat: *He is a thin man.* 3. few and far apart: *She has thin hair.* 4. like water; not like glue: *a thin gravy.* **thin ner, thin nest.**

thing any object or material you can see, hear, touch, taste, or smell. **things.**

think 1. have ideas; use the mind: *She will think about our problem.* 2. believe without knowing: *Do you think it will rain?* **thought, think ing.**

thin ly in a thin way: *Paint covered the wall very thinly in some places.*

third 1. next after the second; 3rd. 2. one of 3 equal parts. **thirds.**

thirsty needing water: *The baby is thirsty. Those plants look thirsty.* **thirst i er, thirst i est.**

thir teen three more than ten; 13. **thir teens.**

thir teenth 1. next after the twelfth; 13th. 2. one of 13 equal parts. **thir teenths.**

thir ti eth 1. next after the twenty-ninth; 30th. 2. one of 30 equal parts. **thir ti eths.**

thir ty three times ten; 30. **thir ties.**

this *This* is used to point out some one thing that is near. We often use *that* for the thing farther away from us and *this* for the thing near us: *This coat is mine. That one is yours. Shall we read this book or that book?*

thorn

thorn a sharp point on a tree or plant: *I stuck my finger on a thorn as I picked a rose.* See the picture. **thorns.**

those *Those* is used to point out several persons or things: *Those are my sisters. Do you own those dogs? Those books are yours.*

though in spite of the fact that: *Though it looked like rain, we started on our hike.*

thought 1. what someone thinks; thinking about something: *She had a sudden thought. Give this problem a lot of thought.* 2. See **think.** *We thought it would snow yesterday. He had not thought of the right answer.* **thoughts.**

thought ful 1. full of thought; thinking: *He was thoughtful for a while and then he laughed.* 2. careful of others: *She is always thoughtful of her friends. That was a thoughtful thing to do.*

thought ful ly in a thoughtful way: *She looked at him thoughtfully.*

thou sand ten times one hundred; 1000. **thou sands.**

thou sandth 1. next after the 999th. 2. one of 1000 equal parts. **thou sandths.**

thrash er a bird somewhat like a thrush. See the picture. **thrash ers.**

thread 1. cotton or silk spun out into a fine cord. You sew with thread. 2. pass a thread through: *She threaded the needle. We threaded a hundred beads.* 3. something long and thin like a thread: *The spider hung by a thread.* **threads; thread ed, thread ing.**

three one more than two; 3. Three and three make six. **threes.**

threw See **throw.** *He threw the paper to me.*

thrill 1. a shivering, excited feeling: *I get a thrill from seeing a parade.* 2. have or give a shivering, excited feeling: *The story thrilled us.* **thrills; thrilled, thrill ing.**

throat the front of the neck; the part through which air goes to your lungs and food goes to your stomach. **throats.**

throne the chair on which a king or queen sits. See the picture. **thrones.**

thrasher

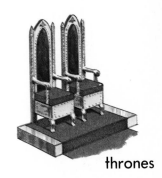
thrones

thrush

through 1. from end to end of: *The truck went through town.* 2. from beginning to end: *She sang every song all the way through.* 3. finished with: *Dad is through work at three o'clock.*

through out 1. all the way through: *The Fourth of July is celebrated throughout the United States.* 2. in every part: *This house is well built throughout.*

throw 1. make something move through the air by the force of your arm: *He threw the ball high.* 2. the act of throwing: *That was a long throw.* **threw, thrown, throw ing; throws.**

thrown See **throw.** *Mother has thrown a sweater over her shoulders.*

thrush a bird that sings. There are many kinds of thrush. See the picture. **thrush es.**

thumb 1. the short, thick finger of the hand. 2. a part that covers the thumb: *There was a hole in the thumb of her mitten.* **thumbs.**

thun der 1. the noise that often follows a flash of lightning. 2. any noise like thunder: *We heard the thunder of the waves on the rocky coast.* 3. make a noise like thunder: *The train thundered out of the tunnel.* **thun dered, thun der ing.**

Thurs day the fifth day of the week. It follows Wednesday. **Thurs days.**

tick et a card or piece of paper that gives whoever has it a right to do something: *We have tickets to the movie.* **tick ets.**

tick le 1. touch lightly, causing little shivers: *He tickled the baby's feet and made her laugh.* 2. have a feeling like this: *My nose tickles from the dust.* 3. amuse: *The joke tickled me.* **tick led, tick ling.**

tide the rise and fall of the ocean about every twelve hours, caused by the moon and the sun: *The tide comes in and goes out.* **tides.**

ti dy neat and in order: *Her room is tidy.* **ti di er, ti di est.**

tie 1. fasten with string or rope: *Please tie this package tightly.* 2. arrange to form a bow or knot: *Mother tied my scarf.* 3. a necktie: *He always wears a red tie.* 4. having the same score: *The game ended in a tie, 3 to 3.* 5. make the same score: *The two teams were tied.* **tied, ty ing; ties.**

ti ger a fierce, striped animal like a large cat. See the picture. **ti gers.**

tiger

tight 1. firm: *Tie a tight knot.* 2. stretched: *The rope was pulled tight.* 3. fitting closely or too closely: *This dress is too tight.* **tight er, tight est.**

tight ly in a tight way: *He held my hand tightly.*

till until.

tim ber 1. a large piece of wood used in building. See the picture. 2. trees; a forest: *Our land is covered with timber.* **tim bers** (for 1.).

time 1. all the days and hours there have been or ever will be. 2. the right time: *It is time to go.* 3. a way of counting time: *What time is it?* 4. choose the right time for: *The batter times his swing right.* 5. **Times,** in arithmetic, means multiply or multiplied by: *2 times 10 is 20.* **times; timed, tim ing.**

timber 1.

tim id frightened or shy. **tim id er, tim id est.**

tim id ly in a timid way: *The mouse peeped timidly out of the hole.*

tin 1. a metal like silver, but softer. 2. made of or lined with tin: *We picked up all the old tin cans.*

automobile tire

toad

ti ny very small; wee: *The new kittens were tiny.*
ti ni er, ti ni est.

tip[1] 1. the end part: *The tip of her finger was cut.*
2. a piece put on the end: *His cane has a rubber tip on it.* **tips.**

tip[2] 1. slope; slant: *Look out, the boat is tipping.*
2. turn over: *Don't tip your glass of milk.*
tipped, tip ping.

tip[3] 1. extra money given for service: *She gave the waiter a tip.* 2. give a tip to: *I didn't tip him at all.* 3. a useful hint: *She gave me a tip on how to clean my shoes.* **tips; tipped, tip ping.**

tip toe 1. the tips of the toes: *I stood on tiptoe to watch the parade.* 2. walk on the tips of the toes: *She tiptoed quietly up the stairs.* **tip toed, tip toe ing.**

tire[1] make weak and sleepy: *The long hike tired the Blue Birds.* **tired, tir ing.**

tire[2] a band of rubber or metal around a wheel. See the picture. **tires.**

tired feeling worn out and ready to rest.

tire some making you tired; not interesting: *We had to listen to a tiresome speech.*

ti tle 1. the name of a book, poem, picture, song: *"Snow White and the Seven Dwarfs" is the title of a fairy tale.* 2. a name showing what you are or do: *Doctor, duke, and Ms. are titles.* **ti tles.**

to 1. in the direction of: *Go to the right.* 2. for: *Mother came to the rescue.* 3. on: *Fasten it to the wall.*

toad a small animal somewhat like a frog. Toads live on land. See the picture. **toads.**

toast 1. slices of bread browned by heat.
2. brown or warm by heat: *Toast your feet by the fire.* **toast ed, toast ing.**

toast er an appliance that toasts bread. Most toasters are electric. See the picture. **toast ers.**

to day 1. this day; now: *Today is Saturday.* 2. on this day: *Are you going swimming today?*

toe 1. one of the five end parts of your foot. 2. the part of a stocking or shoe that covers your toes. **toes.**

to geth er 1. with each other: *The girls work well together.* 2. into one group: *The king called the people together. Sew these pieces together.*

told See **tell.** *She told me. Has she told you?*

tom a hawk a small Indian ax used long ago. See the picture. **tom a hawks.**

to ma to a fruit eaten as a vegetable. See the picture. **to ma toes.**

to mor row the day after today. **to mor rows.**

tone 1. the kind of sound something makes; the way a voice sounds: *The tone of your voice tells how you feel. You can speak in angry or gentle tones.* 2. in music, the difference between two notes: *C and D are one tone apart.* **tones.**

tongue 1. the part inside your mouth that moves: *You use your tongue for tasting and for talking.* 2. anything like a tongue: *a tongue of flame.* **tongues.**

to night the night following today: *I am going to the movie tonight.*

ton sil one of two small, round masses inside the throat: *He's had his tonsils taken out.* **ton sils.**

too 1. also: *The hikers are hungry and tired too.* 2. more than enough: *You gave me too much.* 3. very: *I am only too glad to go along.*

took See **take.** *Who took my book?*

tool an instrument that helps you do work: *Dad carries his garden tools in a bag.* **tools.**

toaster

---

tool

electric toaster

tomahawk

tomato

top²

torch 1.

torch 2.

tortoise

tooth 1. one of the hard, white parts in the mouth, used for chewing. 2. something like a tooth: *Each sharp point on the edge of a saw is a tooth.* **teeth.**

tooth brush a small brush used for cleaning teeth. **tooth brush es.**

tooth paste a very thick liquid used to clean your teeth.

tooth pick a small, pointed piece of wood or plastic for removing bits of food from between the teeth. **tooth picks.**

top¹ 1. the highest part: *the top of your head.* 2. the part that is up; the surface: *the top of the car, a table top.* 3. the highest: *the top drawer, the top shelf.* **tops.**

top² a toy that spins. See the picture. **tops.**

torch 1. a burning stick or a light to be carried: *The king's servants carried torches so that he could see.* 2. an instrument with a very hot flame, used to burn off paint or to melt some metals. See the picture. **torch es.**

tore See **tear**¹. *She tore open the package.*

torn See **tear**¹. *He has torn a branch from the rose bush.*

tor til la a thin cake, usually made of corn meal and eaten hot. A tortilla is often filled with cheese or meat. **tor til las.**

tor toise a turtle that lives on land. See the picture. **tor tois es** or **tor toise.**

toss 1. throw gently with the palm of the hand upward; cast; fling: *She tossed the ball to the baby.* 2. throw about: *The cork was tossed around by the waves.* 3. lift quickly: *The wild horse tossed its head and galloped away over the prairie.* **tossed, toss ing.**

touch 1. put the hand on or against something and feel it: *She touched the towel to see if it was dry.* 2. be against; come against: *Your sleeve is touching the butter.* 3. being touched: *Just the touch of my hand woke the baby.* 4. the sense that lets you know things by feeling or coming against them. **touched, touch ing; touch es.**

to ward in the direction of: *He was walking toward the door.*

tow el a piece of cloth or paper for wiping: *He dried his face with a clean towel.* **tow els.**

tow er a high building or a high part of a building. See the picture. **tow ers.**

town a community smaller than a city. **towns.**

toy 1. something made for a child to play with: *Dolls, tops, stuffed animals, are toys.* 2. made as a toy: *He had a toy truck.* **toys.**

track 1. steel rails for trains to run on: *Be careful crossing the railroad track.* 2. a mark left: *There were tire tracks in the snow.* See the picture. 3. follow by marks or smell: *The dog tracked the rabbit into the woods.* 4. make marks on: *Don't track the floor.* **tracks; tracked, track ing.**

trac tor a sturdy vehicle used for pulling farm machines. See the picture. **trac tors.**

trade 1. getting something in return for giving something: *My kite for her bat was a fair trade.* 2. make a trade. *Will you trade your candy bar for these peanuts?* **trades; trad ed, trad ing.**

traf fic people and vehicles coming and going: *There's lots of traffic in the city.*

traf fic light a signal that changes from a green light to a yellow light to a red light every few seconds. A traffic light shows drivers when to stop or go. **traf fic lights.**

tower

track 1.

track 2.

farm tractor

transom

mouse trap

bear trap

trail 1. a path: *There's a trail through the woods.* 2. look for by its tracks or its smell: *The dogs trailed a raccoon but lost the scent.* 3. anything that follows: *The plane left a trail of white in the sky.* **trails; trailed, trail ing.**

train 1. a line of vehicles or cars that move together: *a freight train, a wagon train.* 2. bring up; teach: *She trained her dog.* 3. become fit by exercise: *The boys trained for the race.* **trains; trained, train ing.**

train ee a person who is receiving training. **train ees.**

tramp 1. walk with heavy steps: *Cows tramped through the garden.* 2. a long, steady walk: *a tramp through the fields.* 3. the sound of a heavy step: *She heard the tramp of marching feet.* **tramped, tramp ing; tramps.**

tran som a window, usually on hinges, over a door. See the picture. **tran soms.**

trans port carry from one place to another. **trans port ed, trans port ing.**

trans por ta tion transporting; being transported; a way of going: *This railroad offers transportation across the mountains.*

trap 1. a thing for catching something: *a mouse trap.* See the picture. 2. catch in a trap: *Settlers trapped animals.* **traps; trapped, trap ping.**

trash stuff of no use; things to be thrown away.

trash man a person who collects and hauls away trash. **trash men.**

trav el go from one place to another: *She is traveling in Europe this summer. I like to travel by train.* **trav eled, trav el ing.**

tray a kind of large plate with a raised edge: *The waiter carried dishes on a tray.* **trays.**

treas ure 1. money and jewels: *The pirates buried the treasure.* 2. something of great value: *A good voice is a singer's greatest treasure.* **treas ures.**

treat 1. act toward: *Be sure to treat your dog kindly.* 2. give something like food, drink, or amusement: *He treated us to ice cream.* 3. try to cure: *The dentist treated my sore tooth.* 4. a gift of food, drink, or amusement: *"This is my treat," she said.* **treat ed, treat ing; treats.**

tree 1. a large plant with a trunk, branches, and leaves. There are many kinds of trees. 2. A **family tree** is a chart with branches showing the members of a family. See the picture. **trees.**

trem ble shake because of being excited, afraid, or weak: *Her hand trembled as she held the book.* **trem bled, trem bling.**

tri an gle a figure having three sides. See the picture. **tri an gles.**

tribe a group of people united by language or family or by the way they live: *an Indian tribe.* **tribes.**

trick 1. something done to play a joke on or to surprise: *Ringing the bell was a trick to get me outside.* 2. an act of skill: *The magician did tricks with cards.* 3. play a trick on: *You tricked me into telling my secret.* **tricks; tricked, trick ing.**

tri cy cle a three-wheeled vehicle that you ride like a bicycle. **tri cy cles.**

tried See **try.** *He tried to carry the chair. He has tried to carry the baby too.*

trike a tricycle. **trikes.**

trim 1. make neat by cutting away parts: *Dad trimmed my hair.* 2. make beautiful: *She trimmed the tree yesterday.* **trimmed, trim ming.**

family tree

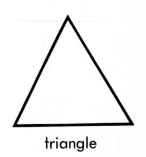

triangle

troll¹

troll²

boy playing
a trombone

trout

trim ming anything used to trim or to make
something look prettier: *The trimming on the
handkerchief was lace.* **trim mings.**

trip I. going somewhere: *a trip to Europe.*
2. stumble: *He tripped on the stairs.* **trips;
tripped, trip ping.**

troll¹ fish by pulling the line behind the boat
near the surface of the water. See the picture.
trolled, troll ing.

troll² in stories, an ugly dwarf or giant. Trolls
often live in caves. See the picture. **trolls.**

trom bone a musical instrument that you play by
blowing into it and sliding a tube. See the
picture. **trom bones.**

tro phy an award, often in the form of a statue
or cup, given as a sign of victory: *Our team
won the baseball trophy.* **tro phies.**

trot go by lifting one front foot and the opposite
hind foot at about the same time. Horses and
some other animals trot. **trot ted, trot ting.**

trou ble I. a problem; something that disturbs: *We
had trouble with the stove. What's the trouble
here?* 2. cause trouble; disturb: *Her son's grades
have troubled her for a long time.* **trou bles;
trou bled, trou bling.**

trou sers a piece of clothing that covers each leg.

trout a fresh-water fish, good to eat. See the
picture. **trouts** or **trout.**

truck a vehicle for carrying heavy loads. **trucks.**

trudge walk in a tired way: *The girl trudged down
the long road.* **trudged, trudg ing.**

true agreeing with the facts; correct; not made up or
make-believe: *This is a true story.* **tru er, tru est.**

tru ly I. in a true manner; exactly: *Tell me truly
what you think.* 2. really: *It was truly beautiful.*

trum pet a musical instrument that you play by blowing into it and pressing keys. See the picture. **trum pets.**

trunk 1. the main stem of a tree. 2. an elephant's nose. 3. a big box for carrying clothes. See the picture. **trunks.**

trust 1. a belief that a person or thing is honest, fair, and true: *I would put all my trust in you.* 2. believe firmly in the honesty, truth, or power of: *The boy trusted his friend. I don't trust that old ladder to hold me.* **trust ed, trust ing.**

truth that which is true: *Tell the truth.*

try 1. set out to do something if you can: *He will try to build a car.* 2. find out about: *Try this game before you buy it.* 3. a chance to try: *The batter has one more try to hit the ball.* 4. judge by law: *The man was tried for robbing the bank.* **tried, try ing; tries.**

tub 1. a large bowl for washing clothes. 2. a bathtub. **tubs.**

tu ba a musical instrument that you play by blowing into it and pressing keys. See the picture. **tu bas.**

tube 1. a long, hollow pipe of metal or other material that carries liquid or gas. 2. a small container for things like toothpaste. 3. an object like a light bulb that is used in radios and TV sets. A TV set has a picture tube. See the picture. **tubes.**

tuck 1. put into a narrow space: *She tucked the letter in her pocket.* 2. put the edge of something into place: *Tuck your shirt in.* 3. cover: *Who will tuck the baby in bed?* 4. a fold sewed in a piece of clothing: *Mother took a tuck in my slacks.* **tucked, tuck ing; tucks.**

trumpet

---

tuck

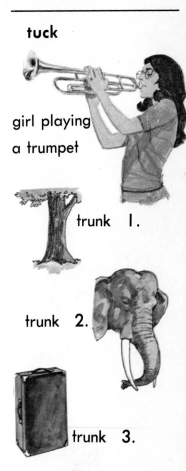

girl playing a trumpet

trunk 1.

trunk 2.

trunk 3.

boy playing a tuba

tube 2.

Tuesday

turnip

tulip

tulip tree

tunnel

turnip

Tues day the third day of the week. It follows Monday. **Tues days.**

tug 1. pull hard. 2. a hard pull: *She gave a tug on the rope.* **tugged, tug ging; tugs.**

tu lip a flower grown from a bulb. See the picture. **tu lips.**

tu lip tree a tall tree with tulip-shaped flowers. See the picture. **tu lip trees.**

tum ble 1. fall: *The child tumbled down the stairs.* 2. a fall: *The tumble hurt him badly.* **tum bled, tum bling; tum bles.**

tum my stomach: *The baby crawled along on its tummy.* **tum mies.**

tune 1. a piece of music: *He played a tune on the violin.* 2. **Out of tune** can mean not producing sounds correctly: *This piano is out of tune.* 3. put in tune; make an instrument sound right: *A man came to tune our piano.* **tunes; tuned, tun ing.**

tun nel a pass under ground: *The road went through a tunnel.* See the picture. **tun nels.**

tur key a large American bird raised for food. **tur keys.**

turn 1. move around a center as a wheel does: *The merry-go-round turned.* 2. cause to move as a wheel does: *I turned the knob three times to open the safe.* 3. motion like that of a wheel: *At each turn of the wheels we went slower.* 4. go in a new direction: *Turn here.* 5. a change of direction: *a turn to the left.* 6. a chance to do something: *It is her turn to read.* **turned, turn ing; turns.**

tur nip a plant. Its large round root and sometimes its leaves are eaten as vegetables. See the picture. **tur nips.**

tur quoise 1. a sky-blue or green-blue stone: *Mom has a turquoise in her ring.* 2. green-blue: *She wore a turquoise sweater.* **tur quois es.**

tur tle an animal having a thick, hard shell. Turtles move very slowly. See the picture. **tur tles.**

tur tle neck a round, high, closely fitting collar on a shirt or sweater. **tur tle necks.**

TV television.

twelfth 1. next after the eleventh; 12th. 2. one of 12 equal parts. **twelfths.**

twelve two more than 10; 12. **twelves.**

twen ti eth 1. next after the nineteenth; 20th. 2. one of 20 equal parts. **twen ti eths.**

twen ty two times ten; 20. **twen ties.**

twice 1. two times: *Twice five is ten.* 2. two times as many: *I have twice as many marbles as my brother has.*

twig a shoot of a tree or other plant. **twigs.**

twin one of two children or animals born at the same time of the same mother. **twins.**

twin kle 1. shine with quick little flashes: *His eyes twinkled when he laughed.* 2. a twinkling light: *There was a twinkle in his eyes.* **twin kled, twin kling; twin kles.**

twirl revolve rapidly; spin; whirl: *Can you twirl a baton?* **twirled, twirl ing.**

twist 1. turn around and around: *She twisted her ring on her finger.* 2. curve: *The road twists around the mountain.* 3. pull or force out of shape: *Don't twist my arm.* **twist ed, twist ing.**

two 1. one more than one; 2. 2. Two and two are four. **twos.**

type writ er a machine for making letters and numerals on paper. See the picture. **type writ ers.**

turtle

typewriter

U u

U or **u** the twenty-first letter of the alphabet.
U's or **u's.**

ug ly 1. unpleasant to look at: *That's an ugly black cloud.* 2. dangerous: *She has an ugly cut on her hand.* 3. cross; not pleasant: *The boy has an ugly look on his face.* **ug li er, ug li est.**

um brel la a folding frame covered with material. An umbrella keeps rain or sunlight off your head. See the picture. **um brel las.**

beach umbrella

um pire a person who judges a game: *The umpire called the batter safe.* See the picture. **um pires.**

un able not able: *A little baby is unable to walk.*

un buck le unfasten the buckle of: *I can't unbuckle my belt.* **un buck led, un buck ling.**

un but ton unfasten the button or buttons of a piece of clothing. **un but toned, un but ton ing.**

un cer tain not certain; full of doubt: *We were uncertain about the time we would get home.*

un chain let loose; set free: *Be sure to unchain the dog before you go away.* **un chained, un chain ing.**

un cle your father's or mother's brother or your aunt's husband. **un cles.**

baseball umpire

un cov er 1. take the cover off: *Uncover the roast so it will get brown.* 2. make known: *The police uncovered a plot.* **un cov ered, un cov er ing.**

un curl 1. make straight. 2. become straight. **un curled, un curl ing.**

un der 1. below: *The ball is under the table.* 2. lower than: *He is under six feet tall.* 3. less than: *Children under five years old go in free.*

un der neath beneath; below; under: *Is that your pencil underneath the desk?*

un der stand 1. get the meaning of: *Now I understand your message.* 2. know well; know how to take care of: *A veterinarian understands horses.* **un der stood, un der stand ing.**

un der stood See **understand**. *She understood what you said. She has always understood what you told her.*

un easy feeling troubled or worried: *She was uneasy about the coming storm. He was uneasy when he couldn't find his pencil.* **un eas i er, un eas i est.**

un fair not fair; unjust: *It was unfair of them to start before the others.* **un fair er, un fair est.**

un fair ly in an unfair way: *We all think you acted unfairly toward us.*

un fas ten loosen; open; take the ties from: *Please unfasten this bracelet for me.* **un fas tened, un fas ten ing.**

un friend ly not friendly: *Don't be unfriendly to the new boy.* **un friend li er, un friend li est.**

un hap pi ly not happily; in an unhappy way: *The girl sighed unhappily.*

un hap py not happy; sad: *The boy's face showed he was unhappy.* **un hap pi er, un hap pi est.**

un healthy 1. not healthy; not having good health: *An unhealthy person isn't strong.* 2. not good for the health: *Wet weather can be unhealthy.* **un health i er, un health i est.**

un hitch unfasten: *Unhitch the horses and let them eat.* **un hitched, un hitch ing.**

uni corn in stories, an animal like a horse, but having a long horn on its forehead. See the picture. **uni corns.**

unicorn

boy and girl
wearing uniforms

man unloading a truck

uni form 1. all the same: *The horses in the circus were uniform in size.* 2. clothes, all alike, worn by the members of a group. Many uniforms are brightly colored. See the picture. **uni forms.**

un ion 1. the joining of two or more people or things to make one. 2. **The Union** is a name for the United States. 3. a group of people joined to protect their jobs. **un ions.**

unit one or a group of something used as a single item. **units.**

unite join; put or be together to make one: *Three choirs united to sing a song.* **unit ed, unit ing.**

Unit ed States U.S.; the United States of America; U.S.A.; the country north of Mexico and south of Canada. See the map on page 380.

un just not fair: *It is unjust to blame him before you know what happened.*

un just ly unfairly: *She was unjustly accused of breaking the vase.*

un kind not kind; cruel: *That was an unkind thing to say.* **un kind er, un kind est.**

un known not known; strange: *Perhaps there are many unknown planets.*

un less if not: *I won't go unless she does.*

un load 1. move a load: *Help me unload the books.* 2. take a load from: *The man unloaded the van.* See the picture. **un load ed, un load ing.**

un lock open the lock of; open anything that is firmly closed. **un locked, un lock ing.**

un lucky not lucky: *She is an unlucky girl. Breaking a mirror might be unlucky.* **un luck i er, un luck i est.**

un pack 1. take out: *Unpack your books and put them on this shelf.* 2. take things out of: *Unpack your trunk.* **un packed, un pack ing.**

un pin take out pins from; unfasten: *She unpinned her scarf.* **un pinned, un pin ning.**

un pleas ant not pleasant; not giving pleasure to: *The medicine has an unpleasant taste.* **un pleas ant er, un pleas ant est.**

un roll 1. open or spread out: *He unrolled his blanket.* See the picture. 2. become spread out: *The yarn unrolled from the ball.* **un rolled, un roll ing.**

un safe not safe; dangerous: *The ice is thin and unsafe for skating.* **un saf er, un saf est.**

un seen not seen: *The roar of an unseen animal scared me.*

un stead i ly not steadily; in a shaky way: *The old man walked unsteadily to the door.*

un steady not steady; shaky: *He was unsteady standing on one leg.* **un stead i er, un stead i est.**

un stuck not stuck; free: *The label came unstuck from the bottle.*

un tie loosen; unfasten: *Please untie the baby's shoe.* **un tied, un ty ing.**

un til 1. till; up to the time when: *He waited until dark.* 2. before: *She will not go until tomorrow.*

un u su al not usual; not common; rare.

un will ing not willing; not ready to or not wanting to.

un wind take from a ball or spool: *Don't unwind the yarn.* **un wound, un wind ing.**

un wise not wise: *It is unwise to get your feet wet in winter.* **un wis er, un wis est.**

un wise ly in an unwise manner: *She acted unwisely when she didn't obey.*

un wrap take off a wrapping; open a package. See the picture. **un wrapped, un wrap ping.**

Cub Scout unrolling
a blanket

girl unwrapping
a present

urn 1.

up 1. to a higher place: *The bird flew up from the water.* 2. to or at the top of: *He went up the hill.* 3. out of bed: *Get up.* 4. at an end: *Time is up.*

up on on.

up set 1. tip over: *Don't upset the glass.* 2. disturb: *Your loud talking upset the baby. Has this bad news upset her?* 3. disturbed: *an upset stomach.* **up set, up set ting.**

up side the upper side.

up stairs 1. up the stairs: *Go upstairs to bed.* 2. to or on a higher floor: *The attic is upstairs.*

up ward toward a higher place: *The smoke drifted upward through the trees.*

urn 1. a kind of large vase. See the picture. 2. a kind of pot for making coffee or tea. **urns.**

us the person speaking plus the persons spoken about: *Our teacher asked us to help her.*

U.S. the United States.

U.S.A. the United States of America; the U.S.

use 1. put to work: *We use our legs in walking. We use spoons to eat soup.* 2. destroy or lose by using: *She used three sheets of paper for her poster. I used five pennies to get one piece of gum.* 3. what a thing is used for: *Can you find some use for this box?* **used, us ing; us es.**

used not new: *a used car.*

use ful of use; giving service; helpful: *This brush is very useful. Make yourself useful.*

usu al 1. common; happening often; not special or rare: *We had our usual Sunday dinner.* 2. **As usual** means in the usual way: *We went to school as usual.*

usu al ly most of the time: *Fran is usually hungry.*

Utah one of the fifty states of the United States. See page 371.

V   v

V or **v** the twenty-second letter of the alphabet.
V's or **v's.**

va ca tion time out of school or away from work:
We took a vacation last week. **va ca tions.**

vac u um clean er an appliance for cleaning
carpets and floors. See the picture.
vac u um clean ers.

val en tine a funny or fancy card sent to someone
on Valentine's Day. **val en tines.**

Val en tine's Day February 14, when some
people send valentines. **Val en tine's Days.**

val ley low land between hills. See the picture.
val leys.

val u a ble having great value.

val ue 1. how useful or important something is;
how much something is worth: *A dime has a*
value of ten cents. This book is of great value.
2. think something is worth a lot: *I would value*
anything my grandmother gave me. **val ues;**
val ued, val u ing.

van a covered truck or wagon: *Our furniture is*
loaded in the moving van. See the picture. **vans.**

vase a container for flowers. **vas es.**

vat a large container for cooking or for liquids.
See the picture. **vats.**

veg e ta ble 1. a plant used for food. 2. anything
that is not an animal or a mineral. 3. made from
vegetables: *vegetable soup.* **veg e ta bles.**

ve hi cle something people can ride in or on:
Automobiles, bicycles, boats, and planes are
vehicles. **ve hi cles.**

vehicle

vacuum cleaner

valley

moving van

lobster vat

plaid vest

view **3.**

vine

vel vet **1.** a kind of thick, soft cloth. **2.** made of velvet: *I wore a velvet hat.*

verb a name for certain kinds of words. In *He is my brother, is* is a verb; in *We danced at the party, danced* is a verb; in *Joe likes pizza, likes* is a verb. **verbs.**

Ver mont one of the fifty states of the United States. See page 372.

verse **1.** a poem or some lines of words that rhyme and have accents at the same place in each line. **2.** one part of a poem or song: *This song has two verses.* **vers es.**

very much; more than usual: *The wind is very cold.*

vest a piece of clothing, like a jacket, but without sleeves. See the picture. **vests.**

vet er i nar i an a doctor who treats animals instead of people. **vet er i nar i ans.**

vi brate move very fast forward and backward; shake rapidly: *A guitar string vibrates when you pluck it.* **vi brat ed, vi brat ing.**

vi bra tion a moving rapidly forward and backward; a trembling motion: *We could feel the vibration of the floor as the truck passed.* **vi bra tions.**

view **1.** the act of seeing: *It was her first view of the city.* **2.** see; look at: *They viewed the ocean without speaking.* **3.** the thing seen: *The view of the lake is beautiful.* See the picture. **4.** a way of looking at or thinking about something: *Children have different views of school.* **views; viewed, view ing.**

vil lage a community, usually smaller than a town. **vil lag es.**

vine a plant that grows along the ground or climbs a wall. See the picture. **vines.**

vin e gar a sour liquid used in some foods.

vi o let 1. a small plant that blooms in the spring. See the picture. 2. blue-purple: *She wore a violet blouse.* **vi o lets.**

vi o lin a musical instrument that you play by moving a bow across strings. See the picture. **vi o lins.**

Vir gin ia one of the fifty states of the United States. See page 373.

vis it 1. go to see; come to see: *Are you going to visit New York?* 2. stay with; be a guest: *I visited my aunt last week.* 3. the act of visiting: *Bobby came for a visit.* **vis it ed, vis it ing; vis its.**

vis i tor a person who visits; a guest. **vis i tors.**

voice sounds made through the throat and mouth: *We could hear voices through the thin wall. His voice is very deep.* **voic es.**

vote 1. say whether you are for or against a thing: *He voted for a new swimming pool.* 2. the act of voting: *Whoever gets the most votes will win.* **vot ed, vot ing; votes.**

vow el 1. an open sound made by the voice. 2. one of the letters *a, e, i, o,* or *u.* **vow els.**

W   w

W or **w** the twenty-third letter of the alphabet. **W's** or **w's.**

wade walk through water or anything that makes walking hard: *Wade through the leaves.* **wad ed, wad ing.**

wa fer a very thin cracker or cookie: *A sugar wafer tastes good with ice cream.* **wa fers.**

waf fle a food like a pancake but cooked in a certain kind of pan. See the picture. **waf fles.**

violet

---

waffle

violet 1.

girl playing a violin

waffle

---

wand

child's wagon

children using
a walkie-talkie

walnut

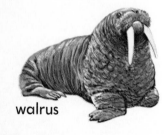

walrus

wag move from side to side or up and down: *The dog wags its tail at everyone.* **wagged, wag ging.**

wag on a four-wheeled cart for riding in and carrying loads. See the picture. **wag ons.**

wail cry loud and long: *The baby wailed until he went to sleep.* **wailed, wail ing.**

wait 1. stop doing something or stay till something happens: *Let's wait for the bus.* 2. the time of waiting: *I had a long wait for the plane.* 3. be ready; look forward: *She is waiting for spring to come.* 4. **Wait on table** means serve food to someone. **wait ed, wait ing; waits.**

wait er a man who waits on table and brings food in a restaurant. **wait ers.**

wait ress a woman who waits on table and brings food in a restaurant. **wait ress es.**

wake 1. stop sleeping: *I must wake at 6 o'clock tomorrow.* 2. cause to stop sleeping: *Don't wake your father.* **waked** or **woke, waked, wak ing.**

walk 1. go on foot: *Walk to the corner with me.* 2. the act of walking: *We took the baby for a walk.* 3. a distance to walk: *It is a short walk to the park.* **walked, walk ing; walks.**

walk ie-talk ie a radio small enough to carry. With it you can hear and talk to someone far away. See the picture. **walk ie-talk ies.**

wall 1. the side of a house or room. 2. a stone or brick fence. 3. anything like a wall: *A wall of water rushed over the dam.* **walls.**

wal nut 1. a large nut. 2. the tree it grows on. See the picture. **wal nuts.**

wal rus a large sea animal, somewhat like a seal. See the picture. **wal rus es** or **wal rus.**

wand a thin stick or rod: *a magic wand.* **wands.**

wan der move about without going any special place: *We wandered through the store looking at things.* **wan dered, wan der ing.**

want 1. wish for: *She wants some candy. Do you want to be an engineer?* 2. need; be without: *Poor people want food.* 3. being without: *Many people are in want.* **want ed, want ing.**

war 1. a long fight between nations or people. 2. any kind of fight: *We have begun a war on mosquitoes.* **wars.**

warm 1. more hot than cold: *Don't drink this warm water. Wear warm clothes to ski.* 2. friendly: *a warm smile.* **warm er, warm est.**

warm ly in a warm manner: *A warmly dressed child enjoys snow. He greeted his friends warmly.*

warn tell of some danger before it comes: *The trooper warned us that the road might be icy.* **warned, warn ing.**

was *He was a giant. I was late for dinner. The sun was shining. She was gone.*

wash 1. clean with water: *Wash your doll's face.* 2. a bundle of clothes to be washed: *Put your socks in the wash.* **washed, wash ing; wash es.**

wash er a machine or appliance that washes clothes. See the picture. **wash ers.**

Wash ing ton one of the fifty states of the United States. See page 374.

Wash ing ton, D.C. the capital of the United States. See page 378.

Wash ing ton's Birth day a holiday every February to honor George Washington. **Wash ing ton's Birth days.**

wash room room where people can wash themselves, usually a public bathroom. **wash rooms.**

was n't was not.

washer

night watchman

wave 1.

waste 1. make bad use of; throw away without using: *Don't waste water. Don't waste milk.* 2. the poor use of something: *Buying these mittens was a waste of money.* 3. material to be thrown away; garbage; trash. 4. not used; to be thrown away: *Is this all waste paper?* **wast ed, wast ing; wastes.**

waste ful not using or saving enough; throwing away or spending too much: *It is wasteful to take more food than you can eat.*

waste ful ly in a wasteful way.

watch 1. look at: *Come and watch this show.* 2. look carefully: *Watch me saw this board so you'll know how to do it. The boy watched for cars at the corner.* 3. keep guard: *I will watch your purse for you.* 4. a small clock. **watched, watch ing; watch es.**

watch ful wide awake; watching carefully: *The dog was watchful even when lying down.*

watch ful ly in a watchful manner: *She led the children across the street watchfully.*

watch man a guard whose business is to watch over and guard property. A night watchman works all night. See the picture. **watch men.**

wa ter 1. the liquid that fills the oceans, rivers, lakes, and ponds, and that falls from the sky as rain. 2. sprinkle or wet with water: *The gardener waters the flowers.* **wa tered, wa ter ing.**

wave 1. a moving hill of water: *We sat on the beach and watched the waves roll in.* See the picture. 2. anything like this: *A wave of laughter rolled through the audience.* 3. move as waves do: *The field of oats waved in the breeze.* 4. move back and forth: *Wave your hand.* **waves; waved, wav ing.**

wax 1. material made by bees to contain honey. 2. any material like this. Some candles are made of wax. 3. made of wax: *wax candles.* **wax es.**

way 1. how to do something; how something is done or can be done: *Scientists are looking for ways to fight germs.* 2. direction: *Go that way.* 3. how to go: *Can you find your way home?* 4. how to get somewhere; a path: *He cut a way through the brush.* 5. a person's wish or desire: *He is a child who wants his own way.* **ways.**

we the persons speaking: *We are coming to visit you. We went riding. We can do it.*

weak 1. easily broken: *There was a weak spot in the tire.* 2. not having power or being strong: *She was weak after her sickness.* **weak er, weak est.**

weap on anything used to fight with. Teeth, claws, hoofs, fists, can be weapons. Spears and guns are weapons too. **weap ons.**

wear 1. have on the body: *Wear a coat today.* 2. last long; give good service: *These shoes will wear well.* **wore, worn, wear ing.**

wea sel a small, quick animal with a thin body. See the picture. **wea sels.**

weath er 1. the state of the air around and above some place: *The weather is cold and rainy here today.* 2. about the weather: *a weather report.*

weath er vane an instrument to show which way the wind is blowing. You may see a weather vane on a roof. See the picture. **weath er vanes.**

weave form threads or strips into an object or a material. You can weave cloth or weave a basket. See the picture. **wove, wo ven, weav ing.**

we'd 1. we had: *We'd left before she came.* 2. we would: *We'd like to see you.*

weasel

weather vane on a roof

girl weaving a rug

311

wedge 1.

wed ding 1. the promises made by a man and woman as they marry each other. 2. the special occasion or celebration when a man and woman marry each other: *They had a large wedding.* 3. of a wedding: *a wedding cake.* **wed dings.**

wedge 1. a piece of wood or metal with one thin edge, used to split wood. See the picture. 2. something shaped like a wedge. 3. squeeze: *His arm was wedged between two logs.* **wedg es; wedged, wedg ing.**

Wednes day the fourth day of the week. It follows Tuesday. **Wednes days.**

wee very, very small. **we er, we est.**

weed 1. a plant without much value that grows almost anywhere: *The yard is full of weeds.* 2. take weeds out of: *It is time to weed the garden.* **weeds; weed ed, weed ing.**

week the time from Sunday through Saturday; seven days. **weeks.**

week ly 1. for a week: *a weekly allowance.* 2. once each week: *This is a weekly newspaper.*

weep cry; sob with tears falling. **wept, weep ing.**

weigh find out how heavy a thing is: *I often weigh myself. How much do you weigh?* **weighed, weigh ing.**

weight how heavy a thing is: *The cat's weight is ten pounds.* **weights.**

wel come 1. a friendly way to greet someone: *Welcome to our party!* 2. greet kindly: *The dog welcomed us with a wagging tail.* 3. You say, "You are welcome," when someone thanks you. **wel comes; wel comed, wel com ing.**

well[1] 1. completely: *He knew the story well.* 2. in good health: *She was sick, but now she is well.* **bet ter, best.**

well² a hole dug in the ground to get water or oil. See the picture. **wells.**

we'll 1. we shall. 2. we will.

went See **go.** *We went home early.*

wept See **weep.** *She wept when her dog ran away. She has wept for an hour.*

were *We were late. Were you late? The children were picking flowers. The flowers were picked by the children. You were right. If I were you, I'd go.*

we're we are.

weren't were not.

west 1. the direction of the sunset; the opposite of east. 2. to the west: *Turn west and go three blocks.* 3. coming from the west: *We could feel the west wind.* 4. **The West** means the western part of the United States.

west ern 1. toward the west: *The western sky is red this evening.* 2. from the west: *I wrote to my western cousins.* 3. A **western** is a story of the West. **west erns** (for 3.).

West Vir gin ia one of the fifty states of the United States. See page 375.

west ward toward the west.

wet covered with water or other liquid; not dry: *Bring me a wet towel, please.* **wet ter, wet test.**

we've we have.

whack 1. a sharp blow: *The lion gave the cub a whack with one paw.* 2. strike with a sharp blow. **whacks; whacked, whack ing.**

whale a sea animal shaped like a huge fish. See the picture. **whales** or **whale.**

wharf a platform out from the shore, so ships can load and unload. See the picture. **wharves** or **wharfs.**

wharves more than one wharf.

well

wharves

well²

whale

wharf

313

what

which

wheat

what 1. *What* is used in asking questions such as: *What are you doing? What happened to him? What is going on here?* 2. *What* is also used in sentences such as: *I don't know what she said. Say what you think. I'll take what cookies you don't eat.* 3. *What* is often used to show surprise or other feelings: *What a ride! What a good party! What noise!*

what ev er any thing at all: *Do whatever you want.*

what's 1. what is: *What's that?* 2. what has: *What's happened to your foot?*

wheat 1. a grain from which flour is made. 2. the plant. See the picture.

wheel 1. a round frame that turns on its center. 2. anything shaped or moving like a wheel. 3. move on wheels: *He was wheeling bricks on a cart.* **wheels; wheeled, wheel ing.**

when 1. at what time: *When does the show begin?* 2. at the time that: *Stop singing when the music stops.* 3. at any time that: *We always laughed when the clown fell down.*

where 1. at what place: *Where does your cat sleep? Where is the money?* 2. to what place: *Where are you taking them?* 3. from what place: *Where did you get those shoes?*

wher ev er any place at all: *Sit wherever you like.*

wheth er *Whether* is used when there are two or more things to choose from: *It won't matter whether we are late or early. He doesn't know whether to wear his coat or his sweater.*

which 1. *Which* is used to ask about persons or things: *Which girl won the game? Which bicycle is yours?* 2. *Which* is also used to connect a group of words with some other word in a sentence: *This book, which I have just finished, is good.*

while 1. a length of time: *We stayed at the library a little while.* 2. during the time that: *While it was raining, he cleaned his room. Vacations are fun while they last.* 3. although: *While it rained all the time, I had fun at the picnic anyway.*

whim per 1. cry with short, low sounds as a puppy cries: *Thunder makes my dog whimper. The sick child whimpered.* 2. the sound of whimpering. **whim pered, whim per ing; whim pers.**

whine 1. make a low, complaining cry or sound: *The dog whined when it heard the noise.* 2. say with a whining, unpleasant tone: *Stop whining or I'll take you home.* **whined, whin ing.**

whip poor will a bird with a strange call that sounds like its name. See the picture. **whip poor wills.**

whirl turn or swing round and round; spin: *The airplane propeller whirled when the pilot turned on the engine.* **whirled, whirl ing.**

whisk er 1. one of the hairs growing on a man's face. 2. **Whiskers** usually means the hair on a man's cheeks and chin. **whisk ers.**

whis per 1. speak very softly and low: *Don't whisper to me in class.* 2. a very soft, low spoken sound: *She spoke in a whisper.* **whis pered, whis per ing; whis pers.**

whis tle 1. make a clear, shrill sound with your lips: *The boy whistled for his dog.* 2. the sound made by whistling. 3. an instrument for making whistling sounds. See the picture. 4. blow a whistle: *She whistled for the band to start playing.* **whis tled, whis tling; whis tles.**

white 1. the color of snow, salt, or cotton. 2. having this color: *Our house is white with a red roof.* **whit er, whit est.**

whippoorwill

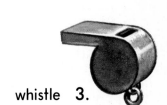

whistle 3.

who 1. *Who* is used in asking questions about persons: *Who is that? Who went with you?* 2. *Who* is also used to connect a group of words with some word in the sentence: *The man who knocked on the door was selling vacuum cleaners.*

who'd 1. who had: *Who'd seen this movie before?* 2. who would: *Who'd believe that?*

who ev er anybody at all: *Whoever gets there first wins.*

whole 1. having all its parts: *This is not the whole set of books because one book is lost.* 2. all of a thing: *Two halves make a whole.* 3. in one piece: *Please cut your sandwich; don't try to eat it whole.*

whole sale the sale of something in a large amount to someone who will sell it again in small amounts: *Grocers buy their stock wholesale.*

who'll 1. who will. 2. who shall.

whom a person spoken about: *Whom do you eat lunch with? She does not know whom to blame. The boy to whom I spoke is new in school.*

who're who are.

who's 1. who is: *Who's going with me?* 2. who has: *Who's taken the paper?*

whose of whom; of which: *Whose sweater is this? Whose mittens are these?*

who've who have.

why 1. for what reason: *Why did she bring two sandwiches? She doesn't know why the dog is barking.* 2. *Why* is sometimes used to show surprise: *Why! the dog is gone! Why, no, I didn't hear the bell.*

candle wick

wick the part of a candle that can be lighted. See the picture. **wicks.**

wick ed bad: *The wicked old witch frightened them.*

wide   1. not narrow; filling much space from side to side: *We crossed a wide river.*   2. far open: *Open the window wide. The children stared with wide eyes at the elephant.*   **wid er, wid est.**

wide ly   far apart; not close together: *The boys gave two widely different accounts.*

width   how wide a thing is; the distance from side to side: *The width of that road is ten feet.*   **widths.**

wie ner   a frankfurter.   **wie ners.**

wife   a woman who has a husband; a married woman.   **wives.**

wig gle   move quickly from side to side: *The child wiggled all through the program.*   **wig gled, wig gling.**

wild   living or growing in forests or fields; not tamed: *The gorilla is a wild animal. Did you see wild roses growing in the field?*   **wild er, wild est.**

wil der ness   a wild place; land with nobody living in it.   **wil der ness es.**

wild ly   in a wild manner: *He rushed wildly out of the burning building.*

will   1. be about to or going to do something: *She will start soon. I will go now.*   2. be able to: *The boat will hold four people.*   **would.**

will ing   ready; wanting to: *She is willing to come.*

wil low   a large tree with slender branches and narrow leaves. See the picture.   **wil lows.**

win   1. succeed over others: *Our team will win the race.*   2. get by work or by skill: *She won a prize for running.*   **won, win ning.**

wind¹   1. air that is moving. Wind can be strong or gentle.   2. breath: *He's out of wind.*   3. put out of breath: *Walking up the hill winded us.*   **winds; wind ed, wind ing.** (Wind¹ rhymes with pinned.)

willow tree

window

wind[2] 1. move in a crooked line: *The road winds up the mountain.* 2. make go by turning: *Wind the clock.* 3. roll into a ball or put on a spool: *Did you wind this yarn?* **wound, wind ing.** (Wind[2] rhymes with find. Wound rhymes with found.)

win dow an opening in a wall or roof to let in light or air. See the picture. **win dows.**

windy having much wind: *windy weather, a windy day.* **wind i er, wind i est.**

wing 1. one of the parts that a bird or insect uses to fly. 2. anything like a wing: *an airplane wing.* **wings.**

wink 1. close the eyes and open them again quickly: *The flashlight made the puppy wink.* 2. close and open one eye as a hint or signal: *Mother winked at me to be quiet.* 3. the act of winking: *Father's wink told me he knew the answer.* **winked, wink ing; winks.**

win ter 1. the coldest of the four seasons; the time of year between fall and spring. 2. of or for winter: *winter gloves, winter storms.* **win ters.**

wipe 1. rub to clean or take away or dry off: *Wipe your hands on this towel.* 2. take away by rubbing: *Wipe the dust from that table. Wipe your tears.* **wiped, wip ing.**

wire 1. metal pulled out into a long thread. You can hang a picture with wire. 2. made of wire: *a wire fence.* 3. put wires in: *The house was wired for electricity.* 4. fasten with wire: *Wire the pieces together.* 5. send a telegram: *He wired his family for money.* **wires; wired, wir ing.**

Wis con sin one of the fifty states of the United States. See page 376.

wis dom being wise; having much knowledge and using good sense.

wise knowing much; not stupid. **wis er, wis est.**

wise ly in a wise manner: *Be sure to spend your money wisely.*

wish 1. need and hope to get something or for something to happen: *I wish I had a new bike. I wish Dad would take me with him.* 2. something wished for: *Her wish for a friend came true.* **wished, wish ing; wish es.**

witch in stories, a woman said to have magic power. See the picture. **witch es.**

with *With* shows that persons or things are or go together: *Go with him. He opened the package with scissors. Do you like cream with cereal?*

with in inside; not beyond: *Please stay within the playground fence.*

with out 1. free from: *My spelling paper was without a mistake.* 2. leaving out: *She went without saying good-by.*

wives more than one wife.

wiz ard in stories, a man said to have magic power. See the picture. **wiz ards.**

woke See **wake.** *I woke early today.*

wolf a wild animal that looks like a dog. See the picture. **wolves.**

wolves more than one wolf.

wom an a female human being. A woman is a girl grown up. **wom en.**

won See **win.** *This team won the game. We have won three games in a row.*

won der 1. a strange and surprising thing: *It's a wonder we got here at all.* 2. wish to know: *I wonder what will happen next.* **won ders; won dered, won der ing.**

witch
on a broomstick

wizard

wolf

woodchuck

woodpecker

won der ful causing wonder: *The ocean was a wonderful sight.* *She has wonderful news.*

won der ful ly in a wonderful way: *The sunset was wonderfully bright.*

won't will not.

wood 1. the hard part of a tree's trunk and of its branches. Wood is used for making many things. 2. made of wood: *a wood handle.*

wood chuck a small animal with a bushy tail. See the picture. **wood chucks.**

wood en made of wood: *That is an old wooden picture frame.*

wood peck er a bird with a hard, pointed bill for making holes in trees to get insects. See the picture. **wood peck ers.**

woods a piece of land covered with trees and bushes: *It is fun to walk in the woods.*

wool 1. the soft coat of a sheep. Wool is made into cloth. 2. something like wool: *You clean pans with steel wool.* 3. made of wool: *wool blankets.*

word 1. a sound or a group of sounds that has meaning: *I can't hear a word you are saying.* 2. the writing that stands for a word: *Can you read that word?* **words.**

wore See **wear.** *She wore her old jeans.*

work 1. something you do: *His work is driving a truck.* *She did beautiful work making that rug.* *Digging is hard work.* 2. do something by trying: *She works hard at her job.* 3. act; operate: *How does this machine work?* **worked, work ing**

work er one who works. **work ers.**

world 1. the earth: *Grandmother took a trip around the world.* 2. everybody on earth: *The whole world waited for the astronauts to land.* **worlds.**

320

worm a small, thin, crawling or creeping animal. See the picture. **worms.**

worn 1. hurt by use: *That rug is badly worn.* 2. See **wear.** *She has worn her boots every day.*

wor ry 1. feel uneasy: *Don't worry about me.* 2. annoy: *Don't worry your dad.* 3. something to worry about: *Her biggest worry is being late.* **wor ried, wor ry ing; wor ries.**

worse 1. not as well: *She feels worse today. She did worse on this test.* 2. less good: *The second story was worse than the first one.* 3. in a less good way: *The child behaves worse when his parents are gone.* See **bad.**

wor ship show great respect and love for something: *Some people go to a church or a synagogue or a mosque to worship.* **wor shiped, wor ship ing.**

worst 1. least well: *This is the worst I've ever felt.* 2. least good: *That's the worst movie I've ever seen.* 3. in the least good way: *The dog acts worst when it's hungry.* See **bad.**

worth 1. good or useful or important enough for: *That TV program is worth watching. Seeing the clowns was worth the whole trip. Is your bike worth ten dollars?* 2. value: *He got his money's worth out of that ball.* 3. how much a certain amount will buy: *a dollar's worth of stamps.*

would 1. See **will.** *They said they would start now.* 2. *Would* is also used to show something done over and over: *The kitten would play for hours.*

would n't would not.

wound¹ 1. a hurt caused by cutting or tearing: *The man has a wound in his side.* 2. hurt by cutting or tearing the skin: *A hunter's arrow wounded the elk.* **wounds; wound ed, wound ing.** (Wound¹ rhymes with tuned.)

worm

***

wound

worm

wound

writer

holly wreath

wren

wrench 4.

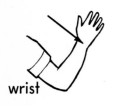

wrist

wound² See **wind².** *She wound the towel around her head. My watch has stopped because I have wound it too tight.* (Wound² rhymes with sound.)

wove See **weave.** *My sister wove a mat for me.*

wo ven See **weave.** *She has woven three towels.*

wrap 1. cover by winding or folding something around: *Did you wrap this present? Wrap up if you're going out.* 2. clothing such as a coat, cape, jacket, that you wear to keep warm. **wrapped, wrap ping; wraps.**

wreath a ring of flowers or leaves. See the picture. **wreaths.**

wren a small bird that sings. Wrens often build their nests near houses. See the picture. **wrens.**

wrench 1. a sudden twist or pull: *He gave his ankle a wrench when he fell.* 2. twist or pull sharply: *He wrenched the handle off when he was trying to open the drawer.* 3. hurt by twisting: *I wrenched my back.* 4. a tool to hold and turn nuts. See the picture. **wrench es; wrenched, wrench ing.**

wres tle 1. try to throw or force someone to the ground. 2. struggle: *He wrestled with the problem all day.* **wres tled, wres tling.**

wres tler a person who wrestles. **wres tlers.**

wrin kle 1. a fold: *My grandmother's face has wrinkles. Why are there wrinkles in this dress?* 2. make wrinkles in: *He wrinkled his nose. She wrinkled her sleeves when she rolled them up.* **wrin kles; wrin kled, wrin kling.**

wrist the joint connecting your hand and your arm. See the picture. **wrists.**

write make letters or words with pen, pencil, or chalk. **wrote, writ ten, writ ing.**

writ er 1. one who writes. 2. an author. **writ ers.**

writ ten See **write.** *He has written a story about a dog.*

wrong 1. not right; bad: *It is wrong to take her bike.* 2. not true; not correct: *I wrote down the wrong answer.* 3. out of order: *What is wrong with the car?*

wrote See **write.** *He wrote three letters.*

Wy o ming one of the fifty states of the United States. See page 377.

X x

X or **x** the twenty-fourth letter of the alphabet. **X's** or **x's.**

X ray a picture that shows what is inside something. See the picture. **X rays.**

xy lo phone a musical instrument. You play it by striking metal bars with small hammers. See the picture. **xy lo phones.**

Y y

Y or **y** the twenty-fifth letter of the alphabet. **Y's** or **y's.**

yard[1] 1. the ground around a building: *You can play in the front yard.* 2. some ground for a special use: *railroad yards, school yard.* **yards.**

yard[2] a measure of length or distance. Thirty-six inches or three feet equal one yard. **yards.**

yarn 1. any loosely spun thread, usually used for knitting. See the picture. 2. a tale; a story: *The old sailors spun some yarns about the sea.* **yarns** (for 2.).

written

yarn

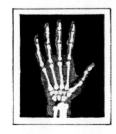

X ray of a hand

boy playing a xylophone

yarn 1.

yellowhammer

yew tree

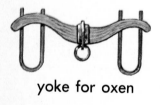

yoke for oxen

yawn 1. open your mouth wide because you are sleepy, tired, or bored: *It isn't polite to yawn at a party.* 2. the act of yawning: *She couldn't hide her yawn during the concert.* **yawned, yawn ing; yawns.**

year 1. a period of time; twelve months. 2. the time from January 1 to December 31. **years.**

year ly 1. once a year: *He takes a yearly vacation.* 2. lasting a year: *The earth makes a yearly trip around the sun.*

yeast a material used in making bread. Yeast makes the bread rise before it is baked.

yell 1. cry with a strong, loud sound: *He yelled when the door shut on his finger.* 2. a strong, loud cry. **yelled, yell ing; yells.**

yel low 1. the color of gold or butter. 2. having the color of gold or butter: *a yellow flower.* **yel lows; yel low er, yel low est.**

yel low ham mer a bird with yellow and brown feathers. See the picture. **yel low ham mers.**

yel low ish looking somewhat yellow: *The sick man had yellowish skin.*

yes 1. a word used to show that you agree. 2. an answer that agrees: *The votes were three yeses and two noes.* **yes es.**

yes ter day the day before today: *Yesterday it rained all day.* **yes ter days.**

yet 1. up to now: *They have not come home yet.* 2. now; at this time: *Don't go yet.* 3. still: *She is working yet.*

yew an evergreen tree. There are many kinds of yew. See the picture. **yews.**

yoke 1. a wooden frame to hitch oxen. See the picture. 2. the part of a dress fitting the neck and shoulders. **yokes.**

yolk the yellow part of an egg. **yolks.**

yon der over there; within sight but not near.

you 1. the person or persons spoken to: *Are you there? I see both of you. I'll give you a book.* 2. anybody: *You have to be friendly to make friends. You always study arithmetic in school. How do you make this go?*

you'd 1. you had: *You'd better hurry.* 2. you would: *You'd like to go, wouldn't you?*

you'll 1. you will. 2. you shall.

young 1. in the early part of life; not old: *Young people like to run.* 2. young ones: *The mother bear fought to protect her young.* **young er, young est.**

your of you or belonging to you: *your head, your shoes.*

you're you are.

yours something of you or belonging to you: *My hands are cleaner than yours. The red book is mine; the blue one is yours. Are these cookies yours?*

your self *Yourself* is used instead of *you* when *you* has already been used in the sentence: *Did you hurt yourself? Can you carry that heavy box yourself?* **your selves.**

your selves the plural form of *yourself*: *Did you boys hurt yourselves? Can you children do this by yourselves?*

you've you have.

yo yo a toy shaped like a wheel. It has a hollow place around its edge. You wind a string around it, then drop it. The yoyo will move up and down the string. See the picture. **yo yos.**

yuc ca a plant having large white flowers. See the picture. **yuc cas.**

yolk

---

yucca

yoyo

yucca

Yu kon Ter ri to ry one of the two territories
of Canada. See the map on page 382.

Z   z

zebra

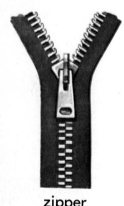

zipper

Z or **z** the twenty-sixth letter of the alphabet.
Z's or **z's.**

ze bra a wild animal somewhat like a horse or
a donkey but striped with dark bands on white.
See the picture. **ze bras.**

ze ro 1. nothing; the figure 0. 2. a very low
point: *It is so cold it must be below zero.*
ze ros or **ze roes.**

zip 1. fasten or close with a zipper: *She zipped
up her jacket and put on her mittens.* 2. move
quickly: *Zip down to the store for me.* **zipped,
zip ping.**

zip per a kind of sliding lock that fastens
together two edges. Zippers are used to fasten
clothes and other things. See the picture.
zip pers.

zoo a place where wild animals are kept. **zoos.**

zoo keep er a person who is hired to take care
of animals in a zoo. **zoo keep ers.**

Gazetteer

A **Gazetteer** is
another kind of dictionary.

This gazetteer gives the names of
American states. The states are given
in alphabetical order. The gazetteer tells
something about each state.

Alabama

The Heart of Dixie

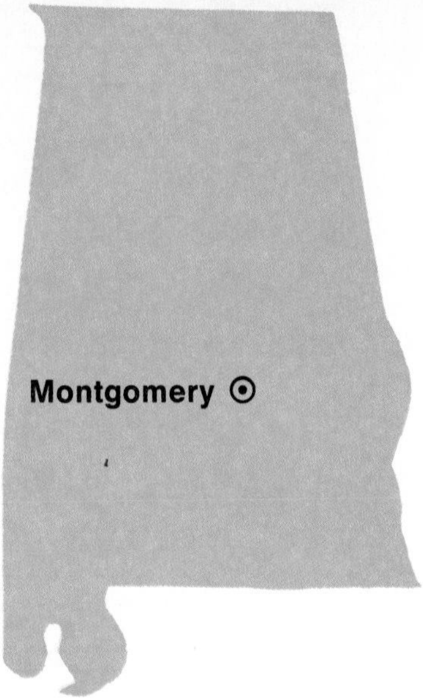

Montgomery ⊙

STATE FLOWER

Camellia

STATE BIRD

Yellowhammer

STATE TREE

Southern (longleaf) Pine

STATE FISH

Tarpon

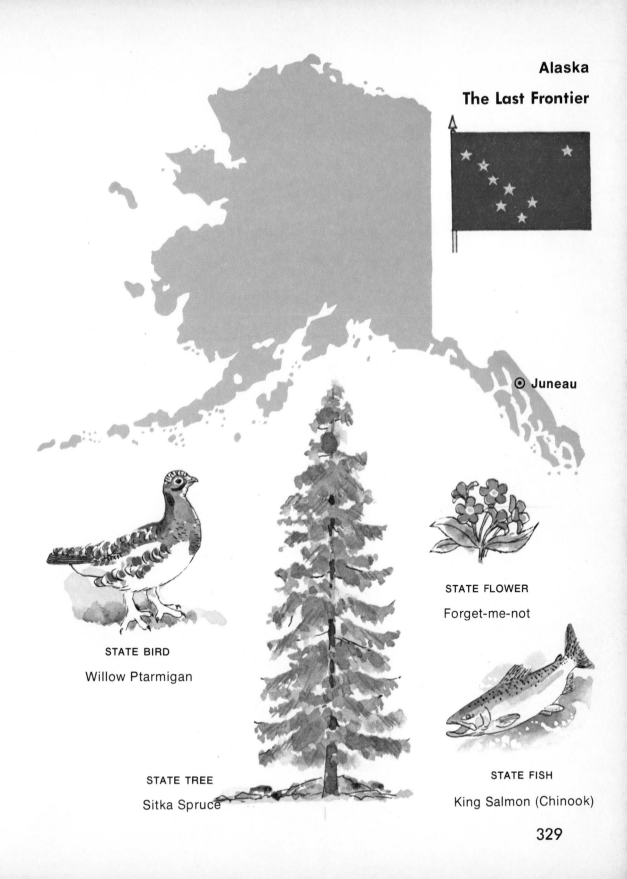

Alaska

The Last Frontier

⊙ Juneau

STATE BIRD

Willow Ptarmigan

STATE TREE

Sitka Spruce

STATE FLOWER

Forget-me-not

STATE FISH

King Salmon (Chinook)

Arizona

The Grand Canyon State

⊙ **Phoenix**

STATE BIRD

Cactus Wren

STATE TREE

Paloverde

STATE FLOWER

Saguaro Blossom

⊙ **Little Rock**

STATE FLOWER

Apple Blossom

STATE BIRD

Mockingbird

STATE TREE

Pine

California

The Golden State

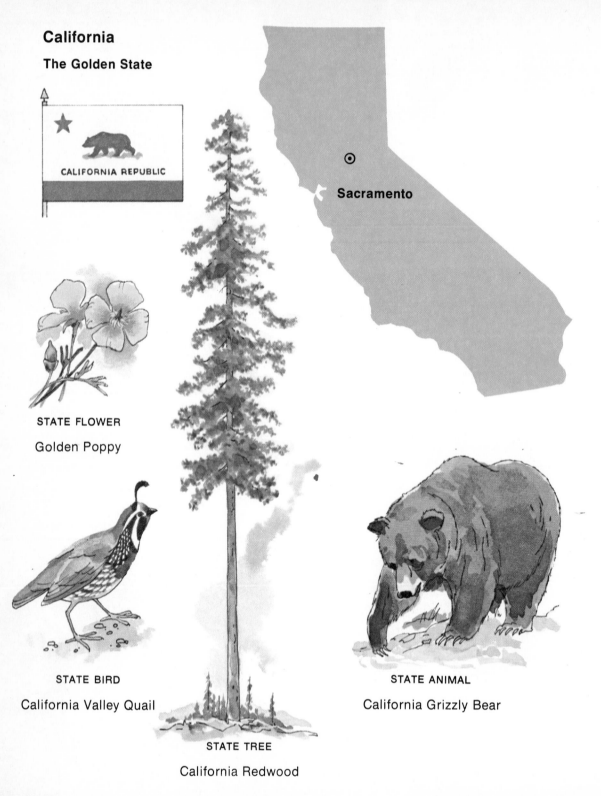

CALIFORNIA REPUBLIC

Sacramento

STATE FLOWER
Golden Poppy

STATE BIRD
California Valley Quail

STATE TREE
California Redwood

STATE ANIMAL
California Grizzly Bear

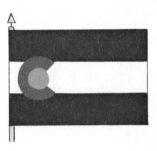

Colorado

The Centennial State

⊙ Denver

STATE TREE

Colorado Blue Spruce

STATE FLOWER

Rocky Mountain Columbine

STATE BIRD

Lark Bunting

STATE ANIMAL

Rocky Mountain Big Horn Sheep

Connecticut

The Constitution State

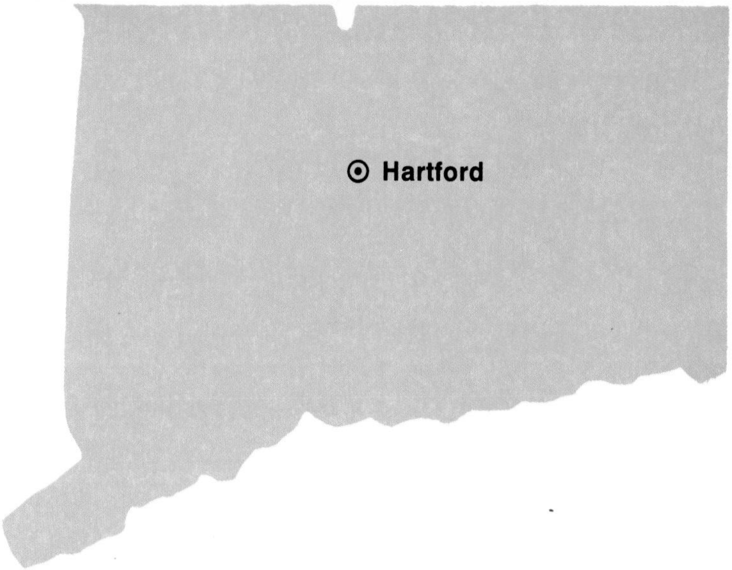

⊙ Hartford

STATE TREE

White Oak

STATE BIRD

American Robin

STATE FLOWER

Mountain Laurel

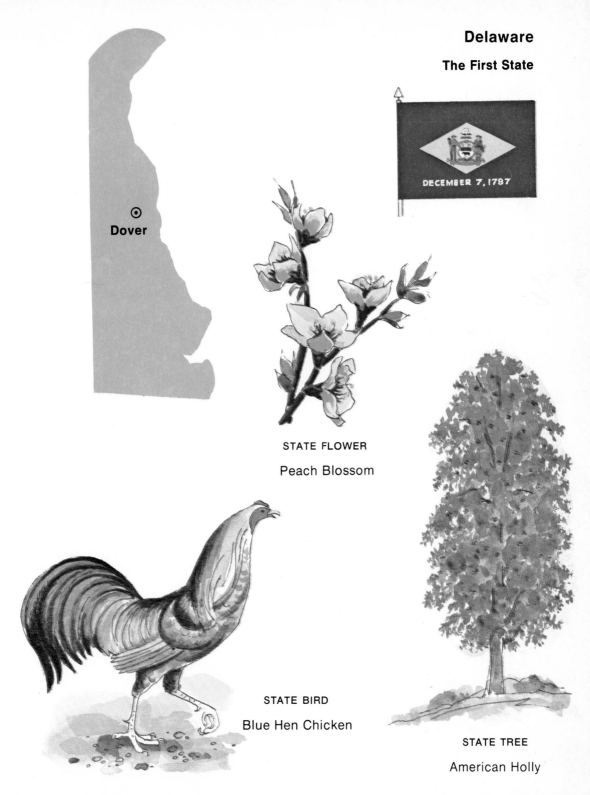

Delaware

The First State

DECEMBER 7, 1797

Dover

STATE FLOWER

Peach Blossom

STATE BIRD

Blue Hen Chicken

STATE TREE

American Holly

335

Florida

The Sunshine State

⊙ **Tallahassee**

STATE FLOWER

Orange Blossom

STATE BIRD

Mockingbird

STATE TREE

Sabal Palmetto Palm

Georgia

The Empire State of the South

⊙ **Atlanta**

STATE BIRD

Brown Thrasher

STATE FLOWER

Cherokee Rose

STATE TREE

Live Oak

Hawaii

The Aloha State

Honolulu

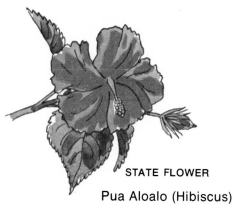

STATE FLOWER

Pua Aloalo (Hibiscus)

STATE TREE

Kukui (Candlenut)

STATE BIRD

Nene (Hawaiian Goose)

338

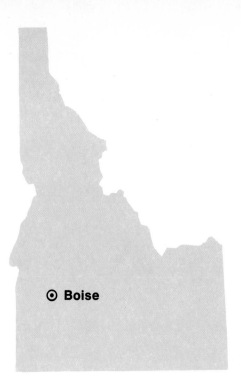

Idaho

The Gem State

⊙ **Boise**

STATE BIRD

Mountain Bluebird

STATE FLOWER

Syringa

STATE TREE

White Pine

339

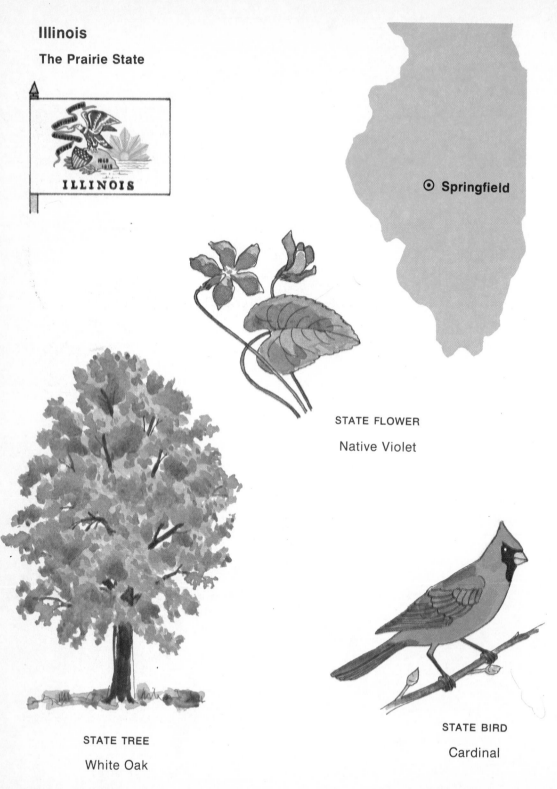

Illinois

The Prairie State

⊙ **Springfield**

STATE FLOWER

Native Violet

STATE TREE

White Oak

STATE BIRD

Cardinal

Indiana

The Hoosier State

Indianapolis

STATE BIRD

Cardinal

STATE FLOWER

Peony

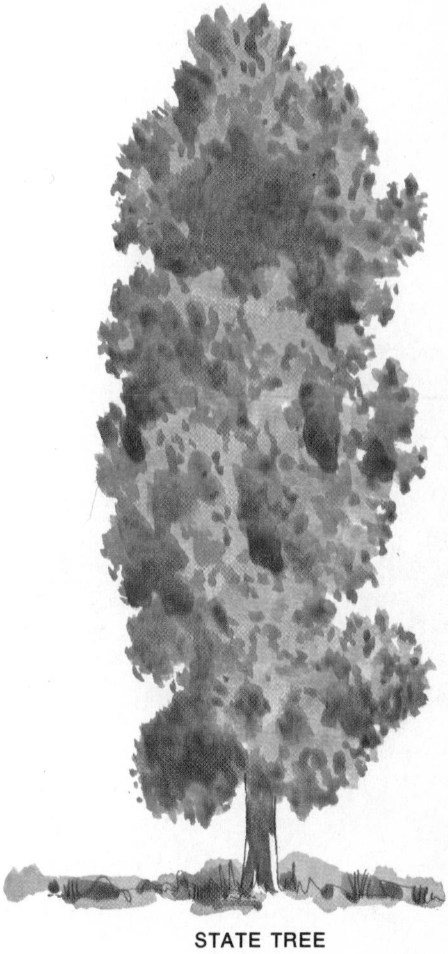

STATE TREE

Tulip Poplar

Iowa

The Hawkeye State

⊙ **Des Moines**

STATE TREE

Oak

STATE BIRD

Eastern Goldfinch

STATE FLOWER

Wild Rose

Kansas

The Sunflower State

⊙ **Topeka**

KANSAS

STATE BIRD

Western Meadowlark

STATE FLOWER

Native Sunflower

STATE ANIMAL

American Buffalo

STATE TREE

Cottonwood

Kentucky

The Bluegrass State

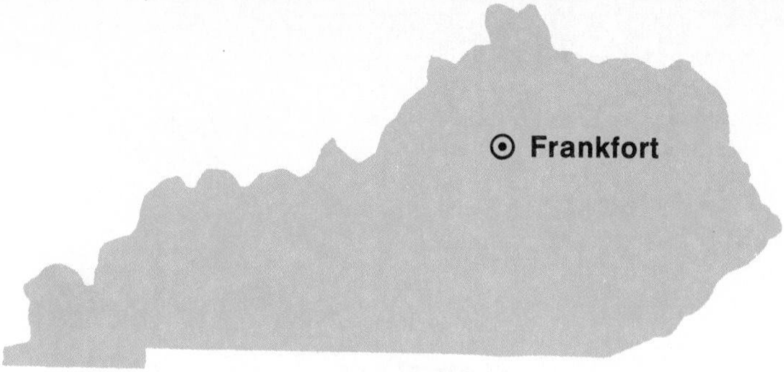

⊙ Frankfort

STATE BIRD

Kentucky Cardinal

STATE FLOWER

Goldenrod

STATE TREE

Kentucky Coffee

STATE FISH

Kentucky Bass

Louisiana

The Pelican State

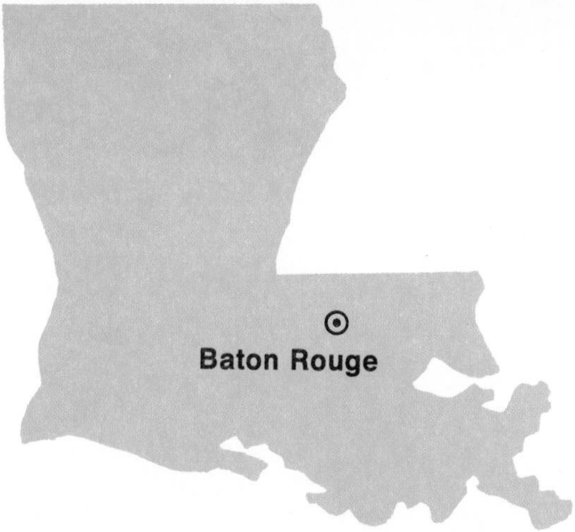

Baton Rouge

STATE FLOWER

Magnolia

STATE BIRD

Eastern Brown Pelican

STATE TREE

Cypress

Maine

The Pine Tree State

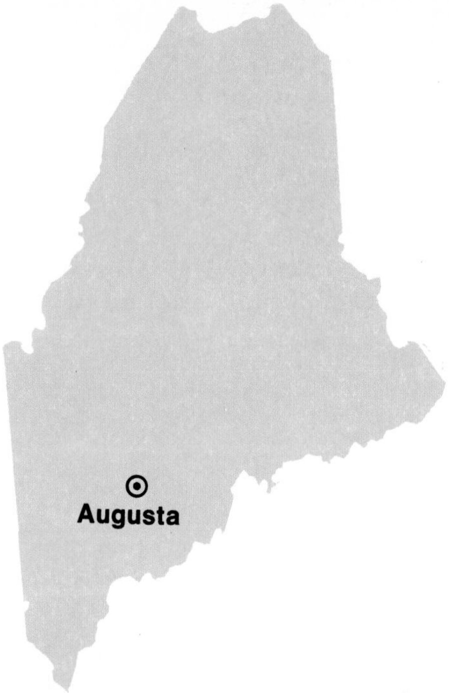

STATE BIRD

Chickadee

⊙
Augusta

STATE FISH

Landlocked Salmon

STATE TREE

Eastern White Pine

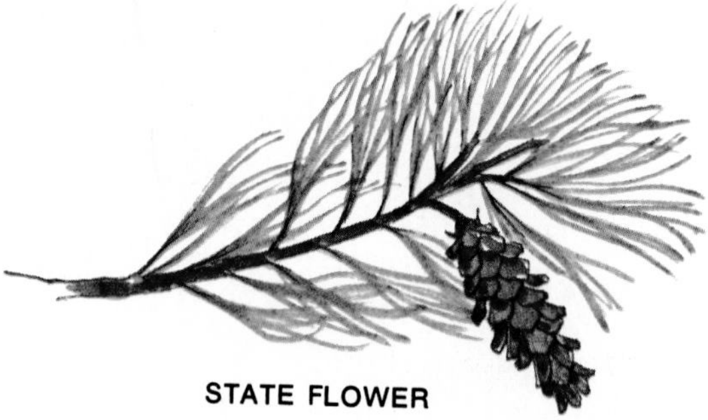

STATE FLOWER

White Pine Cone and Tassel

346

Maryland

The Old Line State

Annapolis

STATE BIRD

Baltimore Oriole

STATE FLOWER

Black-eyed Susan

STATE FISH

Rockfish

STATE ANIMAL

Chesapeake Bay Retriever

STATE TREE

Wye Oak

347

Massachusetts

The Bay State

Boston ⊙

STATE TREE

American Elm

STATE BIRD

Chickadee

STATE FLOWER

Mayflower

348

Michigan

The Wolverine State

⊙ **Lansing**

STATE BIRD

Robin

STATE FLOWER

Apple Blossom

STATE FISH

Trout

STATE TREE

White Pine

349

Minnesota

The North Star State

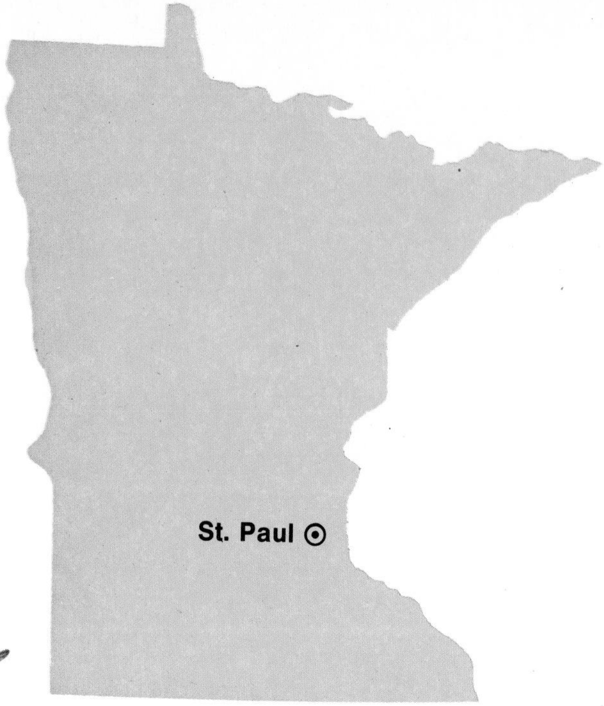

St. Paul ⊙

STATE TREE

Norway Pine

STATE FLOWER

Pink-and-white Lady's-slipper

STATE FISH

Walleye

STATE BIRD

Common Loon

Mississippi

The Magnolia State

⊙ Jackson

STATE FLOWER

Magnolia

STATE BIRD

Mockingbird

STATE TREE

Magnolia

351

Missouri

The Show-Me State

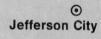
Jefferson City

STATE FLOWER

Hawthorn

STATE TREE

Dogwood

STATE BIRD

Bluebird

Montana
The Treasure State

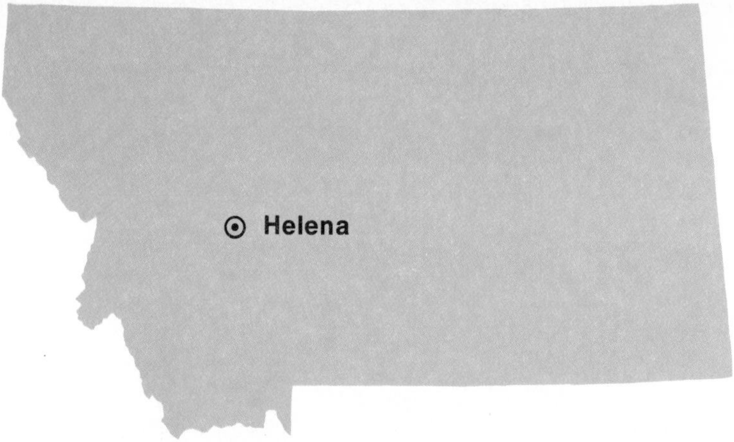

⊙ **Helena**

STATE BIRD

Western Meadowlark

STATE FLOWER

Bitterroot

STATE TREE

Ponderosa Pine

Nebraska

The Cornhusker State

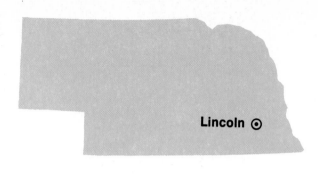

Lincoln ◉

STATE BIRD

Western Meadowlark

STATE TREE

Cottonwood

STATE FLOWER

Goldenrod

Nevada

The Silver State

⊙ **Carson City**

STATE BIRD

Mountain Bluebird

STATE TREE

Single-leaf Piñon

STATE FLOWER

Sagebrush

New Hampshire

The Granite State

STATE BIRD

Purple Finch

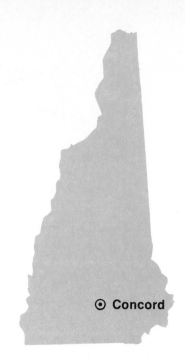

⊙ **Concord**

STATE TREE

White Birch

STATE FLOWER

Purple Lilac

New Jersey

The Garden State

⊙ Trenton

STATE BIRD

Eastern Goldfinch

STATE FLOWER

Violet

STATE TREE

Red Oak

New Mexico

The Land of Enchantment

⊙ **Santa Fe**

STATE BIRD

Road Runner

STATE FISH

Cutthroat Trout

STATE FLOWER

Yucca

STATE TREE

Piñon

STATE ANIMAL

Black Bear

358

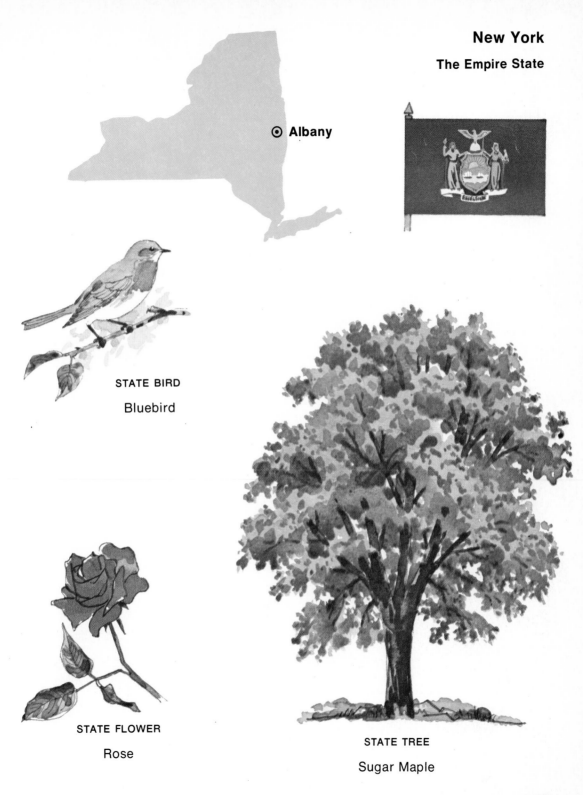

New York

The Empire State

⊙ Albany

STATE BIRD

Bluebird

STATE FLOWER

Rose

STATE TREE

Sugar Maple

North Carolina

The Tar Heel State

Raleigh

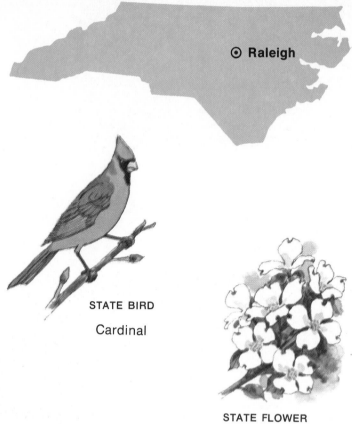

STATE BIRD

Cardinal

STATE FLOWER

Dogwood

STATE TREE

Pine

STATE ANIMAL

Gray Squirrel

North Dakota
The Sioux State

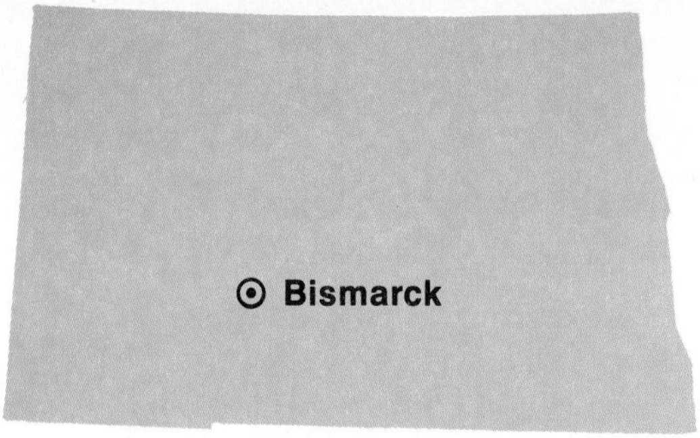

⊙ **Bismarck**

STATE BIRD

Western Meadowlark

STATE FLOWER

Wild Prairie Rose

STATE TREE

American Elm

361

Ohio

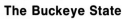

The Buckeye State

⊙ **Columbus**

STATE BIRD

Cardinal

STATE TREE

Buckeye

STATE FLOWER

Scarlet Carnation

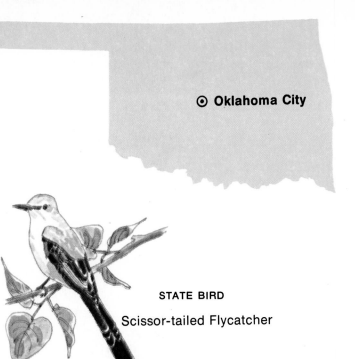

Oklahoma

The Sooner State

⊙ Oklahoma City

STATE BIRD

Scissor-tailed Flycatcher

STATE FLOWER

Mistletoe

STATE TREE

Redbud

Oregon

The Beaver State

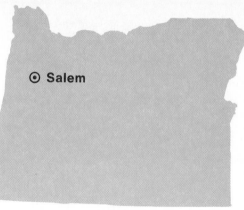

⊙ **Salem**

STATE FLOWER

Oregon Grape

STATE ANIMAL

Beaver

STATE BIRD

Western Meadowlark

STATE TREE

Douglas Fir

STATE FISH

Chinook Salmon

Pennsylvania

The Keystone State

⊙ **Harrisburg**

STATE FLOWER

Mountain Laurel

STATE BIRD

Ruffed Grouse

STATE ANIMAL

Whitetail Deer

STATE TREE

Hemlock

365

Rhode Island

Little Rhody

 **Providence**

STATE TREE

Red Maple

STATE BIRD

Rhode Island Red

STATE FLOWER

Violet

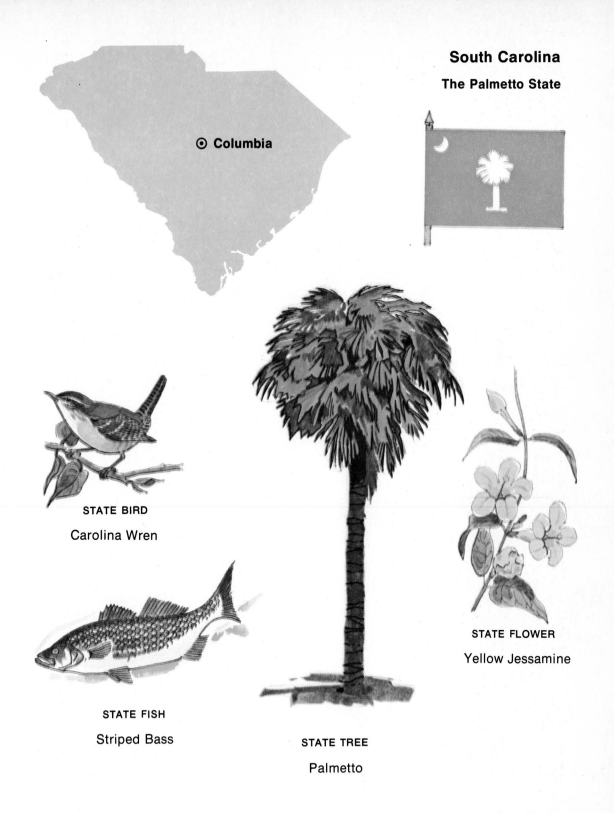

South Carolina

The Palmetto State

◉ Columbia

STATE BIRD
Carolina Wren

STATE FISH
Striped Bass

STATE TREE
Palmetto

STATE FLOWER
Yellow Jessamine

367

South Dakota

The Coyote State

⊙ **Pierre**

STATE BIRD

Chinese Ring-necked Pheasant

STATE FLOWER

Pasqueflower

STATE TREE

Black Hills Spruce

STATE ANIMAL

Coyote

⊙ **Nashville**

Tennessee

The Volunteer State

STATE BIRD

Mockingbird

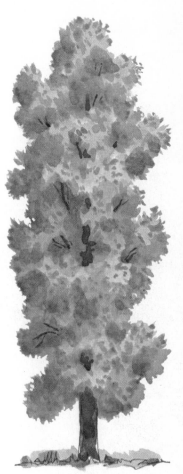

STATE TREE

Tulip Poplar

STATE FLOWER

Iris

Texas

The Lone Star State

⊙ **Austin**

STATE TREE

Pecan

STATE FLOWER

Bluebonnet

STATE BIRD

Mockingbird

The Beehive State

Salt Lake City

STATE FLOWER

Sego Lily

STATE BIRD

Seagull

STATE TREE

Blue Spruce

Vermont

The Green Mountain State

⊙
Montpelier

STATE FLOWER

Red Clover

STATE BIRD

Hermit Thrush

STATE TREE

Sugar Maple

STATE ANIMAL

Morgan Horse

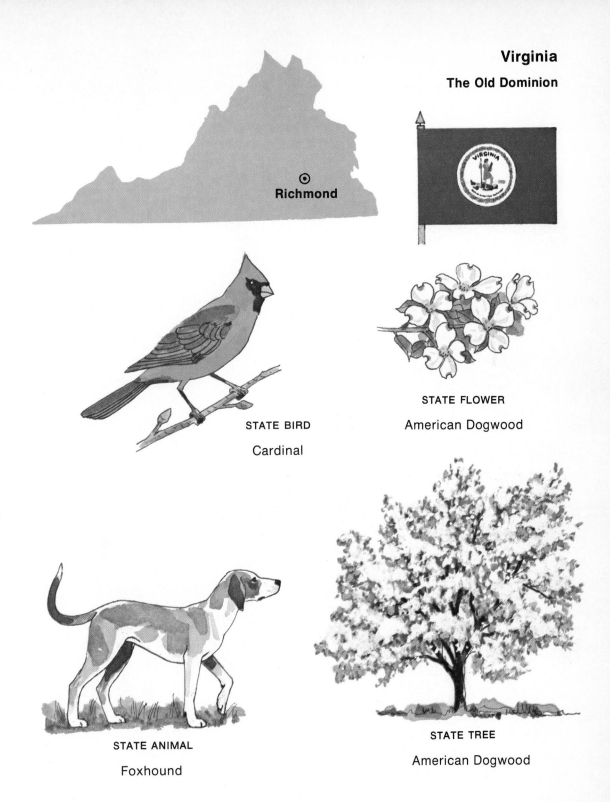

Virginia
The Old Dominion

Richmond

STATE BIRD

Cardinal

STATE FLOWER

American Dogwood

STATE ANIMAL

Foxhound

STATE TREE

American Dogwood

Washington

The Evergreen State

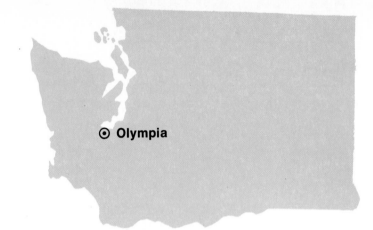

⊙ **Olympia**

STATE TREE

Western Hemlock

STATE FLOWER

Coast Rhododendron

STATE BIRD

Willow Goldfinch

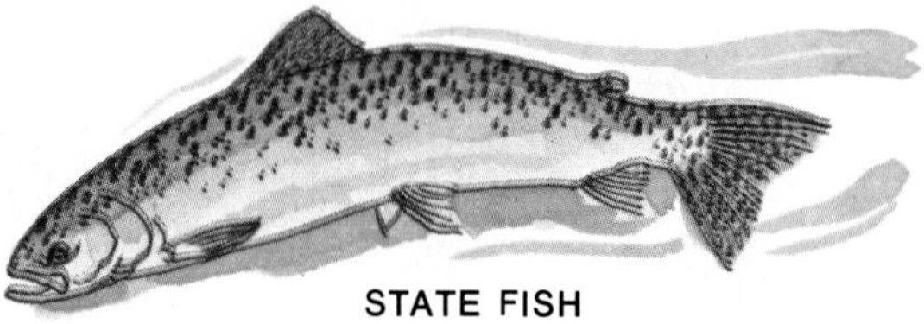

STATE FISH

Steelhead Trout

West Virginia

The Mountain State

⊙ **Charleston**

STATE BIRD

Cardinal

STATE FLOWER

Big Rhododendron

STATE ANIMAL

Black Bear

STATE TREE

Sugar Maple

Wisconsin

The Badger State

STATE BIRD

Robin

⊙ **Madison**

STATE FLOWER

Wood Violet

STATE TREE

Sugar Maple

STATE FISH

Muskellunge

STATE ANIMAL

Badger

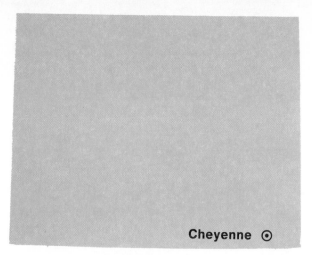

Cheyenne ⊙

Wyoming

The Equality State

STATE BIRD

Meadowlark

STATE FLOWER

Indian Paintbrush

STATE TREE

Cottonwood

District of Columbia

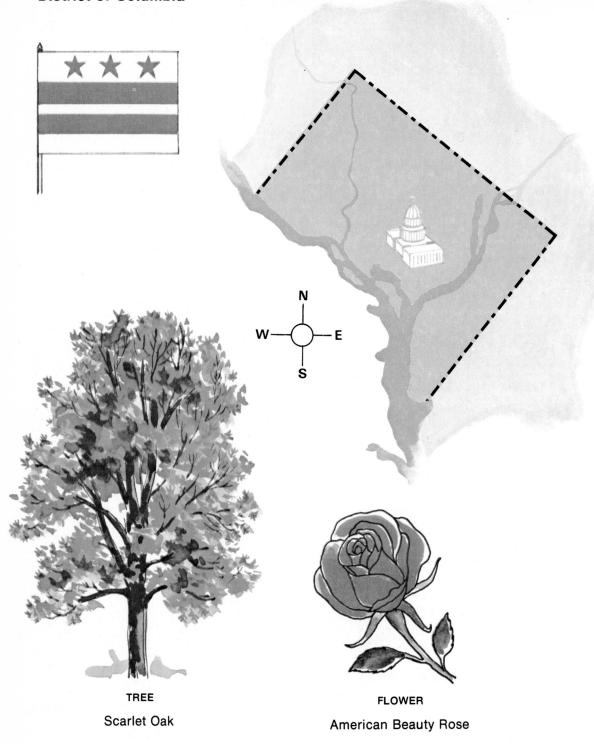

TREE

Scarlet Oak

FLOWER

American Beauty Rose

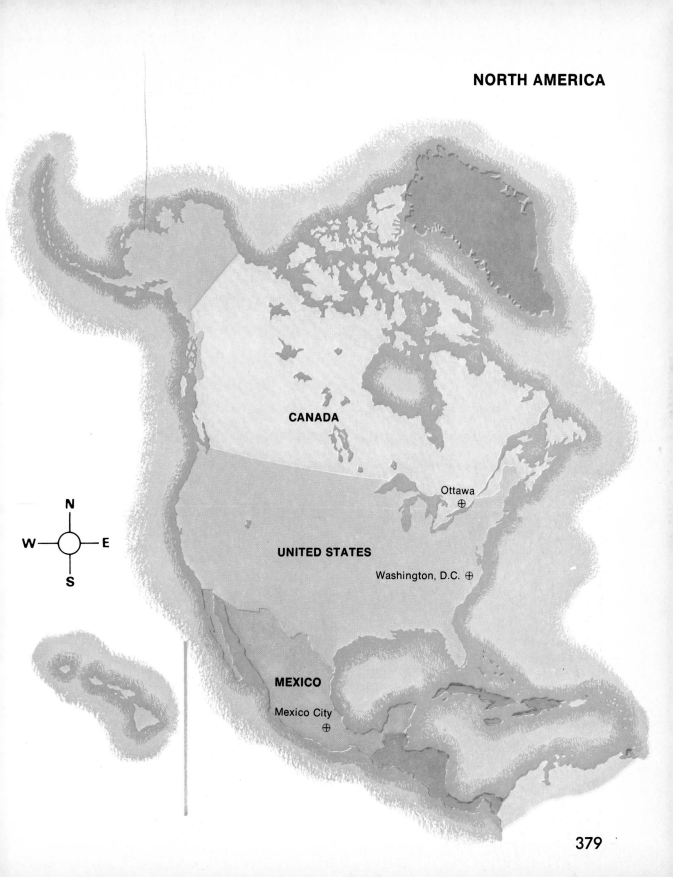

NORTH AMERICA

CANADA

Ottawa ⊕

UNITED STATES

Washington, D.C. ⊕

MEXICO

Mexico City ⊕

N
W — E
S

UNITED STATES

WASHINGTON

MONTANA

OREGON

IDAHO

WYOMING

NEVADA

UTAH

COLORADO

CALIFORNIA

ARIZONA

NEW MEXICO

ALASKA

HAWAII

N
W E
S

NORTH DAKOTA

MINNESOTA

SOUTH DAKOTA

WISCONSIN

MICHIGAN

NEW HAMPSHIRE

MAINE

VERMONT

MASSACHUSETTS

RHODE ISLAND

CONNECTICUT

NEW YORK

NEW JERSEY

NEBRASKA

IOWA

ILLINOIS

INDIANA

OHIO

PENNSYLVANIA

DELAWARE

MARYLAND

Washington

DISTRICT OF COLUMBIA

WEST VIRGINIA

VIRGINIA

KANSAS

MISSOURI

KENTUCKY

NORTH CAROLINA

TENNESSEE

SOUTH CAROLINA

OKLAHOMA

ARKANSAS

MISSISSIPPI

ALABAMA

GEORGIA

TEXAS

LOUISIANA

FLORIDA

CANADA

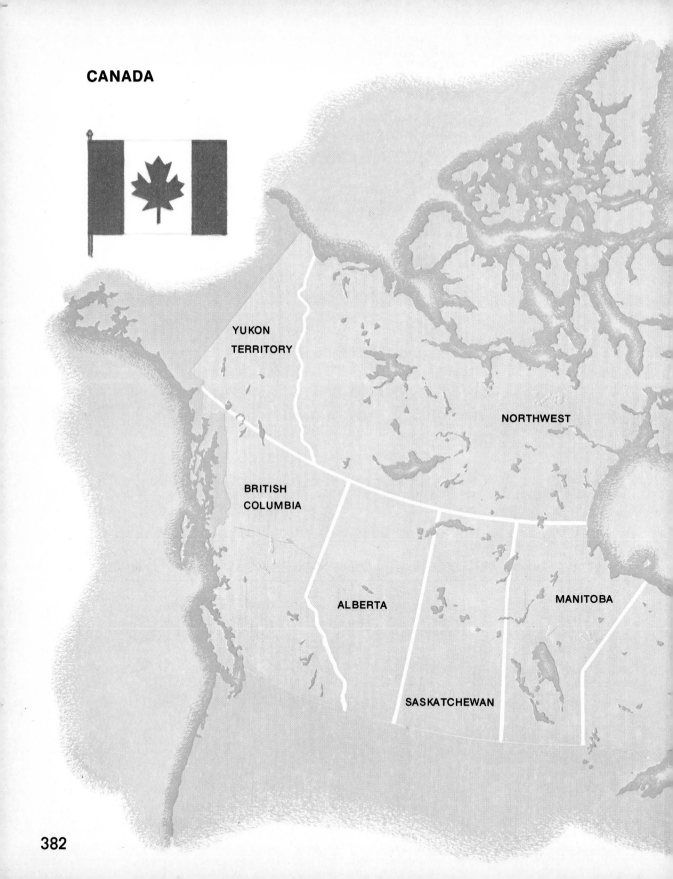

YUKON
TERRITORY

NORTHWEST

BRITISH
COLUMBIA

ALBERTA

MANITOBA

SASKATCHEWAN

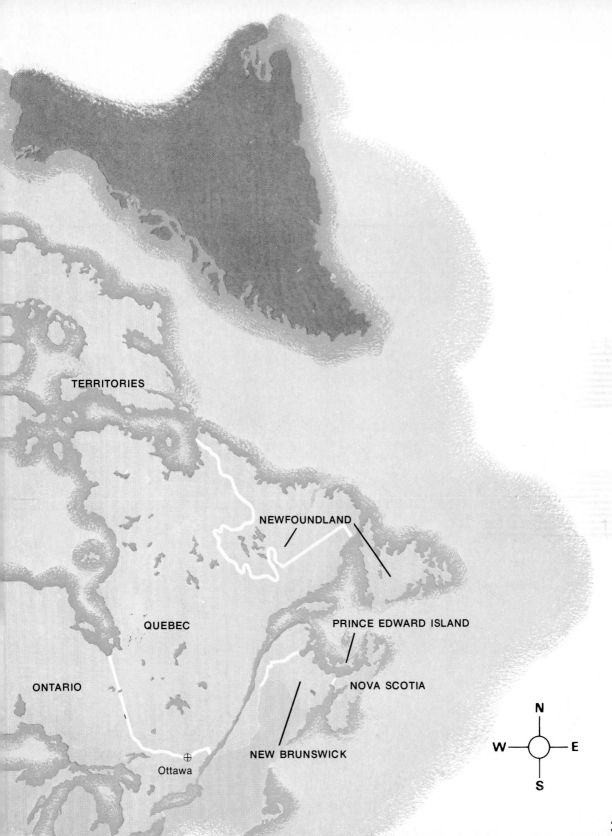

ONTARIO

QUEBEC

TERRITORIES

NEWFOUNDLAND

PRINCE EDWARD ISLAND

NOVA SCOTIA

NEW BRUNSWICK

Ottawa

N
W E
S

MEXICO

Mexico City

N
W   E
S